I0126967

NEW DEVELOPMENTS in ANARCHIST STUDIES

Thought | Crimes

2015

NEW DEVELOPMENTS IN ANARCHIST STUDIES

First published in 2015 by

Thought | Crimes

an imprint of punctum books * brooklyn, ny

punctumbooks.com

ISBN-13: 978-0988234093
ISBN-10: 0988234092

and the full (color!) book is available for download at

www.thoughtcrimespress.org

a project of the
Critical Criminology Working Group,
publishers of the Open Access Journal:
RADICAL CRIMINOLOGY:
journal.radicalcriminology.org
Contact: Jeff Shantz (Editor),
Dept. of Criminology, KPU
12666 72 Ave. Surrey, BC V3W 2M8

NAASN :: North American Anarchist Studies Network /
La Red Norteamericana de Estudios Anarquistas /
Le Réseau Nord-Américain d'études Anarchistes

This collection is based on contributions compiled from the open
call for papers for the 5th Annual NAASN Conference
(held January 2014, in Surrey, on unceded Coast Salish territories)

NAASN . ORG Conferences:

2009: Hartford, CT | 2011: Toronto, ON | 2012: San Juan,
Puerto Rico | 2013: New Orleans, LA | 2014: Surrey, BC
(Coast Salish Territories) | 2015: San Francisco, CA

This 2014 conference was organized by the
Critical Criminology Working Group (including
faculty, students & comrades of the KPU
Criminology Dept.) AND with the support of a grant
from the **Faculty of Arts, Kwantlen Polytechnic
University** AND with the support of the

Kwantlen Student Association

and the KPU
Criminology Student Society

KWANTLEN STUDENT ASSOCIATION

CRIMINOLOGY
STUDENT
SOCIETY

— n a a s n 2 0 1 4 . o r g
& 2 0 1 4 . n a a s n . o r g —
built with free, open source software,
'**Open Conference Systems**' from the Public Knowledge
Project @ Simon Fraser University—**http://pkp.sfu.ca/ocs}**

[design & open format publishing by **pj lilley**]

NAASN 5

North American Anarchist Studies Network 5th Annual Conference, January 16-18, 2014

Surrey, Kwantlen Polytechnic U.

Contents

1 | Anarchism from the Margins: Introducing New
Developments in Anarchist Studies 1
Jeff Shantz

2 | Social Capital In Anarchist Movements................11
Dana M. Williams

3 | Marginalization of Anarchism within Mainstream
Criminology: A Content Analysis.........................37
Christopher Howell

4 | Sexuality, Assault, Police Infiltration and Foucault:
Notes for Further Inquiry.............................63
Dr. Michael Loadenthal

5 | Abolition Journal, Introduction & Manifesto 89
Introduced by Brian Lovato & Eli Meyerhoff

6 | In Defense of Counterposed Strategic Orientations:
Anarchism and Antiracism........................97
Jakub Burkowicz

7 | Anti-State Resistance On Stolen Land: Settler
Colonialism, Settler Identity And The Imperative Of
Anarchist Decolonization.........................145
Adam Gary Lewis

8 | A Diversity of Media Tactics: Grassroots
Autonomous Media in Montreal 187
Sandra Jeppesen, Anna Kruzynski, Aaron Lakoff and →

Rachel Sarrasin—Collectif de recherche sur l'autonomie collective (CRAC)

9 | Radical Politics in a Conservative Capital: Anarchist Groups and Projects in Edmonton............199
Robert Hlatky

10 | The Right to the City Begins on the Street...............249
Dr. Katherine Dunster

11 | Anarchist Surrealism & Canadian Apocalyptic Modernism: Allusive Political Praxis in Elizabeth Smart's *By Grand Central Station I Sat Down And Wept*..331
James Gifford

12 | ¡Mesoamerica Resiste! Excerpts from the companion guide to the graphic narrative.........................357
with the Beehive Design Collective

Appendix 1: NAASN Statement of **Purpose**.............363
Appendix 2: NAASN5 **Call for Papers** (Fall, 2013)...366
Appendix 3: NAASN5 Full **Schedule** +
+ Forum on Indigenous Food Sovereignty
+ Surrey Anarchist Bookfair 369
Appendix 4: A few words about **Surrey**....................372
Appendix 5: **Indigenous Food Sovereignty Forum**..374
Appendix 6: **Surrey Anarchist Bookfair** Poster.........382
Appendix 7: Surrey Anarchist Bookfair Tablers.........383

1| Anarchism from the Margins: Introducing *New Developments in Anarchist Studies*

Jeff Shantz[1]

A narchism is enjoying a rather remarkable renaissance, in theory and in practice, through the first decades of the twenty-first century. Notably this renaissance is taking place simultaneously in the streets and in the schools, in activism as well as in academia. The reasons for the resurgence of anarchism are varied but without question the primary impetus has been the community opposition to neoliberal capitalist globalism and associated regimes of austerity and repression along with the pressing fact of ecological crisis. Many are inspired to act by the enormity of current social and ecological harms and the

---

1   Jeff Shantz teaches in the criminology department at Kwantlen Polytechnic University, Surrey

growing realization among wider sectors of the population that these are not problems that can be resolved within the framework of state managed capitalist development. At the same time many among newer generations of activists, and some of the earlier generations, have seen or learned from the failures of previous frameworks of resistance politics, particularly the statist forms of the various Marxisms and social democracies. For many, anarchism stands as the most promising basis for analyzing and understanding contemporary capitalist societies and for informing an opposition to capitalist arrangements in such as way as to pose a realistic, positive, liberatory alternative.

In the North American context it is reasonable to suggest that anarchism, both as social movement and as social theory, is presently at the highest level of activity and influence it has achieved at least since the flourishing of New Left politics in the late 1960s and early 1970s. It is also safe to say that the diversity and depth of anarchist ideas, and the range of research and scholarship, are well beyond that achieved in that earlier wave (which does not detract from the great quality of many of those works of the 1960s and 1970s). Not only areas of study for which anarchism has a more ready association, such as sociology or politics, but fields such as horticulture, literary criticism, aeasthetics, urbanism, and technology studies among others have seen developments in anarchist research.

Impetus

Significantly, social developments in terms of struggle and resistance have intersected with developments in terms of academic research and scholarship at various levels. Younger people engaged in struggles in the streets against capitalist globalization and neoliberal austerity have entered the post-secondary classrooms bringing their critique of existing structures with them and turning their critical eye toward academic disciplines that too often re-inforce or sustain existing relations of power rather than, as scholarship should anyway, contesting them. At the same time current students are faced with the political im-potency and inaction of the recent challengers to radical theory, notably postmodernism and postructuralism and various cultural theories that have lost attentiveness to political and economic structures of power, exploitation, and inequality, and which have substituted detached per-sonalistic cynicism for engaged collective action. And such "critical" theories have proven of little use as tools in the most pressing struggles of the day, particularly against neoliberal austerity and the new enclosures of land and labor. Indeed, the trajectory of postmodernist theorizing has shown it to be too easily rendered an apo-logy for or facilitator of such processes.

The new scholars have sought alternatives to moribund mainstream and orthodox theories and, as they may have in the streets, found overlooked, forgotten, discarded his-tories of critical and radical theory that provide better, more insightful answers to their questions—they have found anarchism. Notably they have found that not only does anarchism address important contemporary concerns, they have also found that anarchist theory was often present at the inception of the academic field they are studying yet has been written out of the disciplinary record with only status quo political motivations to answer why. Attention, thus, has been given to applying anarchist analysis to understanding and advancing social struggles but also to rethinking the narratives framing recognized academic disciplines and scholarly practices.

From the Margins: The NAASN Conference

In the present context there is growing interest in anarchism as an important area of scholarly activity. In the current period anarchism has emerged as a vital critical perspective within disciplines as diverse as criminology and literary studies, geography and communications. At the same time many community members involved in community organizing have become interested in anarchism as offering relevant perspectives on social justice. This is reflected, in part, in the emergence of the North American Anarchist Studies Network itself and the success of the five annual NAASN conferences. NAASN brings together activists and academics, anarchist and non-anarchist scholars, all with interests in anarchism.

From January 16 to 18, 2014 the Fifth Annual North American Anarchist Studies Conference was held at

Kwantlen Polytechnic University (KPU) in Surrey, British Columbia. As part of the conference the First Annual Surrey Anarchist Bookfair was held in the Conference Centre on January 18. Thursday, January 17 also included parallel sessions on Indigenous Food Sovereignty. These events saw more than 300 people attend the Surrey campus and participate in a range of events from panel discussions to workshops to roundtables.

These facts alone represent something of a significant development, both in terms of the wide interest in anarchist scholarship and research, involving community members as well as students and faculty, and in terms of local community organizing, in a suburban working class context outside of mainstream activist spheres in Metro Vancouver. As suburbs of Vancouver go Surrey is perhaps the least well regarded. It is a place many downtown Vancouver activists simply will not go, at least willingly. Surrey has had an undue reputation as a bit reactionary, despite histories of union activism and broad social democratic politics that would hint otherwise. Still the idea of an anarchist conference and bookfair in Surrey was greeted by many activists and community organizers with a good deal of scepticism. Yet, and this shows something of the contemporary draw of anarchist ideas, it worked and worked wonderfully. People showed up. And stayed. Many asked if there would be another event the following year (there will be).

One of the great benefits of developments like the North American Anarchist Studies Network and its annual conferences is an opportunity for mutual aid support among academics and activists. It provides new venues in which unique cross fertilizations and hybridities can occur. In NAASN the boundaries between disciplines dissolve somewhat and real multi (anti-) disciplinarities can occur. New projects too emerge. In Surrey it was a curious, but welcomed, occurrence that several anarchist scholars lived in Surrey but were unknown to each other, despite having lived nearby for years. The conference introduced them, revealed them to each other. Out of this relationships have been built. The conference announced the formation of the Kwantlen Center for Anarchist Studies, a new resource for developing new anarchist works and for hosting and archiving some previous ones.

Perspectives

This book represents works presented for and at the Fifth Annual North American Anarchist Studies Network Conference. Everyone scheduled to present at the conference was invited to submit their final paper the collection. Most did (some were committed to other venues such as specific academic journals).

The papers collected here show a sampling of the great diversity of anarchist research, scholarship, and action. They show a variety of styles and commitments, theoretical emphases and practical approaches, both in the scholarship represented and the anarchist projects engaged with by the authors. A wonderful range of issues are addressed.

It is hoped the collection will provide an important new venue for intellectual and practical, research, engagement, and exchange. Despite the exciting growth in anarchist research and scholarship it is still difficult to find venues for anarchist works within traditional academic publishers and journals. This collection provides an important opportunity for publications by a variety of practitioners which might otherwise not find a venue for publication given the still limited opportunities for such critical, even radical, work.

This collection should make clear the vitality and vigor of contemporary anarchist scholarship. These are incisive, engaging, and engaged works. They pose the potentially profound insights of anarchist thought in various areas of social life and show the contributions to social understanding, broadly understood, of theoretical perspectives still in development. It is hoped that *New Developments in Anarchist Studies* will provide a useful new resource for teaching within the classroom and beyond.

NAASN5

5th Annual Conference of the

NORTH AMERICAN

La Red Norteamericana de Estudios Anarquistas / Le Réseau Nord-América

ANARCHIST STUDIES N

Panel Presentations & Discussion, featuring local & international scholars, from a variety of disciplines—teaching & independent

|Schedule subject to change: Please register on our website for final conference details: *http://naasn2014.org*|

Thursday afternoon 2pm: ANARCHY & SOCIETY (sociological approaches): Liberation & Symbolic Interaction; | Anarchistic Social Capital: Envisioning & Measuring Orientations Towards Horizontalism; | Marginalization of Anarchist Criminology: a Content Analysis of Introductory Criminology Textbooks
3:30pm: The POLITICS of VIOLENCE: Stumbling in the Dark: Anarchism & Terrorism Research; | Statecraft & Sexual Trust: Infiltrating the Revolutionary Left; | Aesthetics & Revolutionary Violence

Welcome/SOCIAL, 5pm, Grassroots Cafe

Friday Morning, 9am: Opening Welcome
10am: ANTI-RACISM & ANTI-COLONIALISM: Presenting *Abolition: A Movement-Relevant Journal of Politics;*| In Defense of Counterposed Strategic Orientations: Anarchism & Anti-Racism; | Anti-State Resistance on Stolen Land: Expanding Anarchism's Anti-Colonial and Decolonizing Potentials Through Anarcha-Indigenism
@ 11:30am: LAND IS LIFE FORUM -------->>>
LUNCH @ 1pm
Friday afternoon NAASN5 panels:
2pm: GRASSROOTS NETWORKS: Media, Cities & Spaces: Activist Media Toolkits: a diversity of media tactics | The Right to The City Begins on the Street | Anarchism in a Conservative Capital: Groups & Projects in Edmonton;
3:30: ART & CULTURE of RESISTANCE: Language of Struggle, Struggle with Language: situationists & "the dangerous classes"; | Anarchist Surrealism, Canadian Apocalyptic Modernism | MESOAMERICA RESISTE! w/Beehive Collective

JANUARY 16-18 • http://NAASN2014.ORG
KWANTLEN POLYTECHNIC UNIVERSITY

Conference Centre (CEDAR Bldg.)
Kwantlen Polytechnic University
12666 72 Avenue, Surrey

Wheelchair accessible (including washrooms)

to VOLUNTEER: Contact *Jeff Shantz, Dept. of Criminology* <jeffrey.shantz@kpu.ca>

...in d'études Anarchistes **& on Saturday, January 18th** 10 AM-3:45PM

NETWORK

+ on Friday ↓

↓ Surrey's 1st!

INDIGENOUS FOOD SOVEREIGNTY

ANARCHIST BOOKFAIR

FREE WORKSHOPS,
practical AND radical: resisting surveillance & anarchist tech support; using "access to information" for investigative research; anarchist interventions in academia; midwives & alternative health practitioners speak out; **decolonization:** mind, body & land

Who is your family? Stories of First Nation Food Sovereignty in the Tla-o-qui-aht Ha-houl-thee
A narrative addressing environmental dispossession, environmental degradation, racism, and food security in the traditional territory of the Tla-o-qui-aht First Nation-- with Dorothy Manson and Johnnie Manson *(also this track's organizer)*

Fostering Intergenerational Resilience through the Decolonization of our Food Systems (with Galen Illerbrun, Similkameen Nation; & Jeska Slater, Cree Nation and YOUNG ARTIST WARRIORS)

Real Talk: on Food security, Sovereignty, and what that means to us (with Xhopakelxhit & Gwaiina of Ancestral Pride, a land based movement of Nuu Chah Nulth / Ahousaht and Coast Salish / Snuneymuxw First Nations.)

PLUS • 'zines & literature • books • art • free exchange of ideas!
with TABLES by:
• Ancestral Pride • BC Blackout & Inner Island Distro • Black Banner Distro + 38 Blood Alley • Critical Criminology Working Group (*your EVENT HOSTS,* with *Radical Criminology* & books by Jeff Shantz) • IWW Vancouver • Kersplebedeb • KPIRG • MENSES (anarcha-feminists) • PM Press • Robert Graham • Spartacus Books • Shout Back Festival • Upping the Anti • Warrior Publications + more TBA!!
pls. write us at <org@naasn2014.org>

[See Appendix 3 (p.369) for the full text of the 3-day schedule: NAASN5 + Indigenous Food Sovereignty & bookfair workshops]

2 | Social Capital In Anarchist Movements

Dana M. Williams[1]

Introduction and Bourdieu on Social Capital

"Anarchists of the world... unite!"

This tongue-in-cheek joke parodies the commonly-held belief that anarchists do not work well with others. Most people assume anarchists are extreme individualists, unwilling to compromise, or collaborate in groups (i.e., every person is "an island", completely independent of others). In reality, this is far from the truth. Anarchists prefer to work on projects, in groups, or within relationships where their participation (and everyone else's) is voluntary, not coerced, and where the power-relations are equally balanced and power is not monopolized by a

---

1   Dana Williams teaches in the sociology department at California State University-Chico.

small group of people (Ward 1996, Ehrlich 1996, Graeber 2009, Milstein 2010, Shantz 2010). This is not only possible, but is the standard mode of existence in anarchist movements. The social phenomenon at the crux of this conception of organization is social capital.

Defining social capital can be challenging, but the French sociologist Pierre Bourdieu's (1986) conception of social capital may be the best. Below, I consider how social capital applies to social movements, particularly anarchism. According to Bourdieu, capital of any form "takes time to accumulate" (p. 241). In doing so, it can take on a variety of forms, including economic, human, social, and symbolic. Social capital consists of social obligations or connections, which can be converted into economic capital. It is "the aggregate of the actual or potential resources which are linked to possession of a durable network of more or less institutionalized relationships of mutual acquisition and recognition" (pp. 248-249). By being members of a group, people have a degree of access to the "collectively-owned capital" of that group.

One's possession of social capital depends on the size and complexity of the network that people can mobilize, as well as the quality and quantity of capital that people in that network have available to them. This network is a series of relationships that is premised upon efforts to socially invest in each other (whether consciously or not), all in ways that help to grow and sustain these relationships for use in the future. Consequently, anarchist movements have greater capital to the extent that anarchist networks possess complex, diverse, and strong social connections. Bourdieu writes: "The reproduction of social capital presupposes an unceasing effort of sociability, a continuous series of exchanges in which recognition is endlessly affirmed and reaffirmed" (p. 250).

Since organizations are arguably one of the most important scales of analysis for studying social movements (McCarthy and Zald 1977), it is reasonable to try applying social capital theory to social movement organizations (SMOs). Some scholars have already begun to do so, with intriguing results (Diani 1997, Mayer 2003, Paxton 2002, Smith 1998). Thus, the breadth of social capital theory offers great opportunities to assist in understanding social movements and SMOs. In addition, anarchist movements ought to seriously consider how to improve their social capital in order to improve their chances of goal-achievement, especially within the context of anarchist organizational forms (e.g., affinity groups, collectives, syndicalist unions, federations, or other projects).

Forms of Social Capital According to Coleman

The various forms of social capital theorized by James S. Coleman can help to clearly define the important factors that contribute to social capital. For those lacking economic and financial capital, social capital is a key means to not only individual agency, but also *social* change, particularly within SMOs. Social capital theory applied to social movements suggests that the common denominator of any movement is usually its raw, collective people power—both bodies and minds.[2]

Sociologists and activists alike have long debated the contradictory degree to which social action is facilitated by agency and restricted by social structure.[3] For Coleman (1988), social capital is one immediate means of agency and it is created by people within the relationships they share. "[S]ocial capital is productive making possible the achievement of certain ends that in its absence would not be possible... Unlike other forms of capital, social capital inheres in the structure or relations between actors and among actors" (p. S98). Coleman describes (1988) three important forms social capital can take: (1) trust, (2) information channels, and (3) norms and sanctions.[4] Seen through these varieties, it is clear that social capital is an important "thing" created within social movements. Coleman's conception of social capital may be seen as akin to a particular operationalization of social resources, as described by resource mobilization theory (Edwards & McCarthy 2004); the very strength of move-

2   Charles Tilly notes the importance of mass participation; he emphasizes the importance of WUNC (worthiness, unity, numbers, and commitment; Tilly 2004).

3   Anthony Giddens (1984) proposes a solution to this supposed dichotomy, through his theory of structuration.

4   Later, in his magisterial work *The Foundations of Social Theory* (1990), Coleman elaborates upon three additional elements of social capital, the first two of which are far less relevant here; these include authority relations, appropriable social organization, and intentional organization.

ments themselves may derive from the accumulation and application of *social* capital. In other words, movements build social capital as a resource and then mobilize when appropriate. According to Coleman (1988), individually-useful resources like human capital (e.g. knowledge, skills, credentials) necessitate the acquisition and deployment of social capital in order to make an impact. Thus, people need each other in order to pursue social goals as well as their own private ends. Taken to its logical conclusion, social capital helps people working in movement organizations, groups, and networks to acquire collective power that they would not possess as mere individuals.

The first form of Coleman's (1988) social capital is trust, which facilitates the exchange of expectation and obligation. The ties between individuals are stronger when there is greater expectation—people know they can rely upon others to follow-through on important or necessary tasks. Stronger ties foster a more intense sense of obligation, as friends, comrades, fellow participants, and activists feel they have to support each other. This obligation may appear to be rooted in common values, shared experiences, or promises. Social capital is clearly an unspoken component of the anarchist theory and practice of "mutual aid": the free exchange of physical, monetary, or political support with the expectation that others will in-turn feel obligation to support them if and when necessary (c.f. Kropotkin 1972). This activity feels very "natural" to most people and they seek out relationships in which they can practice mutual aid with others. Movements that encourage the practice of mutual aid are likely to have greater social capital and people are more likely to trust one another. Anarchists also place trust in others in ways that are contingent upon a person's hierarchical position. Thus, it is generally assumed that most "average" people are worthy of a degree of trust, while those in positions of authority are not worthy of such trust.

Trust is particularly useful in revolutionary movements where the risk of state repression is highest. Part of this deep trust is represented in the willingness to plan possibly illegal actions—e.g., property destruction against corporate property, blockading military depots, sabotaging logging equipment, supporting wildcat strikes, or unpermitted marches—with each other and assume that sensitive information will not be conveyed to anyone else, whether loose-lipped associates or police. Sharing secrets in a safe manner is an important practice in radical movements, since anti-authoritarian direct action plans tend to be kept strictly within the immediate social circles that are part of the planning. A key example of such trust is that found within the SMO called an "affinity group," small groupings composed exclusively of people who know, trust, and share common identities with each other. Affinity groups are similar to families, but deliberately built around political commitments that may engage in contentious politics and challenging activities—such as militant protest or other direct action—that require strong trust and support from one's affinity group.

Coleman's (1988) second form of social capital, information channels, can also lead to the empowerment of social movements. By personally knowing people who have valuable information, one has less need to independently gather information. Thus, there is "information potential" in our relationships with others. Social capital is fostered and accumulated when activists create and regularly exercise communication through radical information channels. As the networks of communication broaden within movements, it is easier for those movements to understand the obstacles they face. Even within geographically diffuse networks, people may remain in contact through telecommunications and Internet technologies, such as cell phones, email listserves, and groupware (software that facilitates organizational decision-making via democratic and collective methods[5]). Activists rely upon each other to gather important information, such as on-the-ground observations about the layout of a city's downtown area, which is useful for planning a protest, civil disobedience, and a variety of direct actions. If one's comrades know whom to contact from other communities, this is valuable information when seeking allies and broader solidarity. Most importantly, anarchist networks are premised upon the free access to information, whether it is mere data, facts, analysis, ideas, or theory. Consequently, anarchists place an emphasis on lowering the cost—economic and social—to information (via free 'zines, leaflets, Internet essay archives, or guerrilla radio

---

5   The Riseup Collective's "CrabGrass" software project is a prime example.

programs), the democratic creation of movement analyses (such as with the Independent Media Center model), and mass distribution of news (for example, the A-Infos News Service and its accompanying free radio project). To the extent that these information channels permeate every sector of anarchist movements, the more likely participants will be highly engaged in important movement debates and theorizing, will have up-to-date understanding of current events and movement activity, and will feel a sense of unity with each other (even if sometimes nuanced or contingent). The quality of information people can acquire in these networks will determine the level of social capital and thus influence the potential of movement personnel's ability to achieve their goals. Movements can aspire to accomplish their goals by wielding information as a tool to combat ignorance, confusion, censorship, and seclusion.

Coleman's final social capital form manifests in social norms, which facilitate certain actions while constraining others. If a movement norm exists that calls on participants to help each other out, even in extreme situations, then the movement will be stronger. Norms can facilitate social capital in all manner of situations. For example, if police attempt to place a fellow demonstrator under arrest during a physically confrontational protest, a common anarchist norm encourages other demonstrators to assist the person facing arrest. The norm of "de-arresting" exists when using "black bloc" tactics, which involves demonstrators physically pulling such an arrestee away from police officers, removing that demonstrator from police "custody." If the de-arresting is successful, the targeted person is pulled deeper into the bloc's ranks and helped to disappear from observing or pursuing police. This anarchist norm contributes to the social capital of all participants, as they understand that others will "have their back."

The norms—and potential sanctions—lobbied against those who deviate from these expectations within SMOs help to create and sustain a radical culture of both internal and external criticism. For instance, acting in the interest of the collective is often a SMO norm. Therefore, meetings and events are managed collectively, open-endedly, or with popular input—this fosters greater social trust. Also, as mentioned earlier, if illegal activities (civil disobedience, direct action, property destruction, etc.) are potentialities for the anarchist movement, participants tend to make broad, general statements in support of such actions, but withhold relevant details from individuals not within one's own affinity group. This norm of "security culture" prevents law enforcement from gaining accurate or useful information about an organization or action. To violate this norm, would result in informal sanctions from other anarchists. A "loose-lipped" individual (1) will be educated and pressured by others to understand the accompanying risks of sharing private information, (2) is unlikely to be trusted as much in the future, and (3) may perhaps be asked to leave the organization. A regular violation of such a norm (especially by multiple individuals) is apt to harm the social relations upon which social capital rests. For example, intervention by government and corporate actors (in the form of subversion, spying, and disruption) is more successful when the security culture norm is weak or nonexistent. In such instances, agent provocateurs may be used to disrupt, frame, or set-up activists (see Boykoff 2007). Thus, movement sanctions are important methods for improving adherence to important movement norms. Strong social trust in an organization may seem to enable the state's use of agent provocateurs, as people may unwisely place trust in a new member who is actually interested in spying or subversion. But, equally strong social norms against dangerous SMO behaviors could bulwark against misplaced trust, too.

Social capital benefits can also be generalizable. Arguably, a key objective of movements is to achieve changes that benefit a group of people larger than the movement's immediate participants. Thus, the social capital acquired by a particular movement can benefit members within an entire social category. For example, feminist movements create benefits for all women in society, not just participants in that movement. Anti-racist movements benefit the members of all disadvantaged groups (such as racial, ethnic, or religious minorities), not just those who populate anti-racist organizations.[6] Gains by anarchist move-

---

6 Additionally, feminist and anti-racist movements also benefit privileged people (e.g., men and whites), as the elimination of domination facilitates egalitarian social relations, happiness, and greater social trust (Williams 2012).

ments—to expand the domains of freedom, to challenge the legitimacy of hierarchical institutions, to create alternative institutions founded on radical values—indirectly benefit others in a society who can use such accomplishments for themselves (this extension may or may not actually enhance social capital itself, for everyone, though, but maybe just extend its immediate benefits). Thus, social capital's democratizing benefits are different from economic capital where usually only those who invest in such capital forms enjoy benefits.[7]

The Dualities and Disappearance of Social Capital

The most recent famous work on social capital in American sociology has been Robert Putnam's *Bowling Alone* (2000), which describes—in incredible detail—the long decline of social capital, community, and participation in American society.[8] His work describes a number of dualities, whose applications are worth exploring here.

A first crucial duality concerns what social capital efforts actually attempt to accomplish. Sometimes people intend to improve the strength of their existing social relationships and in other moments the goal is to expand

---

7   This, of course, introduces the problems of free-riding (see Olson 1965), which may be overcome by value-driven action as opposed to purely "rational" action, social pressures to participate, small-sized groups, and a fair and even distribution of collectives goods in society.

8   Some of Putnam's results are generalizable to other societies, too.

those relationships outward to new groups. Both these efforts are crucial for the long-term vitality of social capital and human communities. Putnam (2000) describes these two efforts as bonding and bridging, respectively. Social capital bonding aims to improve the capital amongst those who already share relationships, enhancing their ties to each other. Bonding is an internally focused social capital effort. For anarchists, bonding helps to create intra-movement solidarity. By hooking-up and bringing closer together those who identify as anarchists, a movement enhances the connections amongst individuals and the trust within that movement. This bonding is crucial, since without internal social capital, coordination is difficult—if not impossible. Various groups within a poorly-bonded movement will not feel a sense of solidarity for each other, nor extend mutual aid when needed.

Social capital bridging attempts to create connections between otherwise unconnected people and groups. Bridging crosses divides that may exist and bring diverse groups into closer contact and affinity. It is an externally- or outwardly-focused effort to enhance social capital. For example, anarchists may seek to improve relations between anarchists with divergent ideological orientations, such as anarcho-syndicalists and anti-civilization anarchists. Additionally, anarchist movements regularly pursue bridging whenever speaking to or working with non-anarchists. Thus, any broader organizing effort involves social capital bridging. For example, the 1999 demonstrations in Seattle against the World Trade Organization brought diverse people together, uniting them under a radical critique of corporate-led globalization and, eventually, capitalism. By connecting anarchists to non-anarchists, the connections multiply and trust grows across movements and in relation to the general population. For any movement to grow and spread its ideas, bridging is a crucial prerequisite. It thrusts movements into contact with those with different ideas or those who are not yet "converted" and hopes to gain new adherents, allies, sympathetic audiences, or at least to not make new enemies.

A second duality Putnam explores is between those who either choose to do formal or informal social organizing. He identifies "machers" as those who invest lots of time in formal organizations. These people are the heart-and-soul of community groups and the driving forces that make things happen. As such, machers are more organized and purposeful with their actions. Many anarchists engage in macher activity: doing community organizing with diverse non-anarchist populations (homeless rights organizations, immigrant populations, pro-choice clinics, militant trade unions and workers, and others). Other machers consciously form organizations—explicitly "anarchist" or not—through which further activities and campaigns can occur. Transparency, outreach, and formality are key efforts of anarchist machers. When acting openly, machers are displaying values to others, clearly declaring their intentions, and are making themselves accountable to others. The extent to which macher anarchists speak and act reliably, they will likely incur trust from others.

Another population, called "schmoozers", spends much of its time engaged in informal conversation and communion, eschewing efforts to wade through formal organizations. Schmoozers are more spontaneous and flexible in their schedules and efforts, and more willing to relate to people individually as opposed to groups of people in formal settings. Many anarchists, of course, pursue these activities, too. Anarchists often hangout with each other and meet people in informal scenes, socializing at parties, squats and social centers, after political rallies, or at other meeting places. The anarchist schmoozer may give intense attention to a small number of people or maybe even just one person; this creates a strong bond, although typically fewer overall connections. Schmoozers create more spaces for private trust to emerge, independent of formal decisions made in organizations and public coalitions. Schmoozers exchange political analysis, ideas, and values in intimate settings, especially when such information is of a private nature. The sharing accomplished in these informal environments enhances individual trust. Both the machers and schmoozers seem to reflect qualities of Etzioni's (1965) categories of instrumental and expressive leaders, respectively—the first contributes in practical and clearly defined ways, while the second contributes to the overall mental well-being and motivation of groups.

A key concern to Putnam (2000) is the comprehensive decline in social capital in the US (changes elsewhere in the world have not been investigated as thoroughly as by Putnam). He considers this decline in social capital to be detrimental for civil society and for representative democracy. For American anarchists, other severe consequences result from declining social capital, which does not bode well for revolutionary social transformation.

According to Putnam, there are various, general sources of this decline in social capital. With each source, it is worth considering how they affect anarchist movements and such movements' capacities to pursue a revolutionary agenda. First, the pressures of time and money, have forced people to work more, work longer, and have less time for community and social activities. This is particularly true for middle-class women who have traditionally had more opportunity to pursue these activities because male-breadwinners' salaries allowed them to stay out of the labor market. There is a seemingly endless drive to and economic imperative for work in order to pay bills, consume products, and build individual careers; all of this detracts from the ability of people to focus on others and, thus, foster transformative social capital.

If the anarchist movement still had a strong anarcho-syndicalist orientation, this increased focus on work might serve as an entry point into radical workplace and union politics. However, this ideological subvariant within anarchism (at least in the US) is about as weak as the overall labor movement's community organizing efforts. Consequently, everyone—including many anarchists—spends more time doing things that do not directly result in greater political awareness, class-consciousness, or radicalism. A possible counter-balance to the destructive results of this factor decreasing social capital is potentially simple: work less. Instead of spending so much time engaged in wage labor, an anarchist could—indeed, many already are—find alternative ways to have their economic needs met. Whether through house cooperatives, food-sharing networks, and other mutual aid projects, people could further extract themselves from labor markets and capitalist enterprise. To do so, would require developing economic survival mechanisms that transcend anarchist subcultures. The benefit for social capital would be two-fold: people would have more non-employed time available for community and social capital building, and the necessities of alternative survival would themselves reinforce stronger social ties with people.

A second source of decreased American social capital is mobility and sprawl. For decades, urban dwellers have been up-rooted (willing and unwillingly) from their traditional, more-or-less organically-created neighborhoods. The clearest indicator of this is the dramatic growth of suburbs, which are generally more affluent, white, and inaccessible to other groups. This suburbanization—as well as the block-busting, red-lining, white-flight, and other racial dynamics that helped drive it—has created relatively homogeneous neighborhoods, in terms of both class and race. But, as a permaculturalist would argue, monocultures are not only devastating for nature and food systems, but so too for communities. Impoverished people and people of color residing in central cities lack the economic and cultural capital that affluent individuals took with them to the suburbs. People in the wealthier suburbs lose contact with people un-alike them, develop callousness towards the problems of "others", and simply do not understand what is going on a few miles from where they live. Since many Americans move regularly (even every year), there is little chance for people to develop long-term, stable relationships with neighbors or to feel responsibility for one's community. The sprawling nature of suburbs makes it more difficult for residents to reach other areas they seek to go, thus requiring long periods of travel, usually solitary in cars. None of these factors bode well for maintaining social capital.

The solution to this problem is simple to state, but harder to accomplish. Anarchists argue there is no easy way to create community—it is hard work, which requires establishing long-term trust. To do this, people must be brought into closer contact together. Classic community organizing approaches do this: bring diverse people that share common interests together in a room and allow them to see each other's human worth, figure out how to trust each other, and articulate a shared vision and course of future action. This is, unfortunately, easier said than done, of course. But, anarchists often advocate clustering together in communities. During the early-2000s, after the protests against the Republican National Convention, I heard rumors that there were entire anarchist neighborhoods in Philadelphia. And other cities have communities like this: the Exarchia neighborhood of Athens, Greece has a strong anarchist presence, as do many areas with squatted social centers in cities like Barcelona and Rome. In my own experience, the Akron Catholic Worker (which was not necessarily anarchist) had four houses on a single city block, which allowed for residents and volunteers to share resources, do communal activities, and maintain strong face-to-face lines of communication. Living in community does not require living communally, of course, although group-houses, squats, intentional communities, and other co-living options help. Close proximity is itself a partial solution to the malaise that long distance inflicts upon social capital.

Third, Putnam observes that technology and mass media has helped to destroy social capital. A key culprit is television. There are numerous reasons why TV has had a detrimental impact upon social ties, but two bear repeating. First, even though people may watch TV in groups, it is usually viewed alone. Moreover, although TV can be viewed collectively, it does not mean that it is a collective activity, since the focus is upon the TV, not each other. It is difficult to communicate, share, and focus upon anything else except the TV program. Since TV watching has been shown (Kubey & Csikszentmihalyi 2004) to induce a cognitive state comparable to sleep, TV viewing numbs our abilities to interact with others. A second reason why TV is detrimental pertains to the portrayals typical to TV. Deviance, law-breaking, extreme personalities and behaviors, violence, individualism, and other programming themes suggest to viewers that people in the outside world cannot be trusted.[9] The more TV people watch, the less they believe others can be trusted.

The anarchist solution to the scourge of hierarchical TV programming is not for the insertion of anarchist TV programming on mainstream channels. Instead, most anarchists have advocated a solution similar to that for overworking: turn-off the TV! It is impressive how much extra time can be liberated in people's days when it is not wasted-away with idle TV viewing. While this is a hard sell to audiences who are seduced by highly sophisticated and well-funded programming (the purpose, of which is to deliver advertisements to audiences), it is still a much-needed prognosis. Instead of relying upon stupefying TV news to convey information, anarchists ought to pursue and expand upon the strategies already used by many anarchist newspapers (and within other media), like the UK's *Freedom*, which engages directly with on-going events, adding a subtle anarchist-spin, analytical perspective, and aesthetic. The key is engagement: one of the benefits of Indymedia was that people could participate in the creation and propagation of media, but do so directly with each other and discuss it without proxy (something that TV has never allowed for).[10] By communicating with people about things that matter—during days that have

---

9   This is particularly true for some TV programming, but less true for other programming (Lee at al. 2003). Additionally, TV viewing done with non-strangers (e.g., family members) further reduces social trust (Patulny 2011).

far more time and less propaganda—there is a greater likelihood of growing social capital. Then, in lieu of individualized activities (like TV-watching), collective activities deserve encouragement: neighborhood sports, potluck meals, festivals, collective work projects, and participatory entertainment.

Lastly, one of the most serious sources of declining social capital, according to Putnam, was an inter-generational one. From generation to generation, ever since those who came of age during the Great Depression and World War II, people have had less and less involvement in community. Newer generations have been more severely affected by the above phenomenon and have not had the same crucial community-building opportunities that earlier generations have. Baby Boomers were considered highly individualistic by their parents, as was the so-called "me generation" of those growing-up in the 1980s. Current cohorts will likely be even more individualistic, as they rely upon personal consumption and technology to differentiate them (often remotely) from each other.[11]

Radical socialization was one of the main ways that classical age anarchists kept inter-generational ideas and

---

10 Of course, another reason for high rates of activist participation... ...with Indymedia, pertains to its organizational structure which imitates desired anarchist social relations.

11 Recent American generations have become more narcissistic and less empathetic (Twenge & Foster 2010, Konrath et al. 2011).

values strong (see Williams 2011). Anarchist families and communities kept anarchism alive in order to pass it along to youth. A strong, capitalist-adversarial, working-class culture enabled this. However, with the deliberate destruction of working-class culture, the buying-off of class allegiances, and the elimination of whole sectors of the economy that employed working-class people, these cultures of resistance disappeared. Combined with political repression with the Palmer Raids and the McCarthy era, new radicals often had to re-discover older traditions for themselves, independent of an older generation who would have otherwise taught them directly (see Cornell's (2011) study of anarchism in-between the classical and contemporary periods). By focusing on inter-generational anarchist socialization, the ideas can persist and possibly strengthen overtime. But focusing on maintaining anarchism over the life-course, by continual, on-going socialization and education projects, anarchist movements can keep adherents connected to movements as they age and change their roles in society (especially become parents). Making sure that anarchism does not remain the domain of a youthful age group is key. Designing movement activities supportive of people's familial obligations by providing childcare and having safe, family-friendly events, will further this end (Law & Martens 2012). Also, giving older people a role in anarchist movements will keep people around longer; thus, a static movement that exclusively emphasizes militant street protest is unwise, as it will exclude people with reduced physical capacities, whether due to ability or age.

Taken together, these strategies suggest ways to reinvigorate social capital, especially for anarchist movements. Future research could focus on a number of related issues and questions. First, how did classic age anarchists speak of and write about social trust? What do contemporary anarchists do that consciously bonds and bridges social capital? And, who are the likely recruits for anarchist movements? In other words, who has a positive orientation toward generalized social trust, but does not have political trust in authority figures? Existing survey data could be used to determine which types of people tend to be horizontalists or hierarchicalists.

References

Bourdieu, Pierre. 1986. "The Forms of Capital". Pp. 241-258 in *Handbook of Theory and Research for the Sociology of Education*, edited by J.G. Richardson. New York: Greenwood.

Boykoff, Jules. 2007. *Beyond Bullets: The Suppression of Dissent in the United States*. Oakland, CA: AK Press.

Coleman, James. 1988. "Social Capital in the Creation of Human Capital". *American Journal of Sociology*, 94: S95-S120.

Cornell, Andrew. 2011. "A New Anarchism Emerges, 1940-1954". *Journal for the Study of Radicalism*, 5 (1): 105-131.

Diani, Marco. 1997. "Social Movements and Social Capital: A Network Perspective on Movement Outcomes". *Mobilization*, 2 (2), September: 129-148.

Edwards, Bob and John D. McCarthy. 2004. "Resources and

Social Movement Mobilization". Pp. 116-152 in *The Blackwell Companion to Social Movements*, edited by D.A. Snow, S.A. Soule, & H. Kriesi. Malden, MA: Blackwell.

Ehrlich, Howard J. 1996. "Anarchism and Formal Organization". Pp. 56-68 in *Reinventing Anarchy, Again*, edited by H.J. Ehrlich. Edinburgh: AK Press.

Etzioni, Amitai. 1965. "Dual Leadership in Complex Organizations". *American Sociological Review*, 30 (5): 688-698.

Giddens, Anthony. 1984. *The Constitution of Society: Outline of the Theory of Structuration*. Cambridge: Polity.

Graeber, David. 2009. *Direct Action: An Ethnography*. Oakland, CA: AK Press.

Konrath, Sara H., Edward H. O'Brien, and Courtney Hsing. 2011. "Changes in Dispositional Empathy in American College Students Over Time: A Meta-Analysis". *Personality and Social Psychology Review*, 15: 180-198.

Kropotkin, Peter. 1972. *Mutual Aid: A Factor in Evolution*. London: Allen Lane.

Kubey, Robert and Mihaly Csikszentmihalyi. 2004. "Television Addiction is No Mere Metaphor". *Scientific American*, 14 (1): 48-55.

Law, Victoria and China Martens. 2012. *Don't Leave Your Friends Behind: Concrete Ways to Support Families in Social Justice Movements and Communities*. Oakland, CA: PM Press.

Lee, GangHeong, Joseph N. Cappella, and Brian Southwell. 2003. "The Effects of News and Entertainment on Interpersonal Trust: Political Talk Radio, Newspapers, and Television". *Mass Communication & Society*, 6 (4): 413-434.

Mayer, Margit. 2003. "The Onward Sweep of Social Capital: Causes and Consequences for Understanding Cities, Communities, and Urban Movements". *International Journal of Urban and Regional Research*, 27 (1): 110-132.

McCarthy, John D. and Mayer N. Zald. 1977. "Resource Mobilization and Social Movements: A Partial Theory". *American Journal of Sociology*, 82: 1212-1241.

Milstein, Cindy. 2010. *Anarchism and Its Aspirations*. Oakland, CA: AK Press.

Olson, Mancur. 1965. *The Logic of Collective Action: Public Goods and the Theory of Groups*. Cambridge, MA: Harvard University Press.

Patulny, Roger. 2011. "Social Trust, Social Partner Time and Television Time". *Social Indicators Research*, 101: 289-293.

Paxton, Pamela. 2002. "Social Capital and Democracy: An Interdependent Relationship". *American Sociological Review*, 67 (2): 254-277.

Putnam, Robert D. 2000. *Bowling Alone: The Collapse and Revival of American Community*. New York: Simon & Schuster.

Shantz, Jeff. 2010. *Constructive Anarchy: Building Infrastructures of Resistance*. Burlington, VT: Ashgate.

Smith, Jackie. 1998. "Global Civil Society?: Transnational Social Movement Organizations and Social Capital". *American Behavioral Scientist*, 42 (1): 93-107.

Tilly, Charles. 2004. *Social Movements: 1768-2004*. Boulder, CO: Paradigm.

Twenge, Jean M. and Joshua D. Foster. 2010. "Birth Cohort Increases in Narcissistic Personality Traits Among American

College Students, 1982-2009" *Social Psychological and Personality Science*, 1: 99-106.

Ward, Colin. 1996. *Anarchy in Action*. London: Freedom Press.

Williams, Dana M. 2011. "Why Revolution Ain't Easy: Violating Norms, Re-socializing Society". *Contemporary Justice Review*, 14 (2), June: 167-187.

Williams, Dana M. 2012. "From Top to Bottom, a Thoroughly Stratified World: An Anarchist View of Inequality and Domination". *Race, Gender & Class*, 19 (3-4): 9-34.

Artwork of Beehive Design Collective | Detail of the bees gathering in creative work, from their graphic narrative, ¡Mesoamerica Resiste! (See page 357.)

3 | Marginalization of Anarchism within Mainstream Criminology: A Content Analysis

Christopher Howell

I n learning about anarchist criminology it is important to learn where and what (if anything) is presented about anarchism in academia. In order to learn what is presented, I conducted a content analysis of introductory criminology textbooks in order to measure the quantity and quality of content presented on anarchism in introductory (1st and 2nd year) criminology. Anarchism is a radical approach to criminology that has important ideals (absolute freedoms, mutual aid, and state abolishment). The theory critically analyzes society in a manner significantly different than any other criminological theory. The content analysis measures to what extent (if at all) anarchism is presented in academic criminology.

Measuring the extent that anarchism is depicted in introductory criminology is beneficial to understanding the theory itself. In my experience in academia, I found that the introductory years do not present anarchism at all. Thus, the content analysis helps show the extent that it is missing, and leads to a theory development of anarchism. The content analysis can help create awareness among professors, students, publishers, and others in understanding how anarchism is presented in introductory criminology textbooks.

Introductory criminology classes are a student's initial exposure to the field. These classes provide the foundation or framework for students. The large majority of classes assign textbooks for the class, which provides a framework for the curriculum of what will be studied. Ross (2008) states, introductory textbooks are a crucial function in "framing and interpreting the discussion of important academic disciplines by defining the boundaries for the inclusion and exclusion of appropriate discourse" (p. 447). Naturally not all textbook content is covered and an instructor may place higher importance on some areas over others; nonetheless the textbook provides a good idea of what is likely to be included or at least an understanding of what is available to be covered. From my academic experience, anarchism is not covered in introductory classroom textbooks.

To help understand the extent that anarchism is presented in introductory criminology textbooks, I conducted a content analysis of all the introductory criminology textbooks (8 textbooks) from Kwantlen Polytechnic University (KPU) for the Fall 2013 semester (13 classes) and the six most popular introductory criminology textbooks from Amazon.ca.

The goal of the research is to measure the extent that anarchism is presented in introductory criminology textbooks. The research is both quantitative and qualitative in design: anarchism is quantitatively compared with other relevant criminological theories and anarchism is qualitatively measured for accuracy and depth. The methodology will be further explained later.

Context

The theoretical perspective of anarchism is politically oriented. Similar to Marxism, it aims to reconstruct the socio-political structure. Anarchism promotes individual liberties and follows a do-it-yourself model. It is a radical theory that has historical and contemporary connections to criminology. Historically, there have been exchanges between Peter Kropotkin (an early anarchist) and Cesare Lombroso (an early positivist criminologist) roughly in the late-1800s. Throughout history there have been anarchist critiques of the criminal justice system, suggestions for positive and humanizing changes that have influenced contemporary theories such as peacemaking criminology, and restructuring society in a manner that involves all members of the community. The point here being that anarchism has been involved in criminological issues and theoretical connections for an extensive period of time. The aim of this content analysis is to describe the extent and quality by which anarchism is presented in introductory criminology (1st and 2nd year classes) textbooks.

There was no previous literature found that measures anarchism, but there are other studies that measure introductory criminological theories. Wright's (2000) study found how little critical criminology is presented in introductory criminology by measuring the amount of content in introductory criminology textbooks. Wright (2000) conducted a quantitative analysis of all known American introductory criminology textbooks from 1990-1999 (34 textbooks) and measured them 'per inch' of content, and then compared the textbooks based on the authors' theoretical bias ('consensus,' 'conflict,' 'interdisciplinary,' 'noncritical,' 'other discipline,' or 'no discernible'). Wright (2000) also qualitatively measured the accuracy of the content presented and, again, compared the textbooks based on the authors' theoretical bias. I do not look to the authors' theoretical bias but do think it is important to compare the theory differentiation Wright used; consensus versus conflict (critical).

Wagner (2006) replicated Wright's study of critical criminology instead using the top 10 Amazon.com introductory criminology textbooks as his sample. Both studies (Wright, 2000; Wagner, 2006) found a disproportionate amount of content covered on consensus theories versus critical theories and the findings were compounded when taking into account the authors' theoretical bias. The researchers found that critical criminology is largely excluded in relation to consensus based theories. Thus, I chose to include at least one theory from each.

I look to take a similar approach to measuring the quantity and quality of content, but I do not comparatively analyze textbooks based on theoretical bias. Although quantitatively measuring the amount of content is beneficial for contextualizing and comparing the extent of theories. Measuring the quality of content is, also, important. Length typically equates to amount of time and effort put into an area, however one author may put in a more concise and accurate paragraph that another author takes two pages to write.

Wright (2000) and Wagner (2006) looked at critical criminology in general as well as specific theories within the field. For instance, they (Wright, 2000; Wagner, 2006) both examined the extent that Marxism, feminism, postmodernism, and other theories were presented in introductory criminology textbooks. Notably, Wright (2000) did include anarchism in his research however it was included within a miscellaneous group that contained other theories in the findings. Wagner (2006) did not include anarchism in his analysis. The results of the miscellaneous group were 1.62 pages of coverage, per text (Wright, 2000). Even without isolating anarchism in the study it is apparent that the miscellaneous group is marginalized.

From this research, it is hypothesized that anarchism will be marginalized in introductory criminology. Nonetheless, this research will help provide a clearer understanding of the extent that anarchism is presented in introductory criminology, in addition to it being a part of a larger project that aims to (re-)connect anarchism to criminology. This initial piece helps better understand the extent to which anarchism is excluded, while suggesting that this exclusion is unjustified.

Although my content analysis does not look to explain and/or discover the effects of marginalizing knowledge versus promoting knowledge or the influence that certain societal structures (e.g. capitalist) have on these effects. Reece Walters (2003) explains some reasons for these adverse affects; explaining why certain factions of knowledge are marginalized while others are promoted, and the connection this has to a capitalist society. This argument is important to note but I do not look to pursue finding data for the argument as it is not conducive to my overall thesis. My content analysis looks to measure the extent and quality of anarchist criminology content presented.

Anarchism

Anarchism is a truly radical theory that takes a left-wing approach of crime and criminology, which helps widen the spectrum of thought in criminology. Just as it is important to understand classical views or conservatism (right-wing theories) in criminology. Yet, from my experience in academia, I have extensively read the right-wing approaches, while anarchism has been excluded.

Anarchism has several different forms that derive from differing theorists. The theorist I focus on is Peter Kropotkin. Kropotkin is an early leading anarchist that was involved in historical debates with founding criminologists. Kropotkin wrote on anarchism in the late-1800s in many books and articles that include *"Mutual Aid"* and *"The Conquest of Bread,"* which theorize communal anarchism and conceptualize anarchist ideals. Kropotkin argues for a societal structure without an authoritative power that requires certain ideals: absolute freedoms, mutual aid, and positive progression for humanity. Kropotkin (1939; 2006) argues that persons are generally good (not egoists) and under an appropriate societal structure (anarchist structure), we could work well together to mutually and individually benefit.

The current research focuses on three key areas of potential intersection between introductory criminology textbooks and anarchism: 1) Content on Cesare Lombroso; 2) Within a Critical/Radical criminology section; and 3) Within content on peacemaking criminology. First Cesare Lombroso: there have been historical exchanges between Lombroso, an influential positivist thinker, and Peter Kropotkin, an influential communal anarchist. Lombroso published several works (1890; 1900; 2006) that analyzed anarchists in order to find and measure physical deformities that cause criminality. Lombroso analyzed anarchists because he believed they were "criminal in nature." Kropotkin (1887) objected to Lombroso's findings, methodology, and conclusions. These critiques of Lombroso's work resonate to this day when Lombroso's work is presented. Thus, two potential areas to include anarchism are in Lombroso's research on criminal anarchists or citing Kropotkin in objections to Lombroso's work.

A second potential intersection of anarchism and criminology is in a textbook's section on critical or radical criminology. Introductory criminology textbooks often present one or more sections on critical or radical theories. Critical criminology refers to the unmasking of political assumptions—moral and ideological—that reaffirm power and economic inequalities in society through "the 'science' of criminology" (Taylor, Walton, and Young, 1975, pp. 4/5). Radical criminology incorporates the definition of critical criminology and extends it to more than merely description, "it must engage in theory and research as *praxis*" (Taylor, Walton, and Young, 1975, p. 24, emphasis in original). There is overlap between the two sections, as all radical theories are critical in nature but not all critical theories are radical in nature. For instance Marxist criminology is an example of a radical theory that is also a critical theory, while postmodernism is a critical theory but not a radical theory. Similar to Marxism, anarchism is a radical approach to criminology, thus it could potentially be included in either or both sections of a textbook.

Lastly, a key topic that could potentially intersect or include anarchism is in the presentation of peacemaking criminology. Peacemaking criminology is a nonviolent, collective effort (offender, victim, family, community members, and so on) to criminology that includes restorative justice and empowers individual freedoms to peacefully respond to and work with social harms (Quinney, 2000; Tifft and Sullivan, 1980; 2006). Some presentations of peacemaking criminology doctrines derive from anarchism, particularly from peacemaking criminology presented by Tifft and Sullivan. Tifft and Sullivan have written on both anarchism (1980) and peacemaking criminology (2001; 2004; 2006). In referencing peacemaking criminology and restorative justice (a form of peacemaking criminology), Larry Tifft and Dennis Sullivan (2006) (re-)connect the persons connected to the harm to the community, and work on the healing process. Notably, Tifft and Sullivan directly cite Peter Kropotkin in their work (1980; 2001; 2004; 2006). In addition to citing Kropotkin, Tifft and Sullivan's conceptualization of peacemaking criminology has clear humanizing connections to the community through solidarity, mutual aid, and mutual support.

Tifft and Sullivan are not the only theorists that present peacemaking criminology. Richard Quinney is coined as the founder of peacemaking criminology and his presentation of the theory continues to be influential today. However, Quinney takes a significantly different approach than Tifft and Sullivan in arguing for peacemaking criminology. Quinney focuses on the individual, arguing that in order to work compassionately together, it requires a mind shift, from a western, rational-egoist mind to an eastern compassionate one (2000). Quinney's (2000) conceptualization of compassion and a compassionate mind draws from Buddhism and Zen, which connects heavily to spirituality and metaphysical arguments.

An issue that arises from Quinney's presentation is that it presents a false dilemma or leads to an unmeasurable variable. The false dilemma is that our minds can be either wholly compassionate or wholly rational. This seems to oversimplify the mind's components into being incompatible with one another. You can either be compassionate or you can be rational. However, this statement seems counter-intuitive. For one, I feel that my mind can be compassionate when a friend talks to me about a dying loved one in one situation, and my mind can be rational in planning for a future career. Secondly, I feel that even in one particular situation, my mind can be both compassionate and rational. For instance, if a person was sentenced to the death penalty, I could empathize in a compassionate way with the convicted and their family and the finality of their life. I could also rationally look at the cost/benefit of the death penalty and the state's ability to control one's life. The same subject brings about differing angles to the topic that help in different ways. The point is that it is mistaken to dichotomize the mind to either compassion or rationality, and to assume that our mind is capable of entirely committing to one or the other.

Tifft and Sullivan (1980) argue for peacemaking criminology by demystifying and broadening the concept 'social harm'. Away from the individual blaming focus that the criminal justice system takes to also include institutions (state, business, etc.) that, also, cause social harms, yet are legitimized. For instance, the rise of poverty levels due to a larger income inequality gap, the disproportionate amount of Aboriginals in jails, detaining protestors at the G20 summit in Toronto for expressing free speech, and the list goes on. Tifft and Sullivan (1980) argue that harm breeds further harm, relying on a state that focuses on harm producing responses to crime, as seen in crime control and punitive measures, breeds further harm within society. Hence, humanistic, community based responses such as restorative justice, which do not rely on the state, (re-)connect the victim, offender, and community, which leads to a more humanizing, peaceful result.

I do not believe that Quinney's presentation is inconsistent with Tifft and Sullivan as both presentations argue for compassion and community connection. However, Quinney focuses on the individual and spirituality in his argument, while Tifft and Sullivan focus on the individual and structuring of society. So, it makes more sense why Tifft and Sullivan cite Kropotkin and Quinney does not. Tifft and Sullivan's presentation derives from communal anarchist tenets. In measuring the extent that anarchism is presented within peacemaking criminology, it is important to also note who the authors of the textbooks use for the presentation, as Kropotkin should be connected or cited in Tifft and Sullivan's presentation but not necessarily in Quinney's.

Methodology

Previous literature (Wright, 2000; Walters, 2003; Wagner, 2006) has shown there is a link between knowledge promoted and knowledge marginalized. Walters (2003) argues that the "production of criminological knowledge" is increasingly representative of State and power interests, which are, typically, connected to research funding. Wright's (2000) study supports Walters' argument in finding that critical criminology approaches are often marginalized. I look specifically to measure anarchist criminology, as Wright (2000) merely grouped anarchism within a "miscellaneous" section included in his overall look at critical criminology. I include Walters' argument to show that I have some assumptions on certain results that need to be explicit.

KPU is a Canadian post-secondary institution. My research measures all introductory criminology textbooks (8 textbooks) from introductory criminology classes that present sociological based theories (2 classes) during the Fall 2013 semester at KPU. This research, also, measures the top 6 textbooks from Amazon.ca. The two classes at KPU that introduce sociological based theories are titled "Introduction to Criminology" and "Sociological Explanations of Criminal Behavior." The former is a first year class, the latter is a second year class. Both classes provide students with initial exposure to the broad field of criminology and include sociological based theories in the curriculum. The first year class also includes topics other than criminological theories and areas than merely sociological based theories, and thus must include a broader amount of material than the second year class. The second year class is the earliest level criminology class dedicated to sociological based theories. The second year class is more thorough than the first year class, but is introductory in nature.

If anarchism is to be included in an introductory criminology textbook, it would be included as a sociological based theory in criminology. Sociological based theories of crime and deviant behavior refer to theories that study social order and structure, and their connection to collective and individual deviant behavior, which may include organizations and institutions (Rock, 2006; Sampson, 2000). This definition is not exhaustive of the topic, however it shows that the theories look at society's connection to crime and deviance, whether at a macro- or micro-level.

In addition to the KPU Fall 2013 textbooks, I chose to also measure the top six introductory criminology textbooks from Amazon.ca. Wagner (2006) and Ross and Rothe (2008) used Amazon.com (the American version) for their sample of introductory criminology textbooks. Wagner had similar findings to Wright whom used all known American textbooks from 1990-1999. Ross and Rothe (2008) focused on state crime, thus their findings are not relatable but the methodology is relevant. Since Amazon.ca is a top-selling textbook site in Canada, the sample collected will act as my control group as well as

helping gauge generalizability issues that arise from focusing on only one sample institution.

As per measuring methods, I chose to conduct a quantitative and qualitative analysis of the content. As the research focuses on anarchism, the qualitative analysis is
solely of anarchism. The qualitative analysis looks at the
accuracy and depth of the content. Accuracy will look at
whether the anarchist content presented is true or false.
For instance, if an author accredits a concept to the wrong
theorist or misconstrues the presentation of the theory.
The depth measures how thoroughly the textbook looks at
the theory. This is not merely connected to length, which
the quantitative analysis will help exemplify, as writing
can be shorter, more concise but have more depth on the
topic. The goal is to understand the quality of anarchism
presented in the textbooks.

The content is, also, quantitatively measured by count-
ing the number of lines of content on the relevant theory.
I chose to focus on number of lines as opposed to a word
count, inch measurement, or other measurement because
the content analysis is exploratory in nature and has a low
projection for anarchist content presented. It is likely that
there is such a high content gap that complete accuracy of
the amount of content is unnecessary. In addition, due to
time restraints a line count enables a more expeditious
project. If there is to be a larger amount of anarchist content than predicted, then a more accurate measurement
will be needed. If there is minimal to no content, then a
more general contextualization of the theory is sufficient

to help better understand the extent that anarchism is excluded from introductory criminology textbooks.

As textbooks come in different shapes and sizes, the research ensured to produce results from each textbook first in order to more accurately compare the overall findings based on a relative percentage. Each book will produce differing lengths that do not necessarily mean the textbook covers a theory more relative to other theories. For instance if one book included 100 lines of anarchism and 1,000 total lines of content, while another book included 50 lines of anarchism and 100 total lines of content, the second book includes fewer lines, but more content relative to the other theories which is a focus of the research.

In order to contextualize the presentation of anarchism, I chose to comparatively measure it against strain theory, Marxism, and peacemaking criminology. Strain theory is a prominent consensus based theory. Marxism is a prominent critical and radical theory. Peacemaking criminology is a critical and radical theory that, depending on which theorist is cited, derives from anarchism. The goal is to quantitatively compare anarchism with particular theories; a consensus based theory, a critical and radical theory, and a theory that derives from anarchism.

Findings

The research found that strain theory, the prominent consensus theory, tended to have the largest amount of content, then Marxism, then peacemaking criminology, and finally anarchism. The research does not show whether consensus theories dominate content (or not) in introductory criminology textbooks from the sample researched. Notably, there are typically one or two chapters on critical criminology while there are consistently more chapters on consensus based theories so their findings likely remain true, but further research would need to be done to replicate Wright's study.

As mentioned earlier, there are three key topic areas that anarchism or Kropotkin's work could be linked to: Cesare Lombroso, critical or radical criminology, or peacemaking criminology. All textbooks with the exception of one (Cullen & Agnew, 2011) had content on Lombroso. None of those textbooks had any discussions about Lombroso's research on anarchists nor Kropotkin's objections to Lombroso's research.

▶ TABLE 1: Content Comparison of KPU Criminology Textbooks: Anarchism Compared with: Strain Theory; Marxism; Peace-making Criminology

KPU Text-books	Strain Theory	Marxism	Peace-making Crim-inology	Anarchism
Book 1	247 lines / 60.6%	80 lines/ 19.7%	80 lines/ 19.7%	0 lines/ 0%
Book 2	580 lines / 45.7%	617 lines/ 48.7%	64 lines/ 5.0%	19 lines/ 1.5%
Book 3*	2,835 lines/ 63.3%	965 lines/ 21.6%	678 lines/ 15.1%	0 lines/ 0%
Book 4	76 lines/ 28.2%	128 lines/ 47.4%	66 lines/ 24.4%	0 lines/ 0%
Book 5*	212 lines / 86.9%	32 lines/ 13.1%	0 lines/ 0%	0 lines/ 0%
Book 6	566 lines / 53.5%	427 lines/ 40.3%	66 lines/ 6.2%	0 lines/ 0%
Book 7	122 lines / 27.0%	244 lines/ 54.0%	86 lines/ 19.0%	0 lines/ 0%
Book 8	506 lines / 38.1%	486 lines/ 36.6%	337 lines/ 25.3%	0 lines/ 0%
Average %	50.4%	35.1%	14.3%	.19%

* Book is in both KPU and Amazon.ca sample.

▼TABLE 2: Content Comparison of Top 6 Amazon.ca Criminology Textbooks: Anarchism as Compared with: Strain Theory; Marxism; Peace-making Criminology

Amazon. ca Top 6	Strain Theory	Marxism	Peace-making Crim-inology	Anarchism
Book 1	932 lines / 54.2%	649 lines/ 37.7%	125 lines/ 7.3%	14 lines/ 0.8%
Book 2	205 lines / 56.0%	123 lines/ 33.6%	38 lines/ 10.4%	0 lines/ 0%
Book 3	731 lines / 62.6%	365 lines/ 31.3%	71 lines/ 6.1%	0 lines/ 0%
Book 4	677 lines / 66.5%	341 lines/ 33.5%	0 lines/ 0%	0 lines/ 0%
Book 5*	2,835 lines/ 63.3%	965 lines/ 21.6%	678 lines/ 15.1%	0 lines/ 0%
Book 6*	212 lines/ 86.9%	32 lines/ 13.1%	0 lines/ 0%	0 lines/ 0%
Average %	64.9%	28.5%	6.5%	0.13%

* Book is in both KPU and Amazon.ca sample.

As per anarchist content under the subject heading of critical or radical criminology, there was one Amazon.ca textbook that contained 14 lines of anarchist content for its description of constitutive criminology, which was in a "radical and critical criminology" section (Akers & Sellers, 2013, p. 239). Otherwise, there were no books that included anarchism in the critical or radical section of the textbook and none of the textbooks presented the theory.

In terms of connecting anarchism to peacemaking criminology, most of the textbooks presented peacemaking criminology according to Quinney. One of the few textbooks that presented according to Tifft and Sullivan presented seven lines on "mutual aid" (Siegel & McCormick, 2010, p. 340). Mutual aid is a term conceptualized by Kropotkin yet he was not cited in connection to the term.

The results from the content analysis are slightly worse than projected from the previous literature. Anarchism was presented for a total of 33 lines (19 lines from one KPU textbook and 14 lines from one Amazon.ca textbook). The 19 lines from the one KPU textbook resulted in 1.5% of the total relevant content in the particular textbook and an average of 0.19% for all the KPU textbooks. The 14 lines from the one Amazon.ca textbook resulted in 0.81% of the total relevant content in the particular textbook and an average of 0.13% from all the Amazon.ca textbooks.

As per the qualitative analysis, there was minimal amount of content presenting anarchism, thus minimal content to analyze; 33 lines. First, the 19 lines from the KPU textbook that had content presented on "mutual aid" from a section in peacemaking criminology: Peacemaking criminology was presented according to Tifft and Sullivan's presentation of the theory. The content did not cite Peter Kropotkin nor did it connect the theory explicitly with anarchism. Peter Kropotkin (1939) should be connected to mutual aid, since he dedicated an anarchist book to the topic titled, *"Mutual Aid"*. The presentation of the term is consistent with Kropotkin's presentation of the concept. As the content was only 19 pages, the content did not go in depth about the concept, however it did connect it to a humanizing and community response to crime (Siegel & McCormick, 2010, pp. 340)—peacemaking criminology response—which is consistent with Kropotkin's argument for communal anarchism (Kropotkin, 1927). Thus the 19 lines on anarchism from the KPU textbook are accurate and shallow.

The 14 lines from the Amazon.ca textbook did explicitly state "anarchism" in the textbook, however it was used as an example to help describe a larger field; "constitutive criminology" as presented by Dragan Milovanovic and Stuart Henry (Akers & Sellers, 2013, p. 239). The content was not specifically about anarchism but did provide characteristics that anarchism shares with other constitutive criminological theories. Since the intention of including anarchism is for a larger field, the content included is deemed "not applicable" as it is neither an accurate nor inaccurate description of anarchism. Anarchism is used to describe another field, therefore, the 14 lines of anarchism from the Amazon.ca textbook is neither applicable for accuracy nor depth. Even though anarchism is used to help exemplify features of a broader field, the lines are included in the research because it presents the student with a name of a theory, thus could potentially plant a seed for future interest.

Conclusion

First and foremost, anarchism is not presented as a theory in the introductory criminology textbooks measured. One anarchist concept is mentioned in connection to peacemaking criminology without connecting where the concept derives from. In the other instance, it is used to help exemplify a larger field. Neither textbook that included anarchism described the theory or contextualized it seriously in the field of criminology, while the rest of the textbooks excluded anarchism completely.

Limitations of this research: there are issues with generalizability and validity of the research. The content analysis is a great way to progress anarchist criminology starting with an early anarchist (Peter Kropotkin). The content analysis could benefit from randomizing the sample group and comparing with a sample group from other nations, since, as Walters (2003) argues, different state structures will produce different marginalized and promoted knowledge.

Anarchism is excluded from introductory criminology textbooks. The exclusion may be purposeful or accidental, future research that aims to explain the rationale for this exclusion is necessary. There is likely no single answer, rather several that produce the result. It is also likely that it is due to a combination of publisher influence (Keenan, 2012), author knowledge or bias (Abrutyn, 2013; Ross and Rothe, 2008; Wright, 2000), and the political nature of anarchism (Arrigo, 1999; Walters, 2003).

Notably, Marxism is a theory that criticizes the societal structure with a heavy focus on economy, class structure, and a socialist egalitarian societal structure. Marxism is consistently presented in introductory criminology textbooks. Anarchism is a theory that has similar critiques to Marxism but is further left on the spectrum of thought, yet anarchism is excluded and Marxism is included.

What can be deduced from the exclusion of anarchism is that the theory is *de facto* marginalized. It cannot be the case that a theory is both excluded from presentation and considered important. This marginalization is unjustified. Anarchism has connections to criminology throughout history and the theory brings a unique and important line of thought to criminology that should be included in introductory criminology textbooks.

Appendix A—All Introductory Criminology Textbooks Measured:
KPU Textbooks:

Adler, F., Mueller, G., Laufer, W., & Grekul, J. (2012). *Criminology* (2nd Canadian ed.). Toronto, Ontario, Canada: McGraw-Hill Ryerson Higher Education.

Cullen, F. T., & Agnew, R. (2011). *Criminological Theory: Past to Present* (4th ed.). New York: Oxford University Press.

Gabor, T. (2010). *Basics of criminology*. Toronto: McGraw-Hill Ryerson.

O'Grady, W. (2011). *Crime in Canadian Context: Debates and Controversies* (2nd ed.). Don Mills, Ont.: Oxford University Press.

Sacco, V., & Kennedy, L. (2011). *The Criminal Event: An Introduction to Criminology in Canada* (5th ed.). Toronto: Nelson Education.

Schmalleger, F., & Volk, R. (2011). *Canadian Criminology Today: Theories and Applications* (4th ed.). Toronto: Pearson Canada.

Siegel, L., & McCormick, C. (2012). *Criminology in Canada: Theories,Patterns, and Typologies* (5th ed.). Toronto: Nelson Education.

White, R., Haines, F., & Eisler, L. (2013). *Crime & Criminology: An Introduction* (2nd Canadian ed.). Don Mills, Ont.: Oxford University Press.

Amazon.ca Top 6 Textbooks[1]:

Akers, R., & Sellers. C. (2013). *Criminological Theories: Introduction, Evaluation, and Application* (6th ed.). New York: Oxford University Press.

Bernard, T., Vold, G., Snipes, J., & Gerould, A. (2010). *Vold's Theoretical Criminology* (6th ed.). New York: Oxford University Press.

Cullen, F., & Agnew, R. (2011). *Criminological Theory: Past to Present* (4th ed.). New York: Oxford University Press.

Hunter, R., & Dantzker, M. (2012). *Crime and Criminality: Causes and Consequences* (2nd ed.). Boulder: Lynne Rienner Publishers.

Linden, R. (2012). *Criminology: A Canadian Perspective* (7th ed.). Toronto: Nelson Education Ltd.

Sacco, V., & Kennedy, L. (2011). *The Criminal Event: An Introduction to Criminology in Canada* (5th ed.). Toronto: Nelson Education.

References

Abrutyn, S. (2013). Teaching Sociological Theory for a New Century: Contending with the Time Crunch. *The American Sociologist, 44*(2), 132–154.

---

1   List was obtained on December 3, 2013 from Amazon.ca under headings "bestsellers", "textbooks", and "criminology". One textbook that would have been #2 of the top six was omitted from the list. The textbook is theories applied to the criminal justice system, not criminology as a whole. I chose to omit the book, because it limits the field of study. Although from looking through the abstract and outline, the textbook does seem to include conflict theories. Nonetheless, since the class focus is CRIM 1100 and CRIM 2331 not CRIM 1101, I decided not to include the textbook in the analyses.

Arrigo, B. (1999). "Critical Criminology's Discontent: The Perils of Publishing and the Call to Action." *The Critical Criminologist* 10(1): 10-13.

Keenan, L. H. (2012). Textbook Pedagogy: Some Considerations. *Classical World* 106(1), 117-121.

Kropotkin, P. (1887). *Are Prisons Necessary?* Retrieved from http://dwardmac.pitzer.edu/Anarchist_Archives/kropotkin/prisons /chap10.html.

Kropotkin, P. (1939). *Mutual Aid*. Harmondsworth Middlesex, England: Pelican Publishing.

Kropotkin, P. (1927). Prisons and Their Moral Influence on Prisoners. In R. Baldwin (Ed.), *Kropotkin's Revolutionary Pamphlets*. Vanguard Press, Inc. Retrieved from http://dwardmac.pitzer.edu/ Anarchist_Archives/kropotkin/revpamphlets/prisonsmoral.html.

Kropotkin, P. (2006). *The Conquest of Bread*. Edmonton, Alberta: Black Cat Press.

Lombroso, C. (1900). A Paradoxical Anarchist. *Popular Science Monthly*. Retrieved from http://www.popsci.com/archive-viewer? id=ByYDAAAAMBAJ&pg=312&query=paradoxical %20anarchist.

Lombroso, C. (1890). Physiognomy of the Anarchists. *The Monist, 1*. Retrieved from http://www.archive.org/stream/monistquart 01hegeuoft#page/n7/mode/2up.

Lombroso, C. (2006). *Criminal Man*. [translated by M. Gibson & N. Rafter] Durham: Duke University Press.

Quinney, R. (2000). *Bearing Witness to Crime and Social Justice*. New York: State University of New York Press.

Rock, P. (2006). *Sociological Theories of Crime*. New York: Oxford University Press.

Ross, J. (2008). Analyzing Contemporary Introductory Textbooks on

Correctional Administration/Management/Organization: A Content Analysis. *Journal of Criminal Justice Education*, 19(3), 446–460.

Rothe, D., & Ross, J. (2008). The Marginalization of State Crime in Introductory Textbooks on Criminology. *Critical Sociology*, 34(5), 741–752.

Sampson, J. (2000). Whither the Sociological Study of Crime? *Annual Review of Sociology* 26: 711–714.

Sullivan, D. & Tifft, T. (2001). *Restorative Justice: Healing the Foundations of our Everyday Lives*. New York, USA: Willow Tree Press Inc.

Sullivan, D. & Tifft, T. (2004). "What are the Implications of Restorative Justice for Society and our Lives" from *Critical Issues in Restorative Justice* ed. H. Zehr & B. Toews. New York, USA: Willow Tree Press Inc.

Sullivan, D. & Tifft, T. (2006). *Handbook of Restorative Justice*. New York, USA: Routledge.

Taylor, I., Walton, P. & Young, J. (1975). *Critical Criminology.* New York: Routledge and Kegan Paul Ltd.

Tifft, L. & Sullivan, D. (1980). *The Struggle to be Human: Crime, Criminology, & Anarchism.* Orkney, U.K.: Cienfuegos Press.

Walters, R. (2003). New Modes of Governance and the Commodification of Criminological Knowledge. *Social & Legal Studies*, 12(1), 5–26.

Wagner, K. (2006). Still Left Out? The coverage of critical/conflict criminology in introductory textbooks. *Academy of Criminal Justice Sciences.* 31(4), 1–15.

Wright, R. (2000). Left out? The coverage of critical perspectives in introductory criminology textbooks, 1990–1999. *Critical Criminology*, 9(1-2), 101–122.

4 | Sexuality, Assault, Police Infiltration and Foucault: Notes for Further Inquiry*

Dr. Michael Loadenthal[1]

---

* These notes (newly published in this collection April 2015) have their basis in on-going research that Michael presented at NAASN5 (January 2014) through his video talk, 'Statecraft & Sexual Trust: Infiltrating the Revolutionary Left' with an accompanying powerpoint presentation. Some slides from the latter are reproduced here as well. Earlier pre-article versions of this talk were delivered collaboratively with anthropologist Dr. Jennifer Grubbs, and presented in 2011 at the Animal Liberation Forum (CSU Long Beach), Anarchist Book Fair (NYC), Public Anthropology Conference (American University), the Graduate Student Sociological Association conference (George Mason University) and Trinity Washington University. Dr. Grubbs also expands upon this inquiry in her 2015 doctoral dissertation entitled, "Que(e)rying the Ecoterrorist: Neoliberal capitalism, political repression as discipline, and the spectacle of direct action."

1   Georgetown University, Program on Justice & Peace *and* George Mason University, School for Conflict Analysis & Resolution

It must be possible to hold the prisoner under permanent observation; every report that can be made about him must be recorded and computed. The theme of the Panopticon—at once surveillance and observation, security and knowledge, individualization and totalization, isolation and transparency—found in the prison and its privileged locus of realization [2].

O ver the past several decades state security and intelligence-gathering forces have found it advantageous and effective to gather information, cause disruption and neutralize social movements through the use of infiltration. While some have noted the decline of such overt methods since the official end to the FBI's Counter Intelligence Program (COINTELPRO), in recent years it has come to light that many of these agents of the state made their activist inroads through sexual misrepresentation; pretending to be someone they were not in order to gain an individual's trust with the aid of sexual contact. I have published biographical accounts of these individuals[3] as well as a lengthier theoretical analysis[4] through the lens of

---

2   Michel Foucault, *Discipline & Punish* (New York: Vintage Books, 1977), 249.

3   Michael Loadenthal, "6 Ways Cops Have Used Sex to Infiltrate and Disrupt Protest Groups," *Green Is The New Red*, January 20, 2015, http://www.greenisthenewred.com/blog/6-ways-cops-used-sex-infiltrate-disrupt-protest-groups/8146/.

4   Michael Loadenthal, "When Cops 'Go Native': Policing Revolution Through Sexual Infiltration and Panopticonism," *Critical Studies on Terrorism* 7, no. 1 (April 2014): 24–42, doi:DOI:10.1080/17539153.2013.877670.

Michel Foucault (1926-1984), the French philosopher and social theorist.

My argument in these inquiries is clear: that the state's use of sexual infiltration as a tactic of intelligence gathering and disruption constitutes a strategic deployment of surveillance technology where activist bodies are observed and policed. The presence and suspicion of police agents from amongst activists' networks is in itself very distracting, serving to cause and exacerbate group conflict. Therefore the police's deployment of small amounts of long-term agents generates incalculable disincentives for social movement participants to transgress the law. If one is to presume that any member of a social network, including intimate partners, can be an agent of the state (e.g. police officer, spy, confidential informant, cooperating witness, private security, etc.), then bonds of human trust break down and divisive issues arise. Moreover, misrepresenting oneself in order to gain sexual access to a person can constitute rape as consent is marred by wrong information.

These themes are explored at length in the previously published materials.

▲ Photo: Christopher Bevacqua (Flickr, CC).

Research Notes: Sexual Assault in Activist Communities

Besides simply using sexuality to gain trust, earn credentials and dispel suspicion amongst activist communities, several police-linked individuals have also been connected to sexual violence. While the role of sexual violence (including rape) within security forces is well documented within the gender studies literature, it is worth mentioning at least two cases where movement infiltrators were linked to sexual assault, showing yet another form of state power wielded through human sexuality. Exemplary for this discussion are the cases of American (former) anarchist activist Brandon Darby and New Zealand informant Robert Gilchrist.

While not explicitly engaging in paid information gathering through sexual infiltration, Darby's case contains within itself additional valuable lessons. Darby was a key organizer with the post-Hurricane Katrina, anarchist-aligned network known as Common Ground Relief (CG). Several well-known local and outside leftist activists, including former Black Panther Malik Rahim, founded CG in 2005. Approximately two weeks after its founding, additional activists, including Darby, arrived in New Orleans and joined in the efforts. During his time with CG, Darby was "notorious for sleeping around the activist scene"[5], sexually assaulting numerous female act-

---

5   Josh Harkinson, "How a Radical Leftist Became the FBI's BFF," *Mother Jones*, October 2011, http://www.motherjones.com/politics/2011/08/brandon-darby-anarchist-fbi-terrorism.

ivists[6], and using his organizational position to resist accountability processes established to seek justice for survivors of sexualized violence. During this time, Darby served to spread disorder and divisiveness amongst the coordinators and volunteers at CG[7], displacing 30 volunteer coordinators and replacing them with his allies[8].

It was through interference efforts such as Darby's that sexual assaults amongst the CG community went unsolved[9] or simply unexamined. Additionally, through dis-

---

6 Diana Welch, "The Informant," January 23, 2009, http://www.austinchronicle.com/news/2009-01-23/729400/; Courtney Desiree Morris, "Why Misogynists Make Great Informants: How Gender Violence on the Left Enables State Violence in Radical Movement," *Make/shift (republished by INCITE!)*, Spring/Summer 2010, http://inciteblog.wordpress.com/2010/07/15/why-misogynists-make-great-informants-how-gender-violence-on-the-left-enables-state-violence-in-radical-movements/; Lisa Fithian, "Lisa Fithian: FBI Informant Brandon Darby: Sexism, Egos, and Lies" (The Rag Blog, March 22, 2010), http://theragblog.blogspot.com/2010/03/lisa-fithian-fbi-informant-brandon.html; Victoria Welle, "Brandon Darby in New Orleans: FBI Informant Was Egotistical Sexist" (The Rag Blog, May 26, 2009), http://theragblog.blogspot.com/2009/05/brandon-darby-in-new-orleans-fbi.html.

7 MJ Essex, "Anarchism, Violence, and Brandon Darby's Politics of Moral Certitude" (New Orleans Indymedia, June 26, 2009), http://neworleans.indymedia.org/news/2009/06/14041.php; Welle, "Brandon Darby in New Orleans: FBI Informant Was Egotistical Sexist."

8 Harkinson, "How a Radical Leftist Became the FBI's BFF."

9 Fithian, "Lisa Fithian: FBI Informant Brandon Darby: Sexism, Egos, and Lies."

placing blame for such occurrences, white activists in CG such as Darby were able to displace responsibility for such assaults onto the non-white, non-activist local community[10]. Not only was Darby complicit in criminal sexual assaults of volunteers and activists, he also furthered a culture of masculinist leadership that served to discourage female and queer leadership and participation[11]. Darby can thus be seen to have utilized a culture of "unrestrained sexual engagements with [activist] volunteers"[12] to disrupt and defame an active anarchist project which at the time was gaining momentum. For this particular FBI informant, sexuality was a weapon deployed like any other to grow discord amongst an organization. To think that his FBI handlers were completely ignorant of this history is rather unlikely. In nearly every account of his personality, authors mention sexist, misogynist and otherwise domineering behaviors that served to alienate collaboration. Following his work with CG, Darby continued his counter-organizing efforts. Three years after the founding

10 Rachel E. Luft, "Looking for Common Ground: Relief Work in Post-Katrina New Orleans as an American Parable of Race and Gender Violence," *NWSA Journal* 20, no. 3 (2008): 5–31.

11 Morris, "Why Misogynists Make Great Informants: How Gender Violence on the Left Enables State Violence in Radical Movement"; Fithian, "Lisa Fithian: FBI Informant Brandon Darby: Sexism, Egos, and Lies"; Essex, "Anarchism, Violence, and Brandon Darby's Politics of Moral Certitude"; Welle, "Brandon Darby in New Orleans: FBI Informant Was Egotistical Sexist."

12 Fithian, "Lisa Fithian: FBI Informant Brandon Darby: Sexism, Egos, and Lies."

of CG, Darby would go on to act as an agent provocateur and paid informant in the case made against anarchists David McKay and Bradley Crowder, accused of planning arson attacks to coincide with the Republican National Convention in St Paul, Minnesota. Darby was the main source of provocation and infiltration into the actions of McKay and Crowder, a case that was profiled in the film *Better This World.*

A second instructive example of sexualized violence from movement informants can be seen in the case of Robert Steven Gilchrist, based in New Zealand. Gilchrist began informant work around 1998 when he participated in demonstrations against the Asia Pacific Economic Development conference. After arousing suspicion amongst activists in the campaign, Gilchrist began making connections in anarchist and anti-poverty networks, and by 2000 was linked to several animal rights (including Auckland Animal Action and the Vegan Balaclava Pixies), environmental (including Greenpeace), anti-war, anti-genetic engineering, anti-capitalist, pro-union and Maori rights networks. During this time he provided frequent reports directly to police via email and responded to their tasks and questions to identify specific individuals, groups and campaigns[13]. Within the animal rights movement, Gilchrist was very active and even allowed himself to be interviewed on TV while participating in a farm raid shown

---

13 Fairfax NZ News, "The Activist Who Turned Police Informer," *Sunday Star Times*, December 13, 2008, sec. Sunday Star Times, http://www.stuff.co.nz/sunday-star-times/features/760466.

on Havoc and Newsboy TV[14]. According to reports, Gilchrist acted as a provocateur, seemingly only interested in confrontational tactics and eager to promote criminal methods[15] and clandestine actions. Like other infiltrators focused on disruption, Gilchrist was said to be outwardly focused on internal conflicts within groups, and at times accused other group members of being police informants, a tactic known as "snitchjacketing"[16]. These methods of promotiting division have been similarly documented throughout the exposure of the British police agents profiled in my prior studies. Intelligence provided by Gilchrist on three individuals was used in Operation 8[17], the 15 October 2007 arrest raids which claimed to have uncovered "paramilitary training camps" in New Zealand.

During his role as an informant, Gilchrist maintained sexual relationships with female activists, one of which lasted for four years[18]. Gilchrist was known as "someone

---

14 Mark Eden, "Police Informer Caught After 10 Years of Spying on Activists," *Peace Researcher*, no. 38 (July 2009), http://www.converge.org.nz/abc/pr38-180b.htm.

15 Fairfax NZ News, "The Activist Who Turned Police Informer"; Eden, "Police Informer Caught After 10 Years of Spying on Activists."

16 Jules Boykoff, *Beyond Bullets: The Suppression of Dissent in the United States* (Oakland, CA: AK Press, 2007), 116–120.

17 Patrick Gower, "'Nice Little Memento' for Police Spy," *New Zealand Herald*, December 20, 2008, sec. National, http://www.nzherald.co.nz/nz/news/article.cfm?c_id=1&objectid=10549050.

18 Fairfax NZ News, "The Activist Who Turned Police Informer."

who would continuously hit on young women, and often make very sexist comments"[19]. According to a female animal rights activist whom he dated, Gilchrist photographed her naked without her consent and then sent these pictures to police counter-terrorism officers. The woman, Rochelle Rees a computer programmer and activist, discovered the pictures as well as troves of email sent by Gilchrist to police while fixing the informant's computer[20]. After developing suspicions, Rees was able to setup monitoring software and observe Gilchrist's email and phone activity. The pictures Rees discovered showed a naked 16-year-old female activist with the subject line "needs a shave"[21]. Reports have also stated that a second set of photographs showing another underage, naked, female activist were located on Gilchrist's computer along with what is described as "disturbing" pornography[22]. In these photographs, the underage female activist is shown posing with Gilchrist's firearms, including poses where she displays a rifle placed against her head and inside of her mouth. Despite Gilchrist sending such defamatory,

---

19 Rochelle Rees, "Police Busted! How Police Spy Robert Gilchrist Was Exposed by His Partner," *Peace Researcher*, no. 38 (July 2009), http://www.converge.org.nz/abc/pr38-180c.htm.

20 Eden, "Police Informer Caught After 10 Years of Spying on Activists"; Rees, "Police Busted! How Police Spy Robert Gilchrist Was Exposed by His Partner."

21 Rochelle Rees, "Gilchrist Sent Naked Photos of Teenager to Police" (Scoop Independent News, December 21, 2008), http://www.scoop.co.nz/stories/PO0812/S00278.htm.

22 Ibid.

misogynist and illegal pictures directly to police, he continued under their employment for an additional three years, receiving $600 weekly plus the cost of expenses. During this period, Gilchrist was observed by Rees trying to solicit sex from other female activists via text messages[23]. In addition, Rees saw evidence that in addition to Gilchrist providing photographs, license plate numbers and other information for police, he also provided social network information such as whom activists were sleeping with and details of ongoing internal conflicts. In total, Gilchrist appears to have served as a police informant from around 1998-2008 in the latter years working largely for the Special Investigations Group that was established in 2004, to investigate national security and terrorism.

In both the cases of Darby and Gilchrist, male activists immersed themselves within radical communities for the purpose of gathering information for police. Both individuals used their position to date and sexually assault female activists likely emboldened by the immunity they could garner from their employment. Not only did both men serve to provide information directly to police, their actions against women also served to disrupt, defame and distract legitimate activists. Through the furthering of infighting and rumors activists' energies were sapped by police agents, energies which could have otherwise been put toward organizing for successful campaigns. While it does not appear that either man used sexuality as an intentional *strategy* within their spy craft, the effects of

---

23 Rees, "Police Busted! How Police Spy Robert Gilchrist Was Exposed by His Partner."

their presence are still key in interpreting the interplay between the statecraft of repression and the voluntary associative properties of radical social movements and networks. Especially in the case of Darby and CG, his exploits allowed the social movement history of the solidarity and aid network to be overcast by accusations of frequent assaults by unaccountable perpetrators. Thus by engaging in unchecked, sexually violent behaviors, Darby was able to re-inscribe a counter narrative atop of an otherwise aid-focused social movement, derailing its hard fought discourse of solidarity and community responsiveness.

...and what does Foucault have to say?

It is important for us to not only recognize the histories, tactics and long-term strategies of police infiltration, but also to begin to build relevant theory as to *why* the state is forging ahead in this manner. Here is where we begin to infuse a bit of guesswork. Without venturing too far into inter-academic irrelevance, I think it is instructive to view the use of sexual infiltration within the discourse on disciplinary power provided by Foucault. Foucault's work throughout his life was to understand the nature of *power*. In Foucault's examination of the changing nature of disciplinary power, he argues that a shift occurs which refocuses punishment on the *disciplinary* and away from the *Monarchical/sovereign* precisely because the former is seen as more effectual, lower costing, and can more readily lead the subject to self-policing in order to avoid pun-

ishment. In other words, at some historical marker it became less efficient to continue hanging criminals in the
town square, and more effective to manage order through
reminding potential criminals that the gallows were just
off stage in the event they transgressed. While the threat
of aggressive surveillance, terrorist labeling and physical
incarceration is a far cry from the guillotine of the Monarch, these methods still serve to dissuade anti-state action through an imagined punishment inflicted on the individual. In *Discipline and Punish*, Foucault argues that a
shift occurs when public punishment, as represented
through Monarchical power, is replaced by self-policing,
as understood through the model of Jeremy Bentham's
Panopticonal prison.

> The transition from the public execution, with its
> spectacular rituals, its art mingled with the ceremony
> of pain, to the penalties of prisons buried in architec-
> tural masses and guarded by the secrecy of adminis-
> trations, is not a transition to an undifferentiated, ab-
> stract, confused penalty; it is the transition from one
> art of punishing to another, no less skillful one. It is a
> technical mutation.[24]

Such a shift occurs, according to Foucault, at "the moment when it became understood that it was more efficient and profitable in terms of the economy of power to
place people under surveillance than to subject them to

---

24 Foucault, *Discipline & Punish*, 257.

some exemplary penalty"[25]. For Foucault, the transition from Monarchical power to disciplinary power is temporally linear, a product of different eras of the state, yet one could argue that while disciplinary power was a latter construction, at times the state may return to public punishment when such a spectacle suits them. The transition described by Foucault—from punishment of the body in public to the creation of docile citizen subjects—exemplifies the learning power of the state yet despite advancements in forms of control, one may at times return to the brutality of days-gone-by to reassert violent consequences for those who challenge authority. In the realm of contemporary social movements, these disciplinary approaches can be seen in prosecutions based around the Animal Enterprise Terrorism Act, state-level eco-terrorism (e.g. Pennsylvania Eco-Terrorism statute 3311) and "ag gag" laws, sentencing involving Terrorism Enhancements, and incarceration in ultra restrictive Communications Management Units. The deployment of such aggressive measures constitutes a disciplinary power wherein the state seeks to reproduce Foucault's "docile bodies" through self-policing.

When the state reaches a certain level of mechanistic regularity and ease with maintaining control over the

---

25 Michel Foucault, *Power/Knowledge: Selected Interviews & Other Writings 1972-1977 by Michel Foucault*, ed. Colin Gordon, trans. Colin Gor et al. (New York: Pantheon Books, 1980), 38, http://www.randomhouse.com/book/55032/powerknowledge-by-michel-foucault.

populace, it no longer requires the gruesome display of power and pain—the gallows, the guillotine and other forms of public bodily disciplining—and can instead inculcate a self-censoring amongst the populace that replicates within the social sphere. This occurs with an omnipresence that is also simultaneously hidden, as the discipline is enacted throughout the public and private spheres, from the political world, to the social world and beyond.

> 'Discipline' may be identified neither with an institution nor with an apparatus; it is a type of power, a modality for its exercise, comprising a whole set of instruments, techniques, procedures, levels of application, targets; it is a 'physics' or an 'anatomy' of power, a technology...On the whole, therefore, one can speak of the formation of a disciplinary society in this movement that stretches from the enclosed disciplines, a sort of social 'quarantine', to an indefinitely generalizable mechanism of 'panopticonism.'[26]

Foucault predicts the creation of a police state society of totalizing surveillance and disciplinary self-regulation. When disciplinary power is no longer "identified with an institution," and is instead "a type of power forming a disciplinary society," the clandestine nature of repression is obscured in the statecraft of rhetoric and juridical violence. Such obscured yet ever-present systems of control establish the deterritorialized nature of state power. Here, the power of the state is to transmit disciplinary power beyond the courts, prisons and police, and into the bodily

---

26 Foucault, *Discipline & Punish*, 215–216.

reality of criminals and those with the potential for criminality.

The power desired by a disciplinary society is one in which "power reaches into the very grain of individuals, touches their bodies and inserts itself into their actions and attitudes, their discourses, learning processes and everyday lives"[27]. In this sense the state must be understood as more than the sum of its parts—the executive, judiciary, legislative, police apparatus, military, civil society —but instead the full management of social, political, economic and personal affairs. This is the site where power, as derived though discipline, inscribes itself upon subjects as the governing logic of life, death and existence—the entire realm of the biopolitical[28]. In a 1979 lecture at the College de France, Foucault states, "The object of the police is almost infinite...there is no limit to the objectives of government when it is a question of managing a public power that has to regulate the behavior of subjects"[29]. Thus the shift in methods of power, or more

---

27 Foucault, *Power/Knowledge: Selected Interviews & Other Writings 1972-1977 by Michel Foucault*, 39.

28 Michel Foucault, *The History of Sexuality, Vol. 1: An Introduction* (New York: Vintage, 1990); *"Society Must Be Defended": Lectures at the Collège de France, 1975-1976*, trans. David Macey, Reprint (Picador, 2003); *Security, Territory, Population: Lectures at the Collège de France 1977-1978*, ed. Michel Senellart et al., trans. Graham Burchell, 1st ed. (New York: Palgrave Macmillan, 2007); *The Birth of Biopolitics: Lectures at the Collège de France, 1978-1979*, First Edition (New York: Palgrave Macmillan, 2010).

29 *The Birth of Biopolitics*, 7.

precisely the establishment of a dual-natured disciplinary power, is illustrative of a totalizing statecraft, not an accidental historical evolution. The Monarch requires both the spectacular violence of the guillotine *as well as* the clandestine violence of the prison's observation tower, as both function in an interdependent matrix of coercion, surveillance and discipline.

▲ Michel Foucault, Paris 1983 (Archive Foucault)

Conclusion

The threat to state power as enacted through radical social movements remains a focus of counter-terrorism programs, and consequently becomes a juridical mission aimed at policing, detaining, and incarcerating any individual or movement that fosters a challenge to ideology, hegemony or property. The state's wedded nature to that of the economy is the foundational assumption of a host of scholars ranging from Marx[30], to Althusser[31], and up until a host of contemporary theorists.[32] Foucault himself identifies the interdependence of state and capital writing that in relation to trade, government is "a particular organization of production and commercial circuits accord-

---

30 "The German Ideology" (republished by Marxist Internet Archives, 1846), chap. 1, 3, http://www.marxists.org/archive/ marx/works/1845/german-ideology/; Friedrich Engels and Karl Marx, "Manifesto of the Communist Party" (republished by Marxist Internet Archives, 1848), http://www.marxists.org/ archive/marx/works/1848/communist-manifesto/index.htm; "Preface to A Contribution to the Critique of Political Economy" (republished by Marxist Internet Archives, 1859), 43, http://www.marxists.org/archive/marx/works/1859/critique-pol-economy/preface.htm.

31 *Lenin and Philosophy and Other Essays* (New York, NY: Monthly Review Press, 1970).

32 see for example David Harvey, *A Brief History of Neoliberalism* (New York: Oxford University Press, USA, 2007); *The Enigma of Capital: And the Crises of Capitalism*, 2nd ed. (New York: Oxford University Press, USA, 2011); Michael Hardt and Antonio Negri, *Empire* (Cambridge, MA: Harvard University Press, 2001); Christian Marazzi, *The Violence of Financial Capitalism (Semiotex*, trans. Kristina Lebedeva and Jason Francis Mc Gimsey (Los Angeles: Semiotext(e), 2011); James C. Scott, *Seeing Like a State: How Certain Schemes to Improve the Human Condition Have Failed* (New Haven: Yale University Press, 1999); Ellen Meiksins Wood, *Democracy against Capitalism: Renewing Historical Materialism* (Cambridge, UK: Cambridge University Press, 1995); *The Origin of Capitalism: A Longer View*, Revised (New York: Verso, 2002); *Empire of Capital* (New York: Verso, 2005); Slavoj Žižek, *First As Tragedy, Then As Farce* (New York: Verso, 2009); *Living in the End Times* (New York: Verso, 2011).

ing to the principle...the state must enrich itself through monetary accumulation"[33]. Foucault[34] also argues that such an interdependence can produce a "crisis" of governmentality if the ideologies presented have a negative economic impact[35]. Within such a crisis of governmentality and liberalism, economic solutions to ward off dangerous ideologies emerge:

> All of those mechanisms which...have tried to offer economic and political formulae to secure states against communism, socialism, National Socialism, and fascism, all these mechanisms and guarantees of freedom which have been implemented in order to produce this additional freedom, or at any rate, to react to threats to this freedom, have taken the form of economic interventions.[36]

Furthermore, once capitalism establishes itself as the creator, distributor and quantifier of wealth, it must subsequently establish itself as a vehicle for the protection of such treasures[37]. Thus the state must create an atmosphere and a socio-political organization that allows for capital accumulation and the protection of private property—two sites where radical social movements seek to intervene

33 *The Birth of Biopolitics*, 5.

34 *The Birth of Biopolitics*.

35 Ibid., 68.

36 Ibid., 69.

37 Foucault, *Power/Knowledge: Selected Interviews & Other Writings 1972-1977 by Michel Foucault*, 41.

and disrupt. One of the ways in which the state seeks to manage such movements and thus mitigate their effects is through the development of *cooperating collaborators*; those movement members that choose to aid security forces in order to leverage their own situation. Commonly these are individuals already under state observation and who are offered a choice: self-preservation in the form of cooperation, or further state estrangement through refusing to aid in the identification, investigation and prosecution of others.

The creation of points of leverage amongst an activist population follows a predictably normative set of processes. First an illegal act is identified and linked to an individual. Then that individual is offered a choice: either accept the juridical consequences for their crime, or provide information and testimony against a second individual in exchange for leniency. This method of producing cooperating defendants has been a cornerstone of the FBI's counter-terrorism strategy. The discovery of an activists' criminality—say for example a small-scale vandalism—is then leveraged to gather far more penetrating facts via typically protected channels. The production of such cooperating delinquents through the leveraging of past criminality is explained by Foucault as a method of creating "perpetual surveillance":

> Delinquency, with the secret agents that it procures, but also with a generalized policing that it authorizes, constitutes a means of perpetual surveillance of the population: an apparatus that makes it possible to su-

> pervise, through the delinquents themselves, the
> whole social field. Delinquency functions as a politic-
> al observatory.[38]

In an interview discussing modes of power, Foucault quite plainly states that "criminals can be put to good use, if only to keep other prisoners under surveillance"[39]. The utilization of such "delinquency" for the purpose of "supervising the whole social field" can be seen in a plethora of cases, but is best exemplified when the state is able to exploit intimate social networks, such as motivating friend to incriminate friend, lover to incriminate lover, and even spouse to provide incriminating evidence against their spouse (as in the case of Frank Ambrose/Marie Mason).

Further research should focus on methods of preventing and responding to incidents of sexual assault in radical communities. Some activists have been involved with these efforts for years and recent inter-movement publications such as *Accounting for Ourselves: Breaking the Impasse Around Assault and Abuse in Anarchist Scenes* by CrimethInc. and *Betrayal: A Critical Analysis of Rape Culture in Anarchist Subcultures* distributed by Words to Fire Press refocus the issue in the contemporary. With the recent joyous release of Eric McDavid, it is important to remember that sexuality was a key tool of the state in this

---

38 Foucault, *Discipline & Punish*, 281.

39 *Power/Knowledge: Selected Interviews & Other Writings 1972-1977* by Michel Foucault, 45.

case as well. Let this case be a reminder of our eternal vigilance and the validity of our often-invoked paranoias. As the saying goes, "Just because you're paranoid does not mean they're not out to get you." With this in mind we must find strategies that allow us to stay safe, remain active, and simultaneously create spaces that are resistant to infiltration and open to allies. This is the task at hand. Wherever we end up in the future, in the interim, while this fight is fought, we stand together and loudly state that whether through violence, the threat of violence, or coercive misrepresentation, those seeking a brighter future all agree that state agents have no business lying their way into our pants!

References

Althusser, Louis. *Lenin and Philosophy and Other Essays*. New York, NY: Monthly Review Press, 1970.

Boykoff, Jules. *Beyond Bullets: The Suppression of Dissent in the United States*. Oakland, CA: AK Press, 2007.

Eden, Mark. "Police Informer Caught After 10 Years of Spying on Activists." *Peace Researcher*, no. 38 (July 2009). http://www.converge.org.nz/abc/pr38-180b.htm.

Engels, Friedrich, and Karl Marx. "Manifesto of the Communist Party." republished by Marxist Internet Archives, 1848. http://www.marxists.org/archive/marx/works/1848/communist-manifesto/index.htm.

Essex, MJ. "Anarchism, Violence, and Brandon Darby's Politics of Moral Certitude." New Orleans Indymedia, June 26, 2009. http://neworleans.indymedia.org/news/2009/06/14041.php.

Fairfax NZ News. "The Activist Who Turned Police Informer." *Sunday Star Times*, December 13, 2008, sec. Sunday Star Times. http://www.stuff.co.nz/sunday-star-times/features/760466.

Fithian, Lisa. "Lisa Fithian: FBI Informant Brandon Darby: Sexism, Egos, and Lies." The Rag Blog, March 22, 2010. http://theragblog.blogspot.com/2010/03/lisa-fithian-fbi-informant-brandon.html.

Foucault, Michel. *Discipline & Punish*. New York: Vintage Books, 1977.

———. *Power/Knowledge: Selected Interviews & Other Writings 1972-1977 by Michel Foucault*. Edited by Colin Gordon. Translated by Colin Gor, Leo Marshall, John Mempham, and Kate Soper. New York: Pantheon Books, 1980. http://www.randomhouse.com/book/55032/powerknowledge-by-michel-foucault.

———. *Security, Territory, Population: Lectures at the Collège de France 1977--1978*. Edited by Michel Senellart, François Ewald, Alessandro Fontana, and Arnold I. I. Davidson. Translated by Graham Burchell. 1st ed. New York: Palgrave Macmillan, 2007.

———. *"Society Must Be Defended": Lectures at the Collège de France, 1975-1976*. Translated by David Macey. Reprint. Picador, 2003.

———. *The Birth of Biopolitics: Lectures at the Collège de France, 1978--1979*. First Edition. New York: Palgrave Macmillan, 2010.

———. *The History of Sexuality, Vol. 1: An Introduction*. New York: Vintage, 1990.

Gower, Patrick. "'Nice Little Memento' for Police Spy." *New Zealand Herald*, December 20, 2008, sec. National. http://www.nzherald.co.nz/nz/news/article.cfm?c_id=1&objectid=10549050.

Hardt, Michael, and Antonio Negri. *Empire*. Cambridge, MA:

Harvard University Press, 2001.

Harkinson, Josh. "How a Radical Leftist Became the FBI's BFF." *Mother Jones*, October 2011. http://www.motherjones.com/politics/2011/08/brandon-darby-anarchist-fbi-terrorism.

Harvey, David. *A Brief History of Neoliberalism*. New York: Oxford University Press, USA, 2007.

———. *The Enigma of Capital: And the Crises of Capitalism*. 2nd ed. New York: Oxford University Press, USA, 2011.

Loadenthal, Michael. "6 Ways Cops Have Used Sex to Infiltrate and Disrupt Protest Groups." *Green Is The New Red*, January 20, 2015. http://www.greenisthenewred.com/blog/6-ways-cops-used-sex-infiltrate-disrupt-protest-groups/8146/.

———. "When Cops 'Go Native': Policing Revolution Through Sexual Infiltration and Panopticonism." *Critical Studies on Terrorism* 7, no. 1 (April 2014): 24–42. doi:DOI:10.1080/17539153.2013.877670.

Luft, Rachel E. "Looking for Common Ground: Relief Work in Post-Katrina New Orleans as an American Parable of Race and Gender Violence." *NWSA Journal* 20, no. 3 (2008): 5–31.

Marazzi, Christian. *The Violence of Financial Capitalism (Semiotex*. Translated by Kristina Lebedeva and Jason Francis Mc Gimsey. Los Angeles: Semiotext(e), 2011.

Marx, Karl. "Preface to A Contribution to the Critique of Political Economy." republished by Marxist Internet Archives, 1859. http://www.marxists.org/archive/marx/works/1859/critique-pol-economy/preface.htm.

Marx, Karl, and Friedrich Engels. "The German Ideology." republished by Marxist Internet Archives, 1846. http://www.marxists.org/archive/marx/works/1845/german-ideology/.

Morris, Courtney Desiree. "Why Misogynists Make Great Informants: How Gender Violence on the Left Enables State Violence in Radical Movement." *Make/shift (republished by INCITE!)*, Spring/Summer 2010. http://inciteblog.wordpress.com/2010/07/15/why-misogynists-make-great-informants-how-gender-violence-on-the-left-enables-state-violence-in-radical-movements/.

Rees, Rochelle. "Gilchrist Sent Naked Photos of Teenager to Police." Scoop Independent News, December 21, 2008. http://www.scoop.co.nz/stories/PO0812/S00278.htm.

———. "Police Busted! How Police Spy Robert Gilchrist Was Exposed by His Partner." *Peace Researcher*, no. 38 (July 2009). http://www.converge.org.nz/abc/pr38-180c.htm.

Scott, James C. *Seeing Like a State: How Certain Schemes to Improve the Human Condition Have Failed*. New Haven: Yale University Press, 1999.

Welch, Diana. "The Informant," January 23, 2009. http://www.austinchronicle.com/news/2009-01-23/729400/.

Welle, Victoria. "Brandon Darby in New Orleans: FBI Informant Was Egotistical Sexist." The Rag Blog, May 26, 2009. http://theragblog.blogspot.com/2009/05/brandon-darby-in-new-orleans-fbi.html.

Wood, Ellen Meiksins. *Democracy against Capitalism: Renewing Historical Materialism*. Cambridge, UK: Cambridge University Press, 1995.

———. *Empire of Capital*. New York: Verso, 2005.

———. *The Origin of Capitalism: A Longer View*. Revised. New York: Verso, 2002.

Žižek, Slavoj. *First As Tragedy, Then As Farce*. New York: Verso, 2009.

———. *Living in the End Times*. New York: Verso, 2011.

ABOLITION

A Journal of Insurgent Politics

5 | Abolition Journal

Introduced at NAASN5 by Brian Lovato [1] (with one of the co-editors, Eli Meyerhoff, via video link)

W e are introducing a new journal in the discipline of political science. Our purpose is to counter the existing hegemony within the discipline of liberal, statist, capitalist, and colonial narratives operating under the guise of political neutrality and meritocracy. Inspired by the Black Campus Movement and the American Indian Movement, we seek to continue their insurgency within and against the colonial, white university. In doing so, we are eager to engage with other disciplines strongly shaped by such radical movements (e.g. Black studies, Feminist studies, American studies, etc.) as well as the radical sub-fields of dominant disciplines (e.g. Human Geography, Cultural Anthropology, Critical Education). Rejecting the

---

1   University of California, Santa Barbara; UAW2865; SBDIY; editor, *Abolition*

"policy-relevant" mission of mainstream political science, we seek to support "movement-relevant" research. Taking our cue from the life and scholarship of the late Joel Olson, we strive to construct an "Abolitionist Political Science"—a project that desires to abolish the intersecting regimes of white supremacy, hetero-patriarchy, capitalism, colonialism, ableism, authoritarianism, the carbon economy, etc. Recognizing that the majority of intellectual work in these areas takes place within radical social movements, we see it as our mission to amplify this work by both bringing it into academic conversations and translating academic work into more popular, communicable pieces. Yet, we also recognize that the very institutions in which we are working, academia and universities, are part of the regimes we seek to abolish. Our journal aims to provide a new means of support for radical academics to grapple with the tensions from struggling within, against, and beyond these institutions.

At the conference, we will be presenting the founding manifesto of the *Abolition Journal* in hopes of entering into a productive conversation with scholars, activists, and organizers both inside and outside of the academy.

Abolition Journal: Manifesto

A bolitionist politics is not about what is possible, but about making the impossible a reality. Ending slavery appeared to be an impossible challenge for Sojourner Truth, Denmark Vesey, Nat Turner, John Brown, Harriet Tubman, and others, and yet they struggled for it anyway. Today we seek to abolish a number of seemingly immortal institutions, drawing inspiration from those who have sought the abolition of all systems of domination, exploitation, and oppression—from Jim Crow laws and prisons to patriarchy and capitalism. The shockingly unfinished character of these struggles can be seen from some basic facts about our present. The 85 richest people in the world have as much wealth as the poorest half; more African American men are in prison, jail, or parole, than were enslaved in 1850; we have altered the chemical composition of our atmosphere threatening all life on this planet; female and trans* people are significantly more likely than cisgender men to be victims of sexual and domestic violence; rich nations support military interventions into "developing" countries as cover for neo-colonial resource exploitation. Recognizing that the institutions we fight against are both interconnected and unique, we refuse to take an easy path of reveling in abstract ideals while accepting mere reforms in practice. Instead, we seek to understand the specific power dynamics within and between these systems so we can make the impossible possible; so we can bring the entire monstrosity down.

We must ask questions that are intimately connected with abolitionist movements if we are to understand these dynamics in ways that are strategically useful. How do those in power use differences of race, gender, sexuality, nationality, and class to divide and exploit us? How do we build bridges across these divides through our organizing? Activists on the ground ask such questions often, but rarely do those within universities become involved. Instead, academia has more often been an opponent to abolitionist movements, going back to the co-constitution of early universities with colonialism and slavery, and the development of racial science and capitalist ideologies. Academic journals have functioned to maintain a culture of conformity, legitimated with myths of "political neutrality" and "meritocracy." At the same time, colleges and universities have always been terrains of struggle, as radical organizers have found ways to expropriate their resources: from W.E.B. DuBois's abolitionist science at Fisk University to the Black Campus Movement of the 1960s. Inspired by them, we refuse to abandon the resources of academia to those who perpetuate the status quo.

Instead, we are creating a new project, centered around *Abolition: A Journal of Insurgent Politics*—for research, publishing, and study that encourage us to make the impossible possible, to seek transformation well beyond policy changes and toward revolutionary abolitionism.

Our journal's title has multiple reference points in a tense relation with one another. "Abolition" refers partly to the historical and contemporary movements that have identified themselves as "abolitionist": those against slavery, prisons, the wage system, animal and earth exploitation, human trafficking, and the death penalty, among others. But we also refer to *all* revolutionary movements, insofar as they have abolitionist elements—whether the abolition of patriarchy, capitalism, heteronormativity, ableism, colonialism, the state, or white supremacy. Rather than just seeking to abolish a list of oppressive institutions, we aim to support studies of the entanglement of different systems of oppression, not to erase the tensions between different movements, but to create spaces for collective experimentation with those tensions. Instead of assuming one homogenous subject as our audience (e.g., "abolitionists of the world unite!"), we write for multiple, contingent, ambivalent subjectivities—for people coming from different places, living and struggling in different circumstances, and in the process of figuring out who we are and untangling these knots to fight for a more just and liberated world. With Fanon, we are "endlessly creating" ourselves.

Abolition takes cues from the abolition-democracy espoused by figures like W.E.B Du Bois, Angela Davis, and Joel Olson. Our orientation toward academic insurgency builds upon the struggles of the Black campus movement against the White University, the American Indian movement against the Colonial University, feminist and queer movements against the Hetero-Patriarchal University, and anarchist and communist movements against the Capitalist University. As efforts to revolutionize academia originated and drew their lifeblood from movements outside and across the boundaries of academic institutions, today we recognize that our journal's radical aspirations must be similarly grounded. We must therefore facilitate collaborations of radical academics *with and in support of* movements that are struggling against oppressive regimes and for the creation of alternative futures. Recognizing that the best movement-relevant intellectual work is happening both in the movements themselves and in the communities with whom they organize (e.g., in dispossessed neighborhoods and prisons), the journal aims to support scholars whose research amplifies such grassroots intellectual activity.

In tension with struggles *against* and *beyond* academia, we recognize the desires of academics to survive *within* it, for the access to resources that inclusion can offer. Rather than accepting such desires as eternal necessities, we foresee that the success of abolitionist projects will change the availability of resources for intellectual activity as well as what we understand as a 'resource.' To help academics grapple with transgressing academia's boundaries, our journal aims to provide some legitimacy within the dominant value practices of academia (e.g., publication requirements for hiring, tenure, and promotion), while simultaneously pushing the limits of those practices. All of our publications will be accessible, free, and open access, refusing the paywalls of the publishing industry. We will also produce hard-copy versions for circulation to communities lacking internet access. Yet, we are not abandoning peer review—sharing writing with respected comrades and giving each other feedback before wider circulation—which can be useful for movements to strengthen and amplify their intellectual activities. As peer review is ultimately based on relationships of trust, we ask why academics on the opposite side of our struggles are our "peers." Instead, we commit to building relationships with activist-intellectuals for whom a new kind of peer review can serve as an insurgent tool to expropriate academia's resources for knowledge production.

"Abolition" as a concept, process, and reality becomes the common ground upon which we meet, struggle, and join together in solidarity.

6 | In Defense of Counterposed Strategic Orientations: Anarchism and Antiracism[*]

Jakub Burkowicz[1]

If, as Richard Day's provocatively titled work announces, *Gramsci Is Dead* (2005) then death must by

---

* An earlier version of this chapter appeared as:
Burkowicz, Jakub. 2014. "In Defense of Counterposed Strategic Orientations: Anarchism and Antiracism." *Affinities* 8(1) http://affinitiesjournal.org/affinities/index.php/affinities/issue/current/showToc

1 **Jakub Burkowicz** is a PhD Candidate (ABD) in Sociology at Simon Fraser University. He is currently completing his dissertation entitled: "Peripheral Europeans: The History of the (De)Racialization of Slavs in Canada." Burkowicz's research and teaching interests include sociological theory; sociology of knowledge; sociology of race focusing on racialization and the history of Slavic immigration in Canada; and social movements with emphases on anarchist and antiracist approaches.

extension also enshroud Michael Omi and Howard Winant's hegemonically-oriented racial formation theory and
the various currents of antiracist thought that it informs.
By orienting itself in poststructuralism, this chapter aims
to displace the Gramscian logic of hegemony in antiracism. I will do so by demonstrating that what Day calls
the *hegemony of hegemony* (2005), which refers to "the
assumption that effective social change can only be
achieved simultaneously and *en masse*, across an entire
national or supranational space" (8), [2] is endemic to anti-
racist theory at the risk of making it unable to keep up
with antiracist social movements.

By *antiracism*, I have in mind actors who view their
activism explicitly in terms of a principled opposition to
racism. Although technically this includes liberal, policy-
driven, state-based approaches developed by think tanks,
commissions, councils, and non-profit organizations,
preference in this chapter will be given to radical, street/
underground/ grassroots-based, and autonomous activist
collectives. It must be stressed early on that even among
this more "focused" range of antiracist actors, racism is
conceptualized in different ways. The non-unified, dispersed existence of these social movements invites us to
consider that racism itself is, as Floya Anthias and Cathy
Lloyd characterize it, "a fluid and shifting phenomenon
which evades clear and absolute definition in a once-and-

---

2   Day's witty coinage of "hegemony of hegemony" denotes
    hegemony becoming hegemonic. The phrase must be read in the
    twofold sense of a preference for the large scale revolutionary
    transformation of the entire social order that has itself become
    large scale within social movement theory.

for-all type of way" (2002, 8). If racism only came down to fascist street level violence of groups like the Ku Klux Klan or Aryan Nations, then antifascism alone would suffice as an antiracist response. If racism was just colonialism, then Indigenist, Nationalist, and Third World anti-colonial movements would do. If racism was only about state control over immigration, migration, and refugee flows, anti-border movements, such us No One Is Illegal, would be the answer. And if racism boiled down to white supremacy and assimilation, then networks like Anarchist People of Color would constitute the right response. The fact is that all of these movements are with us right now because racism functions according to many logics. The response to racism is, unsurprisingly, as diverse as racism itself.

The significant distinction developed here is between *counter-hegemonic* and *strategically flexible* antiracist movements. The former aspire to bring about as much total change as possible, and as such they are much more likely to attempt to institute antiracism by working within, what John Holloway describes as, "the state paradigm" (2010, 12). The latter bypass this paradigm as they do not seek to universalize their aims and do not aim their political projects at anything like the complete transformation of the entire range of social relations; rather, following the logic of affinity, they are open to diffusion, fragmentation, and multiplicity. This chapter demonstrates that the hegemony of hegemony has established a firm foothold in antiracist theory from where it identifies an impasse in antiracist social movements, effectively closing off or dismissing affinity-based antiracist projects.

The impasse consists of what Omi and Winant call "counterposed strategic orientations" (1986, 102)—that is, of the fact that antiracist movements employ multiple, even contradictory, approaches in combating racism and generally suffer from "splintered political action" (1986, 102). In light of this "crisis," Omi and Winant's racial formation theory prescribes a counter-hegemonic solution that calls for antiracist movements to abandon their multiple approaches in favor of a single, unified theoretically-sanctioned strategy that would "consolidate a new radical democratic politics with majoritarian aspirations" (Omi and Winant 1986, 140).

As such, I read racial formation theory as partaking in the counter-hegemonic longing for what Pierre-André Taguieff calls "a certain antiracism that still remains to be invented" (2001, 80). This chapter takes a contrary position. Rather than rethink, like Omi, Winant, and Taguieff, about how to get back to the drawing board in order to create an adequate or correct counter-hegemonic antiracist theory with which we could direct and shape the movements (a project that imagines that it is necessary to go from theory to practice),[3] we ought to instead entertain the possibility that contemporary antiracist social movements—and specifically, affinity based movements—have outmaneuvered the drawing board and that what is required is that we pay greater attention to already exist-

---

3   The injunction becomes explicit in Floya Anthias and Cathie Lloyd's, *Rethinking Anti-Racisms: From Theory to Practice*. Its aim, the editors tell us, is "to consider new ways of thinking about anti-racism and how they impact on anti-racist political practice" (2002, 1).

ing social movements as potent reservoirs of antiracist theory. To this end, I will map out the strategic orientations of two contemporary anarchist antiracist movements, anarchist antifascism and Anarchist People of Color. My argument is that these movements bypass the hegemony of hegemony in antiracism by productively utilizing two contradictory strategies. Employing Taguieff (2001), I argue that antifascist anarchists orient their activism according to the strategy of *universalism* (based on an appeal to colorblind ideology), while Anarchist People of Color utilize the strategy of *differentialism* (based on an appeal to race-conscious or colourconscious ideology). However, where, along with Omi and Winant, antiracist theory identifies a limit of "two antiracisms with contradictory values and norms" (Taguieff 2001, 8), I propose to recast antiracist anarchism in terms of a *strategically flexible antiracism* that can only be grasped outside of the logic of hegemony.

Gramsci and Antiracism

A suspicion of Gramsci may at first sight seem unwarranted. His work certainly makes a number of significant contributions, if not advances, to Marxism and continues to play a substantial role in contemporary social movement theory. For one, Gramsci's contribution consists of a theory of history without guarantees. Drawing on Ernesto Laclau and Chantel Mouffe, we may say that Gramsci matters because in his work the "logic of necessity" gives way to "the logic of spontaneism" (1985, 12). This is to say, Gramsci abandons the materialist inspired laws of historical progression. He dispenses with the holdovers of vulgar Marxist history, which see a mechanistic unfolding of history that "does not allow for the possibility of error" (Gramsci 1999, 408). In addition, Gramsci complicates the dialectical materialist account of the social. His work does not rely on the familiar model of the base and super-structure, where the latter strictly functions as an ideolo-gical defense mechanism of the former; rather, for Gram-sci the superstructure itself develops according to its own historical trajectory and cannot be seen solely as some-thing generated by economic conditions in the defense of those conditions. Politics develops in relationship to eco-nomics, but, and crucially, "it is also distinct from it" (Gramsci 1999, 140). Rather than seeing political parties (a superstructural element) as a "mechanical and passive expression of those classes" (Gramsci 1999, 227) whose interests they represent, we are offered a view that main-tains that parties also "react energetically upon them [eco-nomic classes] in order to develop, solidify and universal-ise them" (227). Gramsci thus offers us an indeterminate account of history along with a relatively autonomous political sphere and civil society that act back on their own economic conditions.

With his theory of hegemony, Gramsci effectively challenges the long-standing idea in Marxism that contra-dictions alone assure the direction that history will take. In a move that removes economism from Marxism, he plunges political action and activism into the uncertain terrain of civil society and culture. Thus, not only does

Gramsci present history as open and unpredictable, but his work also advances a theory of revolution without a *pregiven* revolutionary subject. No longer is the proletariat automatically the privileged agent of historical change in the capitalist epoch. Rather than constructing a theory of the agent, Gramsci presents us with a theory of the battleground, where the key actor emerges out of alliances established in the course of struggle itself. This means that the result of political struggles does not inevitably depend, for Gramsci, on any relationship between the forces of production and the relations of production but is contingent on the relationship between various political actors who struggle to achieve the "political articulation of dissimilar elements" (Laclau and Mouffe 2001, 60). This is not to deny that capitalism contains certain contradictions; it is only to say that the outcome of those contradictions ultimately depends on "a strong activity of the will" (Gramsci 1999, 336) of political actors who variously form alliances as they seek to liquidate their opponents. Finally, it is important to note that to succeed, such alliances must attempt to consolidate a large, unified oppositional culture that, in turn, must "aim to replace" (Gramsci 1999, 340) the existing hegemony. Every counter-hegemony is successful to the extent that it becomes hegemonic.

Many social movement and antiracist theorists analyze social movements through the prism of Gramscian hegemony and the contours of Gramsci's theory I have just identified. Gayatri Spivak, for example, considers that any progressive social movement must face "the difficult task of counterhegemonic ideological production" (1988, 275) and that it is the task of theory to identify the way in which variously localized and dispersed movements can successfully do so. With rampant racism in its various forms—Islamophobia, anti-Semitism, systemic racism against people of colour, ongoing colonialism, and the reawakening of fascism—we may ask, is antiracism not after all in crisis, or, following Spivak, at least badly in need of counter-hegemonic refurbishing? Many sociologists and antiracist theorists have done just that. For them, Gramsci holds out the possibility of a unified antiracist theory and a large scale, coherent movement that could deal a final blow to hegemonic racism. Gramsci informs the work of Cathy Lloyd, who frames the problem by asking, "[h]ow will the traditional themes of anti-racism—opposition to racial discrimination, representation of and solidarity with people who experience racism, and the attempt to establish an anti-racist common sense (or hegemony, in the Gramscian sense)—fit into the political discourses of the twenty-first century, marked by post-colonialism and globalization?" (2002, 61). Similarly, Himani Bannerji poses the problem in a Gramscian frame when she argues that "our hegemonic 'subsumption' into a racist common sense... can only be prevented by creating counter-hegemonic interpretive and organizational frameworks..." (2000, 120). Echoing her, Paul Gilroy likewise hopes to overcome inadequate antiracist counter-hegemony by appealing to "new bases for solidarity and *syn-*

chronized action" (2001, 111-2, emphasis mine). The problem that is restated in this current of antiracism is one of turning dispersed minorities and their various movements into effective, which is to say unified, actors who seek to form a counter-hegemonic bloc.

For Gramscian inspired antiracist theory, a large diversity of movements presents itself as something to be overcome. This is to be accomplished by the active reorganization of disparate and unorganized political actors down to a manageable common core. It is in the sense of being dissatisfied with a non-unified diversity of social movement actors that antiracist theory can, in fact, be said to suffer from the hegemony of hegemony—that is, of the desire for large scale, unanimous, concerted action. As Lloyd observes, "[h]istorically anti-racism is associated with movements in support of decolonialisation, anti-fascism and struggles against deportation and for immigrants' rights" (2002, 63). This, however, is not good enough for her; in fact, it indicates a quandary. The desire for a common counter-hegemonic core, a large-scale collective refusal of racism, reasserts itself when, following this observation, she asks: "What are the links between these different aspects and do they make some kind of coherent whole which constitutes anti-racism?" (2002, 64). The problem of unity haunts her work and Gramscian inspired antiracist theory in general.

We encounter with full blown vigor this "dilemma" and the proposed counter-hegemonic solution in the sociology of Omi and Winant. Their magnum opus, *Racial*

Formation in the United States (1986), in its third edition as of 2013, provides a framework that is enjoying considerable popularity with many antiracists. As the editors of the recently published *Racial Formation in the Twenty-First Century* note, "the roots of racial formation continue to develop as scholars addressing topics from gender and sexuality to indigeneity and settler colonialism, and spanning from literary studies and American studies to sociology, adapt the racial formation framework" (HoSang, LaBennett, and Pulido 2012, 19). Given that Omi and Winant draw on Gramsci,[4] their work introduces the hegemony of hegemony into antiracist theory. Keeping this in mind, let us consider in more depth how the direct Gramscian inheritance presents itself in their work in terms of a movement-state nexus, the necessity of a vanguard, and the identification of a central antagonism.

The Movement-State Nexus

Omi and Winant import Gramsci's political ontology, which privileges political action as occurring within a

---

4   The debt is acknowledged openly:

> In our view, the concept of hegemony, through which the dominant social forces acquire the consent of the subordinate ones, in itself presumes and autonomous civil society and a limited capacity for state 'intervention' into the realm of 'micro-politics,' since this 'consent' is not given stupidly or blindly but because the needs, interests and ideas of the subordinate groups are actively incorporated and taken into account in the organization of society (Omi and Winant 1991, 170n. 22).

movement-state nexus. Their theoretical conceptualization of the battleground of political action as involving
two distinct players—social movements and states—is a
direct inheritance from Gramsci. Reflecting on historical
victories, Gramsci notes:

> A study of how these innovatory forces developed,
> *from subaltern groups to hegemonic and dominant
> groups*, must therefore seek out and identify the
> phases through which they acquired: 1. Autonomy
> vis-à-vis the enemies they had to defeat, and 2. Sup-
> port from the groups which actively or passively as-
> sisted them; for this entire process was historically ne-
> cessary before they could *unite in the form of a State*.
> (1999, 53, emphasis mine)

While he did not explicitly address antiracist movements,
any successful counter-hegemony presupposes, as the
above formulation shows, that all movements must defeat
enemies and create alliances in order to form states and
exercise hegemony. This is precisely what is involved in a
subaltern group becoming hegemonic.

The state-movement nexus and the formula of counter-
hegemony seeking hegemony are firmly in place in Omi
and Winant. They explicitly argue that "the trajectory of
racial politics links... two central actors in the drama of
contemporary racial politics—the racial state and racially
based social movements" (Omi and Winant 1986, 82).
For Omi and Winant, racial identities, racism, and antiracism must in fact be grasped in terms of what they call
"movement/state relationships" (1986, 176n. 38). This is

so because the way we see and understand race changes only by virtue of a change in the relationship between social movements and the state, as both engage in *"political contestation over racial meanings"* (Omi and Winant 1986, 69, emphasis in original). The crucial thing to keep in mind here is that while "social movements create collective identity" (Omi and Winant 1986, 83) and "pose new demands originating outside state institutions" (Omi and Winant 1986, 84), it is only by directing themselves toward the state that such movements can transform the racial order. *Racial formation*, in fact, designates the historic equilibrium, the horizon of racial meanings that make up our "common sense" or what we may call our common stock of racial knowledge. The racial categories and the identities they enable, the kinds of things we "know" about racial others, are all established and negotiated by state-movement relations. Racial formation theory thus imagines hegemonic common sense as arising primarily from "a complex system of compromises" (Omi and Winant 1986, 78) between social movements and states.

Besides hinging the social construction of racial identity on hegemonic relations, what we are presented with in racial formation theory is a political formula that maintains that antiracist movements can only succeed to the extent that they capture or merge with state power. Failure is conceptualized by Omi and Winant as the failure to penetrate the state, which occurs when "minority movements could not be consolidated as a permanent radical democratic political force" (1986, 141). We would do well to remember that all this emphasis on the state is justified because, for the theory of hegemony, it is the presumed primary locus of politics. The state, in other words, is the hub from which an antiracist common sense could be elaborated, the centre from which racial relations can be rearticulated. Thus, when Omi and Winant argue that "[t]he state provides a political framework for interest concertation" (1986, 176n. 39), they refer precisely to its capacity, in the Gramscian sense, of universalizing the particular perspective of antiracism as the hegemonically articulated common sense perspective of civil society itself.

The Vanguard

Having identified the political terrain in terms of the movement-state nexus, the theory of hegemony "supposes an intellectual unity" (Gramsci 1999, 333) as a necessary component of successful social movements. Intellectual unity has the presumed advantage of clarifying the task at hand. Such unity identifies the enemy and provides a single, univocal answer to the pressing question, "what is to be done?" Where, we might ask, would social movements achieve such unity? The answer is from a fundamental group that is made up of organic intellectuals who can step in to lead social movements as the "organisers of a new culture" (Gramsci 1999, 5). Gramsci is not shy about the elite status of this group. He argues that any successful counter-hegemony requires strong leadership that would be separate from the masses:

> Critical self-consciousness means, historically and politically, the creation of an *élite* of intellectuals. A human mass does not "distinguish" itself, does not become independent in its own right without, in the widest sense, organising itself; and there is no organisation without intellectuals, that is without organisers and leaders, in other words, without the theoretical aspect of the theory-practice nexus being distinguished concretely by the existence of a group of people "specialised" in conceptual and philosophical elaboration of ideas. (Gramsci 1999, 334)

Gramsci, as such, envisions political struggle taking place on the terrain of culture where an intellectual vanguard, the movements it leads, and the state with which they clash for supremacy, are the vital components of the theory of hegemony.

Incorporating this, Omi and Winant presuppose that "[r]acial movements come into being as the result of political projects, political interventions led by 'intellectuals' " (Omi and Winant 1986, 80). In the Gramscian tradition of championing organic intellectuals, they open the category of the intellectual to include such actors as "religious leaders, entertainers, schoolteachers" (1986, 173n. 11), along with presumably professional intellectuals like Omi and Winant. The assumption in their work is that leaders are clearly needed for what racial formation theory calls the "rearticulation" of racial meanings:

Rearticulation is a practice of discursive reorganization or reinterpretation of ideological

> themes and interests already present in the subjects' consciousness, such that these elements obtain new meaning or coherence. This practice is ordinarily the work of "intellectuals." Those whose role is to interpret the social world for given subjects... may on this account be "intellectuals." (Omi and Winant 1986, 173n. 11, emphasis in original)

The intellectuals are mandated by racial formation theory with the task of finding and formulating the coherent whole of the antiracist movement in order to be able to lead and manage it. Their separation from the masses and assigned task of cultural rearticulation is in Omi and Winant true to Gramscian form.

The Central Antagonism

Despite developing an indeterminate theory of social change, for Gramsci the economy remains the most important site of conflict. Like a good Marxist, he never abandons the presupposition of a central economic contradiction or the base and superstructure model; rather, Gramsci introduces the terrain of culture and civil society in relationship to the economic base. The former may well be read according to the Althusserian logic of being determined "in the last instance" by the latter, which plays the role of what Peyman Vahabzadeh calls *ultimate referentiality*—"a presumed ultimate ground" that is said to manifest itself socially and from which in-turn we claim to derive our knowledge of the social (2009, 458). The economic base, in other words, is the "point of ultimacy…that justifies an entire theoretical approach" (Vahabzadeh 2009, 458) we call Marxism, just as one might regard patriarchy as the point of ultimacy for radical feminism or the psyche as a point of ultimacy for psychoanalysis.

Omi and Winant, similarly, conceive of a central antagonism upon which they pivot social movements and the vanguard. The Gramscian import here is oblique, however, as the economy no longer occupies the central place, as it does in Marxist theory; only the idea of a central antagonism is retained. Omi and Winant abandon the economic base as a central antagonism while preserving all the other basic features of Gramsci's theory. Thus, we have Gramsci's frame without, specifically, Gramsci's Marxism,[5] or it could be said that we still have ultimate referentiality but with a shift in the grounds of ultimacy.

The political universe of Omi and Winant posits race as ultimate referentiality. For them, race serves as a fundamental, deterministic category. As they boldly proclaim, "[c]rucial to this formulation is the treatment of race as a *central axis* of social relations which cannot be subsumed under or reduced to some broader category or conception" (Omi and Winant 1986, 61-2, emphasis in original). Furthermore, for Omi and Winant, race "suffuses" (1986, 90) social relations and "pervade[s] US so-

---

5   It is for this reason that we may prefer to characterize the antiracism of Omi and Winant as "Gramscian influenced" as opposed to "Gramscian."

ciety, extending from the shaping of individual racial identities to the structuring of collective political action on the terrain of the state" (1986, 66). Omi and Winant thus, to draw on Todd May, produce an image of the "world as a set of concentric circles, with the core or base problematic lying at the centre" (1994, 10). All major problems can be reduced to the privileged ultimate ground of race that in their theory is conceptualized "as a fundamental *organizing principle* of social relations" (Omi and Winant 1986, 66, emphasis in original). Placing all their bets on the ahistoric structuralist horse of foundationalism, they announce that "[r]ace will *always* be at the center of the American experience" (Omi and Winant 1986, 6, emphasis in original), and, in what amounts to sidestepping the particular national histories of various nation-states, that "[e]very state institution is a racial institution" (Omi and Winant 1986, 76).

All the elements discussed are, of course, interrelated, and it was only for the sake of conceptual clarity that I separate them. The theory of hegemony tells us that what really matters is a complete transformation of the entire social structure on the basis of a central antagonism. Given that there is a central antagonism in the form of racism,[6] a vanguard of organic intellectuals are, as May puts it, "peculiarly well placed to analyze and to lead the resistance" (1994, 11). Success in this formulation can only

---

6 As we shall see, Omi and Winant also identify only a particular type of racism as the central antagonism. We may deduce that a vanguard is needed to not only identify the centre (racism) of their political universe but to also specify its nature.

be achieved when the vanguard leads the social move-ments in capturing or modifying state power. The theory of hegemony is thus offered as the solution to the crisis of fragmented, leaderless movements that, as I will show next, are strategically held to be at odds.

Toward a Strategically Flexible Antiracism

The hegemony of hegemony looms large in Omi and Winant. While their work has the advantage of offering a coherent and tightly bound theory of, and for, antiracist social movements, it runs against a number of severe lim-its that a poststructural critique makes clear. As Day ar-gues, the theory of hegemony imagines that only large-scale social change is effective, that the goal is one "of a final event of totalizing change" (2005, 9). The limit here is that in privileging this goal, the hegemony of hege-mony blocks alternative interpretations of antiracist social movements that dispense with vanguards; that refuse to see race/racism as a fundamental, central antagonism; and that do not measure success in terms of the capacity for movements to penetrate the state. All of this is to say that racial formation theory allows us to think of movements only in terms of their capacity for counter-hegemony. It evaluates them according to this counter-hegemonic standard. In so doing, it subsumes social movements to the state, potentially bureaucratizing the former. Operat-ing under the hegemony of hegemony, racial formation theory cannot account for social movements outside of the trajectory it proscribes for them: "Racially based political movements as we know them are inconceivable without the racial state" (Omi and Winant 1986, 80). Racial formation theory thus inhibits our ability to think of antiracist social movements according to a more suitable non-hegemonic logic—a logic that Day designates as the *affinity for affinity* (2009), which denotes "non-universalizing, non-hierarchical, non-coercive relationships based on mutual aid and shared ethical commitments" (8). In short, racial formation theory only accounts for counter-hegemonic radical social movements, while dismissing and ignoring non-hegemonic forms of antiracism.

Furthermore, by conceiving the terrain of resistance in terms of hegemony, racial formation theory runs the risk of legitimizing only one type of antiracist strategy, variously ignoring or dismissing the complexity of strategies already in use. Omi and Winant impose such a limit to the extent that they identify as the goal an antiracism that utilizes the concept of race to wrest concessions on behalf of racial minorities. Reflecting on past social movements, Omi and Winant observe that the Civil Rights movement was limited initially by seeking "black integration" (1986, 19) premised on "rhetoric [that] often explicitly appealed to the ideal of a 'race-free' society" (1986, 92), whereas they regard "[t]he real accomplishment of cultural nationalist currents... in unifying and promoting collective identity among the oppressed" (1986, 44). Omi and Winant, as such, deny post-racial society as a goal and privilege the differentialist antiracist use of racial identity. As they openly state, "[t]he central argument of this work... cannot be addressed by 'colorblind' theory or policy" (1986, 143). Taguieff, as a counterexample, takes the opposite side in favor of a colourblind, race-free society. He identifies the antiracist goal as one of "clear[ing] the horizon of the opiated fumes exhaled by the fetishism of difference" (Taguieff 2001, 310). It is important to note that just like Omi and Winant, Taguieff also operates under the hegemony of hegemony in that his work blasts the triumphant tones of a wide-reaching global antiracism. However, unlike Omi and Winant, who see racial identity simply as "difference" or "community," Taguieff identifies it as a handmaiden to cultural nationalism and to "the reign of pure violence" of 20th century totalitarian systems (2001, 306). To get away from racial classification, which for him is in itself problematic, he proposes a rethinking of "founding universalism, which forms the basis of an effective antiracist position" (Taguieff 2001, 305). Taguieff thus advocates universalist antiracist strategy as *the* strategy, while Omi and Winant promote differentialist antiracism.

The above mentioned theorists are not alone. Many antiracists operate under the shadow of Gramscian hegemony and engage in the fatal business of choosing the absolute best strategy for antiracism. Echoing Taguieff, Gilroy claims universalist antiracism as the clear choice of strategy when he argues that "action against racial hierarchies can proceed more effectively when it has been purged of any lingering respect for the idea of 'race' " (2001, 13). Assuming the stance of the intellectual *qua* the vanguard, he stresses that marginalized "groups will need to be persuaded very carefully that there is something worthwhile to be gained from a deliberate renunciation of 'race' as the basis for belonging to one another and acting in concert" (Gilroy 2001, 12). The hegemonic commitment to universalist strategy becomes evident when antiracists reject the race concept as "an intellectual error" and conclude that "enabling people to express their own racial identity and to be accorded equality, and rights, *as races* is problematic" (Bonnett 2000, 7, emphasis in original) or when they, in the same vein, argue that "the most significant… social movements have undermined the viability of the concept of 'race' " (Farrar 2004, 219).

At its core, universalist antiracism eschews racial categories and identities on the grounds that these are the tools with which racists carve up and establish racial hierarchies. For Taguieff, Gilroy, Bonnett, and Farrar, all racism begins with a fundamental, essential difference that is attributed as a "natural" property of the social construct we call race. To be sure, their position is certainly informed by the history of racism. Take, for example, 19th century scientific racism which employed anthropology, anthropometry, craniometry, and other disciplines, in order to construct typologies that supported the classification of human populations into physically discrete human types. We could say that simply differentiating people into various racially defined categories (white, Asian, black, Indigenous, etc.) is an invitation to racism. Judging from racist social movements such as Eugenics, and apartheid states such as pre-Mandela South Africa or Jim Crow era United States, it appears that race is the currency of racism, and it follows that any use of racial identity only lands us deeper into peril. Racial identity, as the lifeblood of various racist movements and states, compromises any antiracism that bases itself on it. For this universalist antiracism, resistance to racism must, there-

fore, aim at humanist, colourblind, and post-racial hori-
zons.

On the other side of the antiracist divide we may observe an unwavering commitment to differentialism. This
current of antiracism often manifests itself in arguments
for the retention of essentialist markers of difference
(variously in the defense of "particularity" or "diversity").
To be sure, differentialist strategy does not naively uphold
racial identity as a biological essence or as something that
occurs naturally. As Agnes Calliste and George J. Sefa
Dei carefully note, "we operationalize the race concept as
a social-relational category defined by socially selected
real or imagined physical, as well as cultural, characteristics" (2000, 20-1). Differentialist strategy recognizes that
even as a social-relational category race essentializes;
however, for differentialist antiracism "the risk of essence" (Spivak 1993, 3) is worth taking since racism can
only, or best, be overcome when "political movements
mobilize around particular forms of identity" (Calliste
and Dei 2000, 28). Such an "oppositional political project
differs from... post-racial perspectives" (St. Louis 2002,
652) of universalist antiracists in that it regards "race...
[as] a conceptual abstraction *with* material effects" (St.
Louis 2002, 666, emphasis in original). It follows here
that given the real social effects (i.e. racism) of what is
admittedly a social construct (i.e. race), we are compelled
to utilize, or at least recognize, racial identity. This current of antiracism takes the social construction of race
seriously enough that it is unwilling to part with race
solely on the grounds that it is a scientifically invalid
concept. Most of the theorists that I have grouped under

the differentialist banner share a suspicion around the easy dismissal of race precisely on the grounds that even as alleged "fictions," racial identities function. Others question the necessary racial privilege involved in being able to sidestep racial identity altogether (Gallagher 2003).

Here too we encounter historic grounds for asserting identity, for retaining it as an antiracist resource, and for demanding the recognition of difference. While examples like scientific racism, Eugenics, and apartheid may readily spring to mind when we consider the history of racism, we would also do well, as this current of antiracism reminds us, to consider that racism also operates by absorbing, including, incorporating, and assimilating difference—in short, by speaking the humanist, colourblind language of universalism. What used to be called "Canadianization" operated precisely according to this dimension of racism in Canada. Duncan Campbell Scott, the Canadian Deputy Minister in charge of Indian Affairs from 1913 to 1932, demonstrated this logic when he stated that the goal of residential schools was "to kill the Indian in the child" (in Truth and Reconciliation Commission of Canada 2012, 81). Residential schools were, according to Scott, to "continue until there is not a single Indian in Canada that has not been absorbed into the body politic, and there is no Indian question, and no Indian Department" (in Truth and Reconciliation Commission of Canada 2012, 12). Today's settler states abide by the logic of universalist racism in adhering to the ideology of meritocracy and in upholding what sociologists call "systemic racism."[7] Unlike differentialist racism, which wants to know the other in order to distance the other, universalist racism wants to know the other in order to erase the problematic signs of their otherness. Universalist racism entertains the fantasy of removing the particular, communitarian markers of Indigeneity and, as Scott illustrates, violently recoding them with markers of an undifferentiated Canadian sameness. Given such forms of racism, the counter-hegemonic commitment to differentialist antiracist strategy, thus, objects in principle "to the use of universal groupings" (Mohanty 2003, 25) that would sub-

---

7 Systemic, or institutional, racism is a kind of racism that takes place in institutions (police departments, colleges and universities, places of employment, etc.) that while appearing to be inclusive and equal, ends up privileging and preserving the interests of the dominant group. Systemic racism has the distinct quality of not looking like racism at first sight. In fact, it works better if those who practice it are not even aware of their role in it. Consider, for example, the current Canadian debate concerning the Parti Québécois' proposed Charter of Quebec Values. In the alleged interest of secularism, the Charter would ban civil servants and public employees from displaying "ostentatious" religious symbols while on the job. To familiarize us with their plan, the party produced a helpful poster that includes illustrations of prohibited expressions of faith. In the interest of being fair, they have included in the poster, along the veiled Muslim woman and Turban-wearing Sikh man, a picture of a chest bearing a large Christian crucifix. On the surface, the Charter seems to fairly target all major religious groups while its systemic racism is obvious when we consider that the ban would not actually affect Christians (other than, of course, Christian monks who actually do wear large crucifixes but who are not likely to apply for jobs in the public sector), but it would adversely affect Muslims and Sikhs. Again, there is nothing blatantly racist about this, and this is the point: systemic racism works best when the employees and party members who institute it are not committed racists but are simply interested in fairly applying the rules to all.

sume difference under a colourblind, post-racial humanism. Instead, it argues for particular racial identity as "as a source of knowledge and a basis for progressive mobilization" (Mohanty 2003, 6).

As I have shown, many antiracist theorists who ground themselves in the hegemony of hegemony can be placed along either differentialist or universalist strategy from where they contest racism while unduly regarding other antiracists with suspicion. My argument is that the choosing of an absolute antiracist aim on the basis of a single antiracist strategy makes sense only within the terms of hegemony itself. After all, if the central antagonism is presumed to be universalist racism (a racism that ignores differences and aims to integrate everyone into a white, but "colourblind," society), it makes perfect sense to propose that movements can only succeed to the extent that they articulate differentialist antiracist aims. To get there it follows that a vanguard is needed to step in and correct the poor analysis of existing movements, to unify fragmented movements, and lead them in struggle against a state. If, on the other hand, the central antagonism is presumed to be differentialist racism (a racism that stresses racial difference, creates racial identities, and aims to segregate/exterminate racial minorities), the same requirements, in terms of a vanguard and engagement with the state, remain in place. My goal, however, is not to argue which strategy is ultimately the correct one but to show that both strategies, when stripped of the hegemony of hegemony, have their place in confronting the various manifestations and symptoms of racism. If we allow that both types of racism can coexist—that states, corporations and other hierarchical institutions and practices, variously embody colourblind and colourconscious racial ideologies—it follows that the choice of strategy ultimately depends on context or on the nature of the racism one is contesting in one's particular location. I am here thus in agreement with Spivak[8] that "strategy suits a situation; a strategy is not a theory" (1993, 4). The choice of antiracist strategy must be made by movements themselves as they adapt themselves to diverse circumstances; it does not lie in any kind of hegemonically oriented theory we may wish for vanguards to impose on social movements.

At this point it becomes necessary to account for strategic flexibility. What exactly is meant by strategy itself, and how is it different from tactics? Let us tease out the difference by way of considering what contemporary social movements mean by the curious phrase "diversity of

---

8　Spivak develops one of the most well-known accounts of the progressive essential uses of identity. She argues in favor of what she calls *strategic essentialism* that pertains to "[t]he strategic use of an essence as a mobilizing slogan or a masterword like *woman* or *worker* or the name of a nation" (Spivak 1993, 3, emphasis in original). Given that she understands that strategic essentialism is only an elaboration of a strategy that is not "good for all cases" (Spivak 1993, 4), I do not place her—despite the fact that she explicitly orients herself in terms of Gramscian hegemony—as a hegemonic proponent of differentialist antiracism. She is, to be sure, under the sway of the hegemony of hegemony, but her nuanced account of strategy falls under my notion of strategic flexibility. Perhaps with Spivak my own argument encounters a limit, or perhaps it is the case that we already have in Spivak a less-than-fully realized contestation of Gramscian hegemony. The fact that she "believe[s] in undermining the vanguardism of theory" (Spivak 1993, 15) certainly should give us cause to consider the latter possibility.

tactics." The concept designates a value among social movement actors. By it, they hint at an open attitude toward the various tactics that actors use in pursuit of social justice. From peaceful assemblies that involve the waving of banners, displaying of signs, and chanting of slogans; to militant barricades that involve black bloc confrontations with state and corporate power; to the subverting of advertisement, which clutters urban landscapes; to the construction of community centres and cooperatives, the diversity of tactics approach opposes the preferential, hierarchical ranking of any of these means of resistance. In the toolbox of the activist *bricoleur*, we find a vast range and combination of such tactics—that is, of means for disrupting and resisting various forms of oppression. Strategy, on the other hand, designates the mode by which such means are arrived at.

I mean by strategy something along the lines of what Michel Foucault means by *discourse*, what Tomas Kuhn means by *paradigm*, and what Karl Mannheim means by *ideology*. I propose that a strategy is an organizing framework that fixes the boundaries of perception and logic toward a certain goal. A strategy is always oriented toward a goal, and it presents us with an overall aim by delimiting the frontiers of intelligibility with that aim in mind. A strategy, strictly speaking, is not a discourse, as it does not join power and knowledge in order to construct subjects (Foucault 2003); nor is it a paradigm, as it does not provide a model for a coherent scientific tradition (Kuhn 1996); nor is it ideology, as it does not designate the underlying political motives and social interests of actors, parties, and movements (Mannheim [1936] 1985). A strategy, however, traverses them all. A strategy *is* possible only as discourse, or only within a certain type of discursive formation, and a strategy *is* also a model (in a loose unscientific sense) that like ideology articulates and contains underlying motives and interest, but it is not any one of these things alone. Rather, a strategy "involves a unitary analysis" (May 1994, 10)[9] that delineates the possible range of tactics toward a predefined aim. Thus, when I argue for a strategically flexible antiracism, this is not the same thing as arguing for a diversity of tactics. It is instead an argument in favor of a wider range of frameworks from which tactics are elaborated and from which they receive their tenor. Lastly, drawing on Jacques Derrida, *strategy* in strategically flexible antiracism is non-teleological; it orients tactics only as a "strategy without finality" (1982:7). In this sense it is compatible only with the non-hegemonic affinity-based principles that characterize contemporary anarchist antiracist movements. As I will show in the next section, these movements, in renouncing hegemony as a goal, renounce finality. They do not chase 19th century chimeras such as freedom, emancipation, and revolution. Without aiming for the complete, total institution of a new world, they work for the radical transformation of the relations in which they find

---

9   I am deliberately misreading May here who speaks of strategy only in terms of *strategic political philosophy*, which unlike me, he does not attribute to theoretical traditions that he defines in terms of *tactical political philosophy* and *formal political philosophy* (1994). To be clear, I accept May's definition of strategy, but I reject his grouping of only certain traditions under this "strategic" heading. For an in-depth critique of May's taxonomy, see Nathan Jun's *Anarchism and Political Modernity* (2012).

themselves, knowing that all that is possible is a trans-formation that will land them into new arrangements of power. As such, they are engaged in the potentially end-less task of challenging and undoing racism, wherever and in whatever form it may arrive.

Given this, a strategically flexible antiracism defends what Omi and Winant identify (if only in passing) as the problem of "counterposed strategic orientations." Where the hegemony of hegemony privileges only either univer-salist or differentialist approaches because it recognizes only a single racial antagonism, a strategically flexible antiracism is open to a deeper complexity, to the bewil-dering possibility that racism itself functions according to contradictory strategies and that any contest with it will necessarily embody contradiction. Following poststruc-tural analysis of the social as "a borderless realm of com-peting and overlapping organization schemes" (Dumont 2008, 18) implies that we recognize the strategic flexibil-ity of racism itself and refuse the reductive interpretation, popular today, of racism solely as a strategy of col-orblindness or colourconsciousness. Poststructuralism de-mands that we abandon the idea of racism as a single structure that can be overcome when we locate its "centre" with recourse to ultimate referentiality. What the plethora of non-unified and non-totalizing antiracist movements designates is not a crisis of a lacking anti-racist core but the fact that racism is too complicated to be reduced to a single, central antagonism. In the face of multiple modalities of racism, contemporary affin-ity-based antiracist movements must be approached, to draw on Foucault's insights on power, as "a plurality of resistances" (1990, 96). The single choice of strategy, therefore, has to be rejected along with the absolute foundationalist grounds that it is predicated on. With Franklin Adler, strategically flexible antiracism identifies a "false choice... between the particularism of the one side versus the universalism of the other" (1999, 493). It also cannot help but reject the preference, characteristic of the hegemony of hegemony, for strong leaders and in-tellectual elites. I next turn to case studies of anarchist an-tifascism and Anarchist People of Color in order to demonstrate how such movements exercise affinity and strategic flexibility, thus bypassing the hegemony of he-gemony in antiracism.

Anarchist Antifascism as Universalist Strategy

Anarchist antifascist collectives confront groups that identify themselves as white supremacist, fascist, nation-alist, or racist. Drawing on a rich history of antifascist resistance during World War II, antifascism designates the activism of North American and European groups such as Anti-Racist Action, Anti-Fascist Action, Arm the Spirit, Antifa, and Red Action. These groups operate on a con-sensus or affinity model in that they are decentralized and leaderless, and they bypass the state as they directly en-gage in antifascist action. Contemporary anarchist antifas-cists employ a tactic that activist K. Bullstreet calls a "physical-force policy" (2001, 3). This entails physical confrontations that sometimes result in hand-to-hand fighting with fascists in the streets. Antifascist groups may therefore show up to rallies, convergences, and other functions of fascist movements in order to disrupt them. As one of Anti-Racist Action's "points of unity" announces, "[w]e go where they go: Whenever fascists are organizing or active in public, we're there. We don't believe in ignoring them or staying away from them. Never let the nazis have the street!" (South Side Chicago Anti-Racist Action 2010, 1). The goal of confronting fascism extends to preventing fascism from developing. As Bullstreet reasons, "[b]y crushing the fascists at an early stage I think it is reasonable to assume that Anti-Fascist Action (AFA) has prevented numerous racist attacks and even saved lives. For if the fascists were given the chance to freely march, sell their papers, and appear as a respectable political force they would just grow and grow" (2001, 1).

Antifascist movements may, as such, be thought of as counter-movements. Their goal is to dismantle already existing movements before these grow and seize the state. It should be pointed out that antifascist activists are aware that, as activist Larry Gambone states, "there is no sort of fascist virus hovering about in contemporary society" (2000, 18) that would see white supremacist groups like the Aryan Nations or the World Church of the Creator seizing state power anytime soon; nonetheless, anarchist antifascists are also aware that fascism emerges out of the same circumstances that engender progressive social movements. It is to the prevention of such a fascist emergence that they dedicate themselves. One could say that they have taken to heart Walter Benjamin's observation that "[b]ehind every fascism, there is a failed revolution" (quoted in Fabry 2012, 39) and that it is the failure of their own movement, and of the Left in general, that will allow fascism to succeed.

For anarchist antifascists, the confrontation with fascism is not solely physical. A considerable amount of their work involves analyzing fascism and prefiguring an antifascist culture. Aside from putting on concerts, visiting local schools to give presentations, and distributing flyers at community events, antifascist activists publish numerous pieces that detail the dimensions of their struggles and offer insight into contemporary forms of fascism. Such analyses are not elaborated by organic intellectuals, party members, or any of the other figures associated with counter-hegemonic movements; they are the work of countless activists themselves who participate on the ground and in front of the computer screen. Antifascists articulate their views in pamphlets, discussion documents, and internet websites, which emerge as participants reflect on their activism. As one series of documents states, stressing the unending nature of analyzing and contesting fascism, "[t]he essays presented here should be taken as part of an ongoing, evolving talk within the movement" (Xtn 2002, 1). Judging from the large quantity of such documents, it can be said that rather than needing intellectual guidance, the movements themselves act as their own intellectuals. Seeking neither to take over/get concessions from state power, nor to lead/unify other movements under a broader antifascist umbrella, anarchist antifascism requires no intellectual elite to lead the cadre.

In terms of strategy, antifascist analyses occupy the space of universalist antiracism. The consensus here is that fascism is a racism that is driven by the need to categorize and hierarchically rank human beings along biologically defined scales of difference. As the activist Don Hamerquist argues, "[t]he physical and social separation of people along racial and ethnic lines is crucial to the fascist worldview" (2002, 62). From his perspective, racism is a deeply divisive practice. It requires the construction of racial categories and our participation in a worldview that maintains that races really do exist. In opposing such a formulation of racism, antifascists understandably adopt a humanist, and even colourblind, perspective. As one pamphlet by a group called Anti-Fascist Forum puts it: "We are acting as citizens to rebuild the ideological and philosophical basis for the liberation of humanity across all borders" (2000, np). In the face of the fascist belief in the "incompatibility of races," the group Anti-Racist Action reacts by upholding a colourblind position: "There is only one 'race'—the human race" (ARA Network 2004). Such a strategy extends to the organizational dynamics and tactics of anarchist antifascist groups, which downplay racial distinctions and present themselves as "multi-racial" crews in composition (The Anti-Racist Action Network 2009).

While the opposition to fascism might form what we could call the "centre" of this current of activism, and while anarchist antifascism operates according to what I

identify as universalist antiracist strategy, antifascist activists understand that the struggle against racism must
take place along many axes of oppression. That is, anarchist antifascism does not treat racism as a central antagonism. As Xtn of Chicago Anti-Racist Action explains,
"[t]aking the fight to fascism—whether in its white supremacist form, in a crypto-fascist fundamentalist variety
or perhaps even in forms we have yet to see—cannot be
sidelined for the larger struggles, or vice versa" (2002,
13). Xtn thus establishes that antifascism should not be
dismissed by radical social movements for "diverting energy away from anti-capitalist struggle" (Xtn 2002, 9) and
neither should other struggles be seen as less important by
antifascists. Rejecting the centrality of any form of oppression, but specifically of economic oppression as the
central oppression from which racism derives, antifascist
activists see their work as addressing the need "to develop
a more complex analysis and, to be blunt, dump workerist
notions that there exists a united proletariat against the
bosses" (Xtn 2002, 10). In fact, antifascism is premised
on an intersectional and interlocking sensibility that displays an affinity for a non-unified plurality of struggles.
Neither class nor race are treated by antifascist activists as
central axes of social relations, and fascism is not considered the only form of racial oppression worth contesting. As the activist Hamerquist observes, "[w]e can't allow a concrete opposition to *the entire range of oppression*, national, sexual, and gender… to be subsumed into
a generalized and abstract opposition to a common en-

emy…" (2002, 63, emphasis mine). Such an orientation, as these activist voices show, removes the need for a single, overarching antiracist approach in favor of strategic flexibility.

Anarchist People of Color as Differentialist Strategy

Anarchist People of Color (henceforth APOC) is not a single group, but a collectivity "created to address issues of race, anti-authoritiarianism [sic], and people of color struggle politics [sic] within the context of anarchism, and to create/increase political safe spaces for people of color" (Anarchist People of Color n.d.). What started as an email list in 2001 by activist Ernesto Aguilar grew in the U.S. into "a loosely organized network of individuals, collectives, and cells" (Anarchist People of Color n.d.). The name APOC, as such, can designate "an individual identity, and a movement. Anyone who is such can claim the acronym apoc" (People of Color Organize! 2011).

Just like anarchist antifascism, APOC is best described in terms of the affinity for affinity. APOC eschews centralization in favor of direct action tactics, which seek neither state power nor to negotiate with it. Direct action marks the preference of APOC to take things into their own hands as they disrupt the flows of state and corporate power and confront racism in its various manifestations. For some APOC, this means standing in solidarity with immigrant workers who are denied services or threatened with further loss of status; for others, it implies opposing racial profiling by the police. The loose organizational structure of APOC means that it can extend like a rhizomatic network into other movements. We can account for this by considering that APOC emerged as discontent mounted over the antiracist approach of the anarchist group Bring the Ruckus. For former members Heather Ajani and Ernesto Aguilar, Bring the Ruckus made their antiracism too dependent on "the participation of white folks, and... [refused] to consider the reality people of color worldwide already understand: masses of whites won't give up their privileges" (2004). Dissatisfied with the way in which Bring the Ruckus made the struggle against racism contingent on the abolishment of whiteness, APOC splintered away; it did so not as a single group, but as a tendency in anarchism itself.

Unlike anarchist antifascism, APOC demonstrates that racism can also be challenged by a differentialist antiracism. To this end, APOC utilizes a highly colourconscious logic—a logic that makes appeals to, rather than downplaying, identity and difference. "There is only one human race" is not a useful rhetorical tactic for APOC. This is because for APOC racism is not only about labeling and dividing people; racism also assumes a liberal-democratic, colourblind tone that neglects "institutionalized, systematic, and historical oppression" of racial minorities (People of Color Organize! 2012). We can therefore say that APOC opposes not divisive but unifying practices of racism, which variously seek integration and assimilation. Its focus is not so much on fascist and nationalist inspired racism as it is on the racism which operates without any easily identifiable racists. I have in mind the racism which marginalizes non-whites in subtle, indirect, and covert ways as it includes them in corporate hierarchies, government bureaucracies, and, even, social movements. It makes sense, as such, that given that there is a racism which pretends not to be racist, or stated differently, that there is a racism which can be experienced without being easily seen, the experiences of people of colour are valued by APOC.

Without recourse to a vanguard and in line with differentialist strategy, APOC draws on what the activist freelark describes as "the epistemic privilege of the oppressed" (2010). That is, APOC privileges "the unique knowledge that an oppressed group has" (freelark 2010) of its own racial subordination. Just as women may recognize the day-to-day experience of sexism, and gays and lesbians have firsthand understanding of homophobia, APOC maintains that people of colour have insights to offer about the everyday, inner-workings of racism. Accordingly, APOC websites and documents are rich in firsthand accounts about what it is like to be a person of colour in a white supremacist society. The differentialist antiracism of APOC implies that identity, even if created by racial discourse, cannot be simply dismissed as a social construct (Law 2010). Instead, racial identity, which operates in a racialized world, is the basis from which radical politics can be elaborated, especially against universalist racism.

As Aguilar observes, "the anarchist movement is a long way from being egalitarian" (2003). From my reading, some of the most progressive work performed by APOC involves challenging racism *within* the anarchist movement itself. Drawing on the epistemic privilege of the oppressed, APOC present a serious challenge to anarchist organizing that goes beyond simply noting that the movement is dominated by white people or that anarchism places whiteness (even as the thing to be abolished!) at the centre of antiracist projects. To this end, APOC has developed micropolitical critiques of the relations of oppression as they play out within the organizational dynamics of radical social movements. In doing so, APOC can be seen to be providing "specific analyses of concrete situations of oppression" (May 2011, 41). Many APOC activists have noted, as activist Bridget Todd observes, that racism within social movements "exists as a kind of pathological denial of the privilege in which white progressive activists are actively rooted" (2011). Self-identified white antiracist activists perpetuate white privilege, as APOC analyses indicate, by "*fetish*[*izing*] people of color struggles" (People of Color Organize! 2011); *tokenizing* people of colour by asking them to join movements in order to make them more diverse (freelark 2010); *expecting to be educated* by people of colour on racism while reveling in white guilt (Toi 2012) and *acting on behalf* of people of colour without obtaining their consent (People of Color Organize! 2011). All of this points to the fact that anarchist movements replicate the very structures of oppression they seek to contest, and that "favoritism toward whites" within social movements (Olson 2012, 50) needs to be contested. To be sure, APOC have challenged white privilege in such movements as Occupy, Bring the Ruckus, Love and Rage, and CrimethInc. When anarchist groups are confronted by the fact that "many people of color do not feel comfortable in almost all-white spaces" (Law 2010), the reactions, as APOC literature attests to, range from *discomfort* and the eventual shifting of topics towards class oppression (freelark 2010); to the *denial* that "anything can be done about POC members feeling unsafe" (Toi 2012), or that white activists are responsible for colonialism (People of Color Organize! 2011); to even *outrage* at what white anarchists perceive as "divisiveness" (Olson 2012, 50) and "reverse racism" (Toi 2012) within the movement.

While "Euro-centric anarchism" (People of Color Organize! 2011) seems to be alive and well, we would do well to end the discussion by noting two promising developments. The first is the emergence of a body of knowledge which, as a result of the work of groups like APOC, provides much needed information on racism and white privilege within the anarchist movement. Although, APOC literature indicates that white anarchists still have a long way to go, we at least have a starting point for how to act in solidarity—that is, for how white and non-white anarchists can work together. It seems the starting point is the willingness to recognize the structural privileges of whiteness. Being able to see that whiteness implies that whites cannot not be racist (at least not while residing in European and white settler societies) is the precondition for further developing anarchist relations across the colour line. The second positive development consists of the very fact that APOC emerged. Historically, such a group designates a new phenomenon on the anarchist scene, creating openings for others like it. With its emergence we finally witnessed APOC conferences and other events organized as "people of color only" spaces, as well as the much needed continuation of resistance against colourblind racism within, and outside of, the anarchist movement.

Conclusion

The antiracist anarchist movements that I have identified here—anarchist antifascism and Anarchist People of Color—are indicative of a displacement of the hegemony of hegemony. Along with poststructural theory, they reveal a way out of Gramscian-inspired antiracism by challenging the idea that racism is the fundamental problem or that there is only one kind of racism; that intellectual vanguards with well-developed analyses are needed to lead social movements; and that the state is the most important site for the contestation of racism itself. In their affinity based prefigurative practices, anarchist antiracist movements show us that resistance to racism can be carried out according to a number of strategies. Affinity in antiracism, as I have shown, is thus best conceptualized in terms of strategic flexibility. Utilizing what, following

Taguieff, I identify as universalist strategy, antifascist anarchist groups oppose colourconscious racist practices, while along the lines of differentialist strategy, APOC brings attention to colourblind racist practices. Both movements, as such, can be seen as operating on the basis of a strategically flexible antiracism that refuses to privilege either strategy as *the* strategy.

The fact that the hegemony of hegemony is firmly in place in antiracism today means that racism cannot be adequately contested or, at least, identified and known in academic theory and analyses. The way that actually existing antiracist social movements engage in strategic flexibility is sidelined in favor of developing "theoretical clarity about racial dynamics" (Omi and Winant 1986, 102). As long as antiracists continue to theorize only from the perspective of differentialist or universalist strategy, mischaracterizations will be reproduced in antiracism. Such mischaracterizations manifest themselves, for example, in a tendency to denounce colourblindness in the United States. The focus for the majority of contemporary American theorists of antiracism seems to be on resisting what they identify as colourblind or post-racial perspectives. To draw on Eduardo Bonilla-Silva, "this new ideology has become a formidable political tool for the maintenance of the racial order. Much as Jim Crow racism served as the glue for defending a brutal and overt system of racial oppression in the pre-Civil Rights era, color-blind racism serves today as the ideological armor for a covert and institutionalized system in the post-Civil

Rights era" (2006, 3). What Bonilla-Silva misses, however, is that both racist and antiracist discourses can make use of colorblindness even in the post-Civil Rights era. By directing our attention solely to colourblind or universalist forms of racism, as American sociology and antiracist theory is wont to do, we lose sight of the complex ways in which racism manifests itself also according to colourconscious strategies, and, equally, how our own antiracism also maintains, and relies on, certain racial myths. The temptation to relegate to the past certain ideologies and strategies of racism, on the basis that these belonged more securely to another era, fails us as such an approach cannot take into account the discontinuities, accidents, and cul-de-sacs of history. A hegemony of hegemony in antiracism, as such, prevents us from considering that it is not a matter of wishing away or using racial identity but, as anarchist antiracist movements show us, of knowing when to use identity in an adequately antiracist way and when to abandon it.

Rather than seeking a coherent antiracist whole, we would do less violence to antiracism if we approached social movements in their already existing complexity. We need to learn to see that by being flexible and employing "counterposed strategic orientations," antiracist anarchists are, in fact, extending the front against racism, and they are doing so precisely by avoiding counter-hegemonic unity. It seems we are, as such, not in need of a unified antiracist theory; what we do need is a lot more of what we already have—that is, non-unified, decentralized, leaderless movements that bypass the need for a single response or a single strategy against racism.

References

Adler, Franklin H. 1999. "Antiracism, Difference, and Xenologica." *Cultural Values 3,* no. 4: 492-502.

Aguilar, Ernesto. 2003. "An Interview with Ernesto Aguilar of the APOC." Common Struggle/Lucha Común. Accessed April 30, 2013. http://nefac.net/node/508.

Ajani, Heather, and Ernesto Aguilar. 2004. "On Donovan Jackson and White Race Traitors Who Claim They're Down." Illegal Voices. Accessed June 23, 2005. http://illegalvoices.org/knowledge/writings_on_anarchism/on_do novan_jackson_and_white_race_traitors.html.

Anthias, Floya, and Cathie Lloyd. 2002. "Introduction: Fighting racisms, defining the Territory." In *Rethinking Anti-racisms: From theory to practice*, edited by Floya Anthias and Cathie Lloyd, 1-21. New York: Routledge.

Anti-Fascist Forum. 2000. *Anti-Fascist Resistance in France* (pamphlet). Np: Arm the Spirit/ Anti-Fascist Forum/ Antifa Info-Bulletin.

Anti-Racist Action Network. 2009. "History." Anti-Racist Action. Accessed September 9, 2013. http://antiracistaction.org/?page_id=30.

Anarchist People of Color. n.d. "Anarchist People of Color." *Anarchist People of Color.* Accessed April 24, 2013. http://anarchistpeopleofcolor.tumblr.com/.

ARA Network. 2004. "About the Anti-Racist Action Network." ARA Network. Accessed June 23, 2005. http://www.antiracistaction.org/pn/modules.php?

op=modload&name=Sections&file=index&req=viewarticle&artid =1&page=1.

Bannerji, Himani. 2000. *The Dark Side of the Nation: Essays on Multiculturalism, Nationalism and Gender*. Toronto: Canadian Scholars' Press.

Bonilla-Silva, Eduardo. 2006. *Racism Without Racists: Color-Blind Racism and the Persistence of Racial Inequality in the United States*. 2nd ed. Toronto: Rowman & Littlefield Publishers.

Bonnett, Alastair. 2000. *Anti-Racism*. New York: Routledge.

Bullstreet, K. 2001. *Bash the Fash: Anti-Fascist Recollections 1984- 93* (pamphlet). Berkeley, CA: Kate Sharpley Library.

Calliste, Agnes, and George J. Sefa Dei. 2001. *Anti-Racist Feminism: Critical Race and Gender Studies*. Edited by Agnes Calliste and George J. Sefa Dei. Halifax, Nova Scotia: Fernwood Publishing.

Day, Richard J. F. 2005. *Gramsci Is Dead: Anarchist Currents in the Newest Social Movements*. Toronto: Between the Lines.

Derrida, Jacques. 1982. "Différance." In *Margins of Philosophy*, translated by Alan Bass, 1-28. Chicago: University of Chicago Press.

Dumont, Clayton W., Jr. 2008. *The Promise of Poststructuralist Sociology: Marginalized Peoples and the Problem of Knowledge*. Albany NY: State University of New York Press.

Fabry, Adam. 2012. "Nach Rechts! Demystifying the Rise of Populist and the Far-Right in Post-Transition Hungary." In *New Populisms and the European Right and Far Right Parties: The Challenge and the Perspectives for the Left*, 39-46. Accessed May 8, 2013. http://transformnetwork.net/uploads/tx_news/NEW_POPULISM S_AND_THE_EUROPEAN_RIGHT_.pdf.

Farrar, Max. 2004. "Social Movements and the Struggle Over 'Race'". In *Democracy and Participation—Popular Protest and New Social Movements*, edited by M. J. Todd, and Gary Taylor,

218-47. London: Merlin Press.

Foucault, Michel. 1990. *The History of Sexuality: An Introduction*, vol. 1. New York: Vintage Books.

—. 2003. *The Archaeology of Knowledge*. New York: Routledge.

freelark. 2010. "Five Things White Activists Should Never Say." People of Color Organize. Accessed February 5, 2013. http://www.peopleofcolororganize.com/analysis/opinion/white-activists/.

Gallagher, Charles A. 2003. "Color-Blind Privilege: The Social and Political Functions of Erasing the Color Line in Post Race America." *Race, Gender & Class* 10, no. 4: 1-17.

Gambone, Larry. 2000. *The Road to Fascism: The Rise of Italian Fascism and Its Relation to Anarchism, Syndicalism and Socialism* (pamphlet). Montreal: Red Lion Press.

Gilroy, Paul. 1990. "The End of Anti-Racism." *Journal of Ethnic and Migration Studies* 17, no. 1: 71-83.

—. 2001. *Against Race: Imagining Political Culture Beyond the Color Line*. Cambridge, Massachusetts: The Belknap Press of Harvard University Press.

Gramsci, Antonio. 1999. *Selections from the Prison Notebooks.* New York: International Publishers.

Hamerquist, Don. 2002. "Fascism & Antifascism." In *Confronting Fascism: Discussion Documents for a Militant Movement,* 15-69. Montreal: Kersplebedeb.

Holloway, John. 2010. *Change the World Without Taking Power: The Meaning of Revolution Today*. New York: Pluto Press.

HoSang, Daniel M., Oneka LaBennett, and Laura Pulido, eds. 2012. *Racial Formation in the Twenty-Frist Century*. Berkeley: University of California Press.

Jun, Nathan. 2012. *Anarchism and Political Modernity*. New York:

Continuum.

Kuhn, Thomas S. 1996. *The Structure of Scientific Revolutions*. 3rd ed. Chicago: University of Chicago Press.

Laclau, Ernesto, and Chantel Mouffe. 2001. *Hegemony and Socialist Strategy: Towards a Radical Democratic Politics*. 2nd ed. New York: Verso.

Law, Victoria. 2010. "People of Color, Class, Diversity & the White Left." People of Color Organize. Accessed February 5, 2013. http://www.peopleofcolororganize.com/analysis/opinion/people-color-class-diversity-white-left/

Lloyd, Cathie. 2002. "Anti-racism, social movements and civil society". In *Rethinking Anti-Racisms: From Theory to Practice*, edited by Floya Anthias and Cathie Lloyd, 60-77. New York: Routledge.

May, Todd. 1994. *The Political Philosophy of Poststructuralist Anarchism*. University Park, Pennsylvania: The Pennsylvania State University Press.

—. 2011. "Is Post-Structuralist Political Theory Anarchist?" In *Post-Anarchism: A Reader*, edited by Duane Rousselle and Süreyyya Evren, 41-5. Winnipeg, MB: Fernwood Publishing.

Mannheim, Karl. [1936] 1985. *Ideology and Utopia: An Introduction to the Sociology of Knowledge*. New York: Harcourt.

Mohanty, Chandra T. 2003. *Feminism Without Borders: Decolonizing Theory, Practicing Solidarity*. London: Duke University Press.

Olson, Joel. 2012. "Whiteness and the 99%." In *We are Many: Reflection of Movement Strategy From Occupation to Liberation*, edited by Kate Khatib, Margaret Killjoy, and Mike McGuire, 46-51. Oakland, CA: AK Press.

Omi, Michael, and Howard Winant. 1986. *Racial Formation in the United States: From the 1960s to the 1980s*. New York: Routledge.

People of Color Organize! 2011. "Anarchist People of Color/Crimethinc Smack a White Boy Eviction Clash." People of Color Organize. Accessed February 5, 2013. http://www.peopleofcolororganize.com/activism/anarchist-people-colorcrimethinc-smack-white-boy-clash/.

——. 2012. "What is White Anti-Racism?: The Win-Win Privilege and the Indulgence of White Guilt." People of Color Organize. Accessed February 5, 2013. http://www.peopleofcolororganize.com/analysis/white-antiracism-winwin-privilege-indulgence-white-guilt/.

Schewidler, Christine, Pablo Rey Mazón, Saba Waheed, and Sasha Costanza-Chock. 2012. "Research By and For the Movement: Key Findings From the Occupy Research General Demographic & Participation Survey (ORGS)." In *We are Many: Reflection of Movement Strategy From Occupation to Liberation*, edited by Kate Khatib, Margaret Killjoy, and Mike McGuire, 69-73. Oakland, CA: AK Press.

South Side Chicago Anti-Racist Action. 2010. "July 31, 2010 Zine." ZineLibrary.info. Accessed April 24, 2013. http://zinelibrary.info/files/chicagoarazine_print.pdf.

Spence, Lester, and Mike McGuire. 2012. "Occupy and the 99%." In *We are Many: Reflection of Movement Strategy From Occupation to Liberation*, edited by Kate Khatib, Margaret Killjoy, and Mike McGuire, 53-65. Oakland, CA: AK Press.

Spivak, Gayatri C. 1988. "Can the Subaltern Speak?". In *Marxism and the Interpretation of Culture*, edited by C. Nelson and L. Grossberg, 271-313. Chicago: University of Illinois Press.

——. 1993. *Outside in the Teaching Machine*. New York: Routledge.

St Louis, Brett. 2002. "Post-race/post-politics? Activist-intellectualism and the reification of race." *Ethnic and Racial Studies* 25, no. 4: 652-75.

Taguieff, Pierre-André. 2001. *The Force of Prejudice: On Racism and Its Doubles*. Translated by Hassan Melehy. Minneapolis: University of Minnesota Press.

Todd, Bridget. 2011. "Racial Fractures and the Occupy Movement." People of Color Organize. Accessed February 7, 2013. http://www.peopleofcolororganize.com/activism/racial-fractures-occupy-movement/.

Toi. 2012. "POC Anti-Racist Organizing and Burnout." People of Color Organize. Accessed February 14, 2013. http://www.peopleofcolororganize.com/analysis/opinion/poc-anti-racist-organizing-burnout/.

Truth and Reconciliation Commission of Canada. 2012. *They Came for the Children: Canada, Aboriginal Peoples, and Residential Schools*. Winnipeg: Truth and Reconciliation Commission of Canada.

Vahabzadeh, Peyman. 2009. "Ultimate referentiality: Radical Phenomenology and the new interpretive sociology." *Philosophy & Social Criticism* 35, no. 4: 447-65.

Xtn. 2002. "Introduction". In *Confronting Fascism: Discussion Documents for a Militant Movement*, 1-13. Montreal: Kersplebedeb.

7 | Anti-State Resistance On Stolen Land: Settler Colonialism, Settler Identity and the Imperative of Anarchist Decolonization

Adam Gary Lewis[1]

Introduction

This chapter argues for increased and sustained analysis and action within anarchist movements of resistance with regard to decolonization and Indigenous struggles against colonization. As individuals and groups committed to anti-oppressive, anti-state and all around lib-

1   Adam's talk was delivered at NAASN5 via a video net link-up, but the room wasn't mic'd back to him, which presented many communication difficulties in the follow-up question and answer/discussion period (our apologies.)

eratory aims, anarchists necessarily must consider the decolonizing and anti-racist dimensions of resistance. This is especially the case for anarchist movements within settler colonial "North America," an entire continent founded on the displacement, dispossession and genocide of Indigenous peoples and one where anarchist movements are most often white settler dominated. As such, we must reconfigure our practice and theory to account for, and actively resist, colonialism, and the ways that it is linked with white supremacy to compound domination and oppression in societies that continue to be premised on the continuation of white-privileged settlers.

Contemporary anarchism, in the settler colonial North American states of Canada and the US, has long had a deep commitment to resist the state, capitalism, and more generally, all forms of oppression and domination, and is placed within the larger scope of Western dominated anarchism (Gordon 2008). The desire to resist all forms of oppression and domination is perhaps one of the hallmarks of anarchism. This often distinguishes anarchism from other radical political projects or political ideologies when coupled with a specific critique and rejection of the state, and allows for an anarchist critique of all aspects of society.

The commitment to a critique of all forms of oppression and domination, therefore, carries with it an enormous responsibility and level of commitment for anarchists. Fighting the state and capitalism is not enough. Anarchism must be against all forms of oppression and domination, and while anarchism generally rejects the view that there is some singular issue or oppression that must be focused on or which is primary (Milstein 2010, 39)[2], it seems imperative to recognize that some forms may come to the fore at specific times and in specific contexts. This chapter argues, first and foremost, for increased recognition of the white supremacist and settler colonial context in which North American anarchism finds itself.

Despite the importance and need for the continued intersectionality of oppression within anarchism indicated above, there are some possible problems or drawbacks to the endless stating of being opposed to all forms of oppression and domination without more concerted action or analysis. One could think here of the anarchist failings in terms of taking on issues of race, racism, white supremacy (as noted by the late Joel Olson, 2009; Lorenzo Kom'boa Ervin, 1994 and more recently by Chris Crass, 2013) and issues of colonization, colonial privilege and decolonization (as noted generally by Simpson, 2011; Lawrence and Dua 2005; and Smith 2005). As Richard Day (2005, 197-202) points out, there is a dangerous tendency within those white anarchists or other radicals on the left to think that, because of their politics, that they are somehow free of oppressive dynamics, while they in

---

2   This perspective has come to the fore in more recent years, and has challenged historic class-centric forms of anarchism that continue to find traction in sectors of the anarchist movement (see in particular Schmidt and Van Der Walt, 2009 for a current representation of this perspective).

fact are intimately involved in maintaining such dynamics. Just because we are anarchists doesn't mean that our politics are actually any more intersectional when it comes to practice. This point is underscored by more general failures and dynamics of white dominance in Left social movement organizing.

In the era after the "Battle of Seattle" in 1999, this critique came to the fore in an article entitled "Where Was the Color in Seattle? Looking for Reasons Why the Great Battle Was So White" by Elizabeth Betita Martinez (2000). Martinez discusses and probes why people of colour were largely unrepresented at the major protests in Seattle, in particular in reference to their voices being at the forefront or core of the movement. This is an especially salient point given that people of colour throughout the world are often both the hardest hit by global economic systems, but also are at the forefront of resistance and organizing. The exclusion of people of colour, and a host of limiting factors that disproportionately affect people of colour (difficulty finding childcare, inability to take off a week from work, financial limitations etc.), meant that resistance in this moment, and in movement-related spaces, was overwhelmingly white dominated. Anarchism, in recent forms, and those who define explicitly as anarchists, or write about anarchism, are still predominantly white in the context of Canada and the US. Anarchism continues to harbor a white-dominated culture, which no doubt continues to suffer from some of the processes and factors of exclusion that Martinez notes more generally, and needs to take the challenges of anti-racism and decolonization more seriously. Perhaps, in part, this is a reflection of the dangerous flattening of social conditions that a theoretical opposition to all forms of oppression and domination might have, where anarchists (among others) can easily oppose "everything" from afar, but fail to grasp the nuances, complexities and particularities of their sites of struggle. Perhaps it is just that anarchists, in this case especially white anarchists, fail to see these important contextual factors because they don't have to engage them given their location as privileged subjects, and thus can choose to overlook them when they are not part of their daily lives and experiences.[3]

I begin by examining some of the anarchist failings in terms of looking at racism, white supremacy and colonization. I chart some of the gaps within anarchism that exists within the context of settler-colonial North America. Next, I problematize the critique of "all forms of oppression and domination" further with a view to taking stock of the settler colonial and white supremacist context that we find ourselves in in North America. This means specifying anarchist theory and practice within the particularities of our context. Finally, I make some initial comments about possible ways of moving forward towards an anti-racist and decolonizing anarchism via anarcha-Indigenism, with particular reference to relationships to land.

---

3   I wish to acknowledge some of the helpful comments from JJ
    McMurtry that brought this point to my attention.

Anarchism, "Strategic Centrality" and the Three Pillars of White Supremacy

Joel Olson (2009, 35), in his significant article "The Problem With Infoshops and Insurrection: US Anarchism, Movement Building and the Racial Order" states rather bluntly that "Anarchism has always had a hard time dealing with race," echoing challenges to anarchism by people of colour like Lorenzo Kom'boa Ervin (1994) or Ajamu Nangwaya (2011). Racism has often been construed as either something to be dealt with after 'the' revolution or something that is understood to be a by-product of capitalism, and thus reducible to class. Both perspectives lead to the view that once capitalism is defeated racism will quietly die as well. Olson argues, however, that racism, as a key aspect of the operation of white supremacy, is one of the core logics that structures capitalism and class consciousness with the US. White supremacy is the "central means of maintaining capitalist hegemony" (Olson 2009, 36) and organizes other forms of oppression in the US context (39). White supremacy has a "strategic centrality" to the US context that other forms of oppression do not. In this sense, he argues, that anarchist critiques of hierarchy are unable to recognize that "various forms of hierarchy are themselves hierarchically organized" while substituting a "moral condemnation of all forms of oppression" for a "political and strategic analysis of how power functions in the US" (37). Olson's argument here is not meant to be interpreted as suggesting that some forms of oppression are in fact more of less oppressive than others. His suggestion flows from a place of being cognizant of the particularities of the context of resistance. In certain contexts, and with certain bodies, different forms of oppression may come to the fore and thus need to be more contextually considered.

Extending Olson's critique further, we might understand both Canada and the US to exist within a strategically central context of white supremacy. Maia Ramnath (2011, 30), focusing on decolonization and anarchism with the Indian/South Asian context makes the argument that I think too applies to the context of settler colonial North America. She argues that racism has been intimately tied to processes of colonization and therefore that the "key to manifesting an anarchist anticolonialism … lies in the intersectionality of those dimensions." A key connection must be made between anti-colonialism and anti-racism (256). Colonialism, connected to white supremacy as a particular pillar among others, again, is "strategically central" for this particular context. Following Andrea Smith (2007), white supremacy can be understood as being bolstered by three pillars of slavery/capitalism, creating racialized hierarchies; genocide/colonialism, rationalizing Indigenous dispossession and destruction; and Orientalism/war, for the purposes of spreading empire abroad. Each pillar, while somewhat unique is also intimately linked to the others, to the point that many are invited to gain privilege in one, while assisting in the oppression of others in another. While Smith's argument is specifically directed to women of colour, to cultivate solidarities across the divisions promoted by the pillars, I think her understanding of the three pillars needs to be extended, to the sorts of privileged, white anarchist subjects that I am primarily focused on in this chapter, in order to further contextualize the terrain of struggle that we find ourselves in.

While there are certainly contextual differences between the settler colonial states of Canada and the US, such as the extent to which slavery and racial hierarchies were constructed, the ways genocide was carried out or the way war is waged and on what scale, the categorical similarities are apparent for the purposes of my analysis here. Whether Canada mediates the continuation of racism and white hegemony through discourses of multiculturalism vs. a US legalist devaluation of black labour, doesn't negate the fact that white supremacy is still the overwhelming framework that structures the context of the settler colonial states of North America (on Canadian colonialism see for ex. Barker, 2009).

Despite the various links between white supremacy and capitalism anarchists are quick to look at classical anarchist theory as a basis for their politics but also for examples of resistance. Olson (2009) suggests that anarchists have had little engagement with the abolitionist, civil rights and Black power movements within the U.S. and continue to repeat anarchist strategies of "infoshops and insurrection" while showing little interest in anti-racist community organizing. These strategies exist primarily outside the context of building mass movements of people that would challenge capitalism and the state and bring forth a new society. They in fact, according to Olson (2009), turn away from movement building with the belief that spaces of autonomy or revolt will be created as examples that will spread spontaneously until a critical mass of such projects eclipse the power of the state. This occurs at the expense of movement building and taking stock of the realities of racism and white supremacy in these particular contexts. Ajamu Nangwaya (2011, 203), writing from the Canadian context, argues further suggesting that if "anarchism is going to make rapid progress in winning over increasing numbers of racialized people under its banner of emancipation it will have to prioritize movement-building and work shoulder-to-shoulder with the racialized oppressed." This includes, in particular, the theoretical deference that anarchism has had to Indigenous struggles and the potentials to learn from historic and ongoing Indigenous movements for resistance.

Chris Crass (2013, 17) makes a similar argument. He argues that movements for "collective liberation" (drawing from bell hooks) need to recognize the need for intersectionality otherwise the work that they take up will continue to be plagued with all forms of oppression and domination. Crass (2013, 18) argues that "If systems of domination are interconnected, then systems of liberation are also interconnected." This means, he argues, that there needs to be particular attention given to anti-racist and feminist[4] work within all movements, but also within anarchism in particular. This is especially the case when looking at the politics of privilege within a mostly white dominated anarchist movement. A turn to anti-racism need to be a conscious effort on the part of anarchists and anarchism (Crass 2013, 55), especially given that white supremacy does not always operate as a conscious set of acts or intentions but rather as a "framework of thought" (134) that "directs the flow of our thoughts" and doesn't require overt forms of racism but only that "we go with the flow of dominant ideology" (131). Or as Ajamu Nangwaya (2011, 202) argues, this "default to whiteness is the hardwired option in the minds of many Whites in North America" and continues to limit the potentials for solidarity and movement-building with people of colour.

Crass (2013) too highlights the need for specific commitments to broad-based social movement organizing that takes seriously the leadership and experiences of people of colour. This movement cannot be afraid to build the capacity for leadership within the movement as well, something that anarchists are often hesitant to take up, on account of seeking to avoid the creation of any and all forms of hierarchy. He argues that for anti-racist and feminist movements to work for collective liberation there

---

4   The feminist implications are obviously important. Anarchism has at times been little better than other movements at dealing with sexism, homophobia or trans*phobia. This needs to be part of an intersectional anarchism, however, discussing the particularities of such a need is beyond the scope of this chapter. I have explored some of the decolonizing implications related to anarcha-feminist and Indigenous feminist perspectives elsewhere, see Lewis (2012a).

needs to be mentors and those ready to engage with others on the complexities of histories of domination and contemporary realities of privilege. The lesson here is that anarchist movements that are interested in living up to their intersectional commitments need to look to Indigenous, anti-racist and people of colour struggles for leadership and be willing to engage with such movements and learn from them, rather than assuming to have the correct answers or ways of pushing resistance forward. This, I think requires that anarchism, at times, step back, and learn from such movements.

Although Olson and Crass, amongst others, both identify the need for anarchists to look to Black freedom struggles in the context of building movements against racism and white supremacy their work doesn't go far enough. Anarchists must also turn to histories and contemporary examples of Indigenous resistance and develop a specific analysis of colonization and a commitment to decolonization and solidarity with Indigenous struggles alongside and connected to struggles against racism and white supremacy. Anarchists must look at the particularities of the context of colonization (in Canada, for example, see Alfred and Corntassel 2005; Barker 2009). Bonita Lawrence and Enakshi Dua have made this argument forcefully in their important work "Decolonizing Anti-racism" (2005). The context of settler colonial states in North America means that colonialism, as it is as a key pillar of white supremacy discussed above, needs to be "strategically central" (Olson 2009) given histories of dispossession and connection of colonialism to settlement and the rise of capitalism and the state.

Recuperating the Settler-Indigenous Binary[5]

Part of the disruption of settler colonialism needs to be in the form of settler identity and its relationship and relevance to anarchist settlers. Lawrence and Dua (2005) in "Decolonizing Antiracism" argue for an anti-colonial orientation within anti-racist theory in order to recognize the complicity of settler populations, and to some degree anti-racism, in the continued colonization of Indigenous peoples. Most clearly they argue that all those who are *not* Indigenous peoples must be understood as settlers, although the power differentials between white people and people of colour are an important backdrop to the complexity of settler identity. They argue that those working within an anti-racist context on the lands of Indigenous peoples need to take up an anti-colonial and decolonizing analysis. They state

> If they are truly progressive, antiracist theorists must begin to think about their personal stake in this struggle [against colonization by Indigenous peoples], and about where they are going to situate themselves (Lawrence and Dua 2005, 126).

They argue that anti-racist scholars, and all those committed to an anti-racist politics, which should include anar-

5   This phrasing comes, in part, from the title of Wolfe's (2013) article—"Recuperating Binarism: A Heretical Introduction."

chists, have failed to take up an understanding of land as a contested space as result of colonization and being bound up with settler identity. They argue that to "acknowledge that we all share the same land base and yet to question the differential terms on which it is occupied is to become aware of the colonial project that is taking place around us" (Lawrence and Dua 2005, 126). Their call is ultimately one for non-Indigenous peoples to recognize their settler histories and the ways that settlers continue to be complicit in colonial processes. This challenge is one that must be taken up specifically within anarchism.

In terms of defining settlers in a more complex way, beyond just being non-Indigenous, Mar and Edmonds argue that:

> In simplest terms, settler colonists went, and go, to new lands to appropriate them and to establish new and improved replicas of the societies they left. As a result Indigenous peoples have found an ever-decreasing space for themselves in settler colonies as changing demographics enabled ever more extensive dispossession. Settlers, in the end, tended not to assimilate into Indigenous societies, but rather emigrated to replace them (2010, 2).

This process continues in settler colonies with increased forms of migration and the theft of Indigenous lands for development and resource extraction projects. As Lawrence and Amadahy (2009) point out, there are certainly histories of slavery, forced migration, oppression and domination that add a large degree of complexity to the definition of settler, most obviously with African-descended populations, but that even with such histories there has been an invitation to participate in the project and processes of colonization of Indigenous peoples, cultures and lands. As Smith argues, the pillar of genocide under white supremacy is what allows non-Indigenous peoples to get away with the assertion, however implicit, of a rightful claim to Indigenous lands, because Indigenous peoples are seen to have disappeared. This allows non-Indigenous inclusion in some of the privileges of colonization, at the expense of Indigenous peoples and their lands (Smith 2007, 68).

Some anarchists may argue that taking up the term settler adds another dimension of specified identity politics to anarchism, which is often interested in breaking down divisions based on identity seeking more general forms of collectivity. This is perhaps fair, to at least some degree, as anarchists are often against the divisions created by other sorts of constructed identity categories such as those based on citizenship. There may also be an argument, voiced by some anarchists, that reverting to a settler-Indigenous binary would only seek to overshadow the class hierarchies that more fundamentally organize hierarchy in a capitalist society. The problem with rejecting the term settler, in this case where we are situated in settler colonial societies, is in part a refusal to engage directly with such realities. It refuses, as Patrick Wolfe (2013, 263) argues, to acknowledge that the relationship between settlers and Indigenous peoples

> is a structural relationship rather than an effect of the will' that precedes those settlers who occupy Indigenous lands now. As he argues further, although wrapped up in their own dynamics of oppression and domination that must be considered, those immigrants who now live on Indigenous lands who 'immigrated against their will...does not alter the structural fact that their presence...was part of the process of Native dispossession (Wolfe 2013, 263).

There is, therefore, a danger that lies in using suggestions of settler dynamics occurring in the past, or no longer applying, or only applying to some non-Indigenous peoples, that can continue processes of colonization, while ignoring that settler colonization is not just an event that has occurred previously, but a structure that continues to exist and narrate relationships and the possibilities of resistance in settler colonial contexts.[6]

Naming something, then, in this case the oppressive reality of settler colonization and the privileges that settlers continue to accrue by holding up such a system or even passively buying into it (which would be part of the complexity of the differences of settler realities with regard to citizenship), performs its own sense of disruption of the colonial norm and multicultural discourse that continues to cast all peoples as equal participants in the state.

---

6 On the topic of settler colonialism as a structure and not an event see for example Wolfe (2013; 2006).

Much like denying the existence of white privilege and the importance of recognizing that those who are defined or seen as white receive such privileges and must therefore be accountable for them, and denying such privileges would be explicitly counter to the development of an anti-racist politics, so too should recognizing the reality of settler identity as linked to settler-colonial privilege be necessary for the development of a decolonizing politics. As Alfred and Corntassel (2005, 601) argue, settler colonialism is a

> narrative in which the Settler's power is the fundamental reference and assumption, inherently limiting Indigenous freedom and imposing a view of the world that is but an outcome or perspective on that power.

Naming settler colonialism, as connected to white supremacy, and the settler identities that grant us privilege, is one step forward to acknowledging that such privilege exists and then actually beginning to do the necessary work of imagining decolonization or "unsettling" in practice. It also serves as an acknowledgement of the Indigenous challenges, from those like Lawrence and Dua (2005) for example, to take the term settler seriously, as something that those with privilege need to, and must, engage with.

Engaging Indigenous Theory and Practice

Further, beyond just examining settler identity, the need for anarchist, and broader left social movement attention to Indigenous struggle is apparent. Indigenous feminist Andrea Smith observes that, in terms of "left" social movements generally, there is a dismissal of Indigenous theory and politics due to a perception that it is endlessly caught up in identity politics or cultural considerations. She argues that Native women's organizing, in particular, has been ignored on account of the perception that Indigenous peoples, and especially Indigenous women, "have nothing to contribute to social justice activism or theory in general...our struggles have no relationship to political economy" (Smith, 2008, xi). This has led, she concludes, to a general under-theorizing of Indigenous activism and resistance and little discussion of its possible contributions to social movement theory and practice more broadly.

Leanne Simpson (2011) argues similarly, suggesting that even if Western theory has been able to consider the particularities of colonialism and how it might operate, such work has been wholly inadequate in finding resonance with Indigenous peoples. She argues that

> western-based social movement theory has failed to recognize the broader contextualizations of resistance within Indigenous thought, while also ignoring the contestation of colonialism as a starting point (Simpson, 2011, 31).

The recognition of colonialism as a starting point for oppression and domination in settler colonial contexts is a key point of analysis that has existed on the periphery of anarchism. A reorientation needs to move towards detailing the complexities of colonialism, the specific efforts of Indigenous peoples to resist its contemporary manifestations and the possible forms that settler decolonization may begin to take. Colonialism, it must be noted, is the historical and ongoing process that structures relationships, power dynamics and social stratification in settler societies like "Canada" and the "US." Colonialism is what, at the most basic level, defines the contexts in which we operate, based upon dispossession and violence for the benefit of settlers. As I have argued above, colonialism is therefore a core logic that underwrites all of the political work, the theory and practice, that we, as anarchists, might seek to implement towards creating cultures of resistance. Therefore, one step forward is for social movement theory as a whole, and anarchist theory in particular, to take Indigenous theory and practice seriously, while paying attention to its own location as a Western-dominated theoretical paradigm.

Andrea Smith (2008, xv), however, argues not for a simple inclusion of Indigenous theoretical perspectives into other disciplines, but rather for a recentring of Indigenous perspectives within other disciplines. This, she argues, requires identifying Indigenous theory and practice as examples that might benefit many others and their work. This is perhaps one step that anarchists might take by reading Indigenous theorists and considering the decolonizing potentials that might be taken up within anarchism. Indigenous theory and practice can disrupt the theoretical and practical assumptions or stalemates within anarchism, as well as shed light on the colonial elephant in the room that has been relatively neglected within anarchist contexts. It also challenges the complacent Eurocentrism that often pervades much anarchist thought and can prompt a reframing and analysis of the complexities of issues of nation, nationalism, self-determination, autonomy and spirituality that are often characterized by anarchists in relatively narrow terms.

Part of this work that Smith suggests might include for anarchists, first of all, actually recognizing Indigenous theory as existing, coming from specific communities, contexts and lands, and itself informing the context of struggle that anarchism finds itself within. Indigenous discussions of the importance of place and land (to which I turn to briefly below); links between capitalism, the state and colonization; between heteropatriarchy, the state and colonization; promotion of traditional governance structures and community relations that exist outside capitalist and statist relations; and a sustained history of militant resistance are but a few points of contact that anarchists would do well to examine. Part of this work within anarchism needs to be to affirm the importance of Indigenous theory itself, as a key contributor to intersectional movements and analysis and to engage with Indigenous theory on its own terms, rather than seeking, for example, to subsume it within anarchism itself, refusing the creeping tendency of appropriation of the wide spectrum of anti-state or "outside-the-state" politics under an anarchist label (although as I discuss below anarcha-Indigenism does provide some possibilities for exchanges and points of connection).[7] This work of engaging Indigenous theory and its theoretical contributions and disruptions has the potential to break open, in part, the boundaries of anarchism, to make its biases and failures of analysis plain and to disrupt the (re)framing of the anarchist canon along rigid class-centric lines (as has been done in the book *Black Flame*, 2009).

Before I move forward it is perhaps important to make a few further comments about the anarchist focus on resisting all forms of oppression and domination and the implications of this sort of politics. There is a very real danger of stating opposition to all forms of oppression being an easy way to put a radical politics forward that may or may not have much substance behind it. It is one thing to add colonialism to the ever-growing list of things anarchists oppose, but it is quite another to actually begin to enact an anti-colonial or decolonizing politics. George Ciccariello-Maher (2011, 21) argues that the "harder work –that of grasping how the capitalist system operates and how it can be brought down through strategic action –remains, despite our declarations of opposition." This point can be extended to the settler colonial system, which is intimately tied to the continuance of both capit-

---

7   I have attempted a process such as this with regard to thinking about bringing forth an anti-colonial and decolonizing research orientation within anarchist and broader social movement research. See Lewis (2012b).

alism and the state, and to the discussion of settler identity above. It is one thing to acknowledge privilege, but another to begin to act. It is one thing, he argues, to commit to anarchist principles in a theoretical way, but quite another to actually figure out how to implement them in practice. Part of this difficulty is sometimes related to the lack of contextualization that anarchists glaze over or reduce to a much more general politics. Citing the work of Joel Olson (2009), discussed above, Ciccariello-Maher reiterates the need for anarchists to see the fundamental ways in which the particularities of context and its "strategically central" components fundamentally structure relations and engagements with capitalism and the state.

The point then, is not to reject a resistance to all forms of oppression but to contextualize theory, strategy, tactics and action, and add colonization and white supremacy to this challenge, as these processes continue to affect and structure relationships in both the settler colonial US and Canada, and that colonization, racism and white supremacy continue to permeate contemporary society and radical movements as well. In the case of settler-colonial North America white supremacy, and the three pillars that uphold it, need to be understood as the core aspects that underwrite all forms of domination on this land. Settler colonization, in particular, structures the relations between settlers and Indigenous peoples and the specific relationship one has to white supremacy and land[8].

---

8   I return to the importance of land later in this chapter.

Anarchism, therefore, must be diverse in its focal points and be willing to expand its critique beyond simply capitalism and the state, but also begin to think carefully about how to attain the ultimate end of a free society without oppression and domination. Anarchism must also be diverse in terms of recognizing that different contexts might require different emphasis or focus and that there are important particular considerations to be made in each case, but should not be rigidly defined from one specific context. This means, very clearly, that anarchism needs to begin to unpack its Euro-centric baggage that dates from classical theorists but continues right into the contemporary. Some possible concepts might include anarchist rejections of "nation" (no borders, no nations), religion, spirituality (no gods, no masters) as being inherently tied to state and hierarchical processes of domination, but which are only understood in a Eurocentric context. Or anarchist forms of economic analysis that understand societal divisions from the stand point of hegemonic conceptions of "working class." Euro-centrism is one of the key processes that set the stage and justification for colonization.

One step in this process, as I suggested above, is to look to Indigenous theory, practice and resistance as a way to disrupt the Euro-centricity and whiteness of anarchism. This would mean, I think, reading and responding to the sorts of Indigenous criticism that I detailed briefly above, as well as Anarchist People of Colour (APOC) perspectives, that contribute to anarchism by

"foregrounding colonialism as a primary category of analysis as well as a primary structure of oppression" (Ramnath, 2011, 256), which echoes the work of Olson discussed above. It means taking Indigenous voices seriously and centering them in our work and our movements. This is especially true within environmental movements that continue to expand against resource extraction
and destruction. Anarchism can continue to attempt to expand its own forms of anti-colonial and decolonizing theory, but without reference to Indigenous theoretical and
movement-based interventions happening now, anarchism
will continue to reside at the level of theory, abstracted
from this context.

Relationships to Land

I have emphasized here, following the likes of Olson,
among others, that anarchist opposition to racism, white
supremacy and colonization needs to be tied to a specific
context in order to be enacted. One of the larger contexts
that requires specific attention, especially by anarchists, is
the colonial context that we continue to live in and the
large amounts of land that have been stolen from Indigenous nations. In this sense, without recognizing and reori-
enting our relationship to land, anarchism carries the
danger of seeking to create alternatives or prefigurative
experiments that reinscribe colonial dynamics (on this
point see also Barker and Pickerill, 2012). This issue has
come up most recently within the broader "Occupy"
movements that have been challenged to "de-occupy" and

decolonize their relationships to land and Indigenous communities.[9] The same challenge needs to be directed at anarchism as well. As Day (2010, 268) argues, as soon as anarchists begin to purchase and accumulate land on which to set up our own autonomous alternatives outside the state, as soon as we begin to create physical infrastructures of resistance, we begin to repeat the logics of colonialism. He summarizes that "it would appear that the resurgence of settler autonomy, our escape from the tyrannies we have foisted on ourselves, once again can only come on the backs of Indigenous peoples."

Relationships to land are connections that settlers have lost when they left lands they were originally "Indigenous" too and took part in the colonial project—connections that settlers have continued to lose as a result of colonial domination that they participate in, hold up and accrue privilege from (see Barker, 2010). Glen Coulthard, citing Vine Deloria Jr., argues that the fundamental difference between settlers and Indigenous peoples comes from the philosophical emphasis that Indigenous peoples place on land. "American Indians," Deloria argues, "hold their lands—places—as having the highest possible meaning, and all their statements are made with this reference point in mind" (1992, 62). Land, most basically understood, is the foundation of Indigenous worldviews, spiritualities and nations. It is also the point of connection that is most important to reassert for the purposes of resurgence and

---

9   See for example Barker 2012; Kilibarda, 2012

resistance to colonization by Indigenous communities (see for ex. Alfred, 2005; Simpson, 2011). From an anarcha-Indigenist perspective, the reconnection to land, as the basis for all other forms of relating and as that which sustains communities, is important to ground our struggles in the intimate contexts of where we are. This is a foundational part of taking up the push for recognizing that white supremacy and its three pillars are at the 'strategically central' part of the context of resistance.

Reconnecting to land also means a move away from the commodification of land and private property relationships predicated on the supremacy of hierarchical economic relationships mediated by the state. Reconnecting with place and landbases and renewing ethical obligations to living in relation to the land might form an initial step in the revitalization and resurgence of Indigenous communities, and as a further element of settler decolonization, as Coulthard (2010) notes. What this looks like in practice will be conditioned by the new forms of relations that settlers form with the landbases they are on and with the Indigenous communities who live there. "The true challenge for anarchists," Barker and Pickerill (2012, 1719) argue, "is to find their own new way of looking at —and being in—place that compliments but does not replicate what Indigenous peoples are attempting to do. Replication of relations, as with appropriation of voice, is an unwelcome and unneeded imposition." So settler anarchists need to consider their own relations to land, and what that might mean in their own particular context, while not relying on Indigenous peoples to "fix" such lack of relations or disconnections for them. All of our relationships, and most especially those associated with land, need to be "unsettled" (Regan, 2010). As I have argued previously (Lewis, 2012b, 236) "[u]nderstanding our position as settlers requires us to take action and commit to a decolonizing and unsettling framework." In short we need to consider, as (anarchist) settlers on stolen lands, how we might "[work] on all these levels in addition to (but not instead of) tackling capitalism and the state, without reducing the struggle to either the material or ideological/discursive plane" (Ramnath, 2011, 27). To fail to look directly at issues of land, as I have argued, does little more than revert to a continuation of processes of colonization.

This chapter has not had the space to detail some of the particular engagements and resonances between anarchist and Indigenous theory and practice, and this needs to be taken up in further work. I have aimed here to chart a course for the need to begin to examine anarchism's decolonizing possibilities as connected to anti-racism. Anarchism needs to take seriously the challenges issued by Indigenous theorists and movements to move towards processes of decolonization, especially with regard to land and prefiguration of alternatives. It must be noted, however, that there is a particular need for openness to contributions and interventions from those who do not rigidly define as "anarchist." While there are similarities between anarchism and Indigenous political theory and practice, as Alfred (2005, 45-46) notes, I have noticed an appropriate wariness on the part of Indigenous peoples to just wholly adopt the anarchist label, or convert to reading and developing anarchist theory in particular, given that the foundation of Indigenous resistance and resurgence comes from within communities and traditions, and can't be fashioned from a Western-dominated political theory. As Barker and Pickerill suggest,

> anarchists must understand that to be truly decolonizing and effective allies to Indigenous peoples, they must step back from attempts to draw Indigenous peoples into movements or insert themselves into Indigenous struggles (1718).

While the potential for solidarities and affinities between anarchist and Indigenous movements might exist, there is a fundamental need for separation and autonomy.

As Ciccariello-Maher (2011, 39) argues, anarchists need to be aware of their own "anarchist imperialism" that privileges self-defined anarchist voices at the expense of all others. He discusses this concept in relation to anarchists from the global North seeking to stand in solidarity with anarchists in the global South rather uncritically. He suggests that there is a tendency for anarchists from the North to *a priori* look to other self-identified anarchists for their solidarity rather than taking stock of the local context and social movement dynamics. In the case of Venezuela, which Ciccariello-Maher focuses on, anarchists have latched onto a localized and typical anarchist critique of Hugo Chavez without attention to the importance that the Bolivarian revolution has had on local peoples and movements. Rather they focus on anarchists for the reason that they are anarchists and fit their own political forms of definition, not because they perhaps actually have a good analysis of the particularities of struggle in that context. Anarchists, we might argue, have a tendency to "anarchize" those that they identify as having affinity with their projects. Maia Ramnath (2011, 6) notes a similar tendency within anarchism and suggests that

> instead of always trying to construct a strongly anarcha-centric cosmology—conceptually appropriating movement and voices from elsewhere in the world as part of "our" tradition, and then measuring them against how much or little we think they resemble our notion of our own values—we could locate the Western anarchist tradition as one contextually specific manifestation a larger—indeed global—tradition.

Anarchists therefore need to engage with other movements on their own terms, but also not just uncritically seek out the most outwardly anarchist aspects to suit their own preferences for solidarity. When engaging with Indigenous theory and practice this would require that settler anarchists recognize that they will not and cannot develop an intimate understanding of Indigenous lifeways, knowledges and teachings. We are outsiders and are not embedded within these lived cultures that are tied closely to relations to land, place and living and non-living things. Everything that we read and engage will be filtered through our own anarchist lens, which often has a Euro-centric glaze and at best we are likely to develop only a surface level understanding. This means, as well, that we need to be accountable to the ways that we centre and take leadership from Indigenous movements.

Another point that warrants brief mention is that while I am arguing here for renewed and specific anarchist attention to the strategic centrality of white supremacy and settler colonialism, the inverse cannot be argued for Indigenous theory and practice. What I mean to say, is that to really live up to its commitment to resist all forms of oppression and domination anarchism "needs" to pay attention to Indigenous and decolonizing theory, while to move towards decolonization and resurgence, Indigenous communities do not need anarchism. Settler interference within Indigenous communities, both historical and continued, is extensive and has done little more than re-inscribe dynamics of colonization. It seems foolhardy to suggest a continuation of this, no matter how well intentioned, in the name of spreading anarchism. While anarchism has much to learn, Indigenous communities do not need anarchist theory for their decolonization and resistance. They don't need settlers at all. And while we might be called upon to create new relations or support projects of resurgence and decolonization, Indigenous communities do not need our theories—they have their own, emanating from traditions, cultural practices and their own Indigenous theorists, practitioners and organizers.

The danger of Eurocentric filtering is present here with my own project, and there is a danger that thinking about anarcha-Indigenism might move in directions that begin to demand anarchism in name and in our forms from Indigenous communities. There are certainly Indigenous peoples who self-define as anarchists and it is important to consider their work, but it is also crucial to look at those who may not be so explicitly defined but who, to use Day's (2005) conception, share an affinity with this anarchist or anarcha-Indigenist project, but may not be familiar with the extensive history of anarchist movements, theorists etc. Following Ciccariello-Maher's caution, Indigenous movements and theorists need to be engaged on their terms and not strictly within the frame of anarchism. The same is true for Black liberation struggles or other people of colour movements. The aim therefore must be to continually seek out exchanges and challenges of anarchism and seek to move towards and enact anti-colonial and decolonizing commitments. Decolonizing anarchism, as Ramnath (2011, 258) argues,

> means making anarchism a force for decolonization, and simultaneously dismantling colonial assumptions within our own understanding and practice of anarchism. That requires us to see anarchism as one locally contextualized, historically specific manifestation of a larger antiauthoritarian tradition.

Conceiving Anarcha-Indigenism

One form of contextual anarchism might begin to emerge under the framework of anarcha-Indigenism. The context of this project exists primarily in the settler colonies of the US and Canada although there has been specific work to connect anarcha-Indigenism to the struggles of the Zapatistas in Mexico as well (see Khasnabish, 2011). Anarcha-Indigenism, in name, might be seen as an emerging and a continually developing theory and practice that has sought to foreground Indigenous critiques of colonialism, but also the state and capitalism. There are no doubt other exchanges that are happening, and have happened, especially at the level of social movements and in even more specific contexts, but anarcha-Indigenism allows for a concerted and explicit focus on colonialism and decolonization within the context of anarchism.

Generally, anarcha-Indigenism might be understood as a coming together of anarchist and Indigenous theory and practice, with also special attention given to the feminist elements within each. In this way anarcha-Indigenism foregrounds a critique of the intersections, overlaps and mutual dependencies that exist between the state, capitalism, colonialism, white supremacy and patriarchy. It seeks though, the much broader anarchist impulse of resisting all forms of oppression and domination (although it is important to note the drawbacks of such an approach, as I have noted above). Its foremost intervention though is the bringing of a decolonizing analysis to anarchism and a push towards locally and contextually rooted strategies for decolonization. This means, quite clearly and importantly that an analysis of settler privilege as linked to settler colonialism, the state and capitalism needs to be continually developed as part of an anarchist analysis. The project of anarcha-Indigenism suggests a problematizing of settler privilege and a push towards decolonization.

The first primary instance of conceiving of anarcha-Indigenism comes from Taiaiake Alfred's 2005 book *Wasase* in which he conceives of his project of Indigenous cultural revitalization and militant warrior ethic in the following terms:

> I might suggest, as a starting point, conceptualizing *anarcho-indigenism*. Why? And why this term? Conveyance of the indigenous warrior ethic will require its codification in some form—a creed and an ethical framework for thinking through challenges. To take root in people's minds the new ethic will have to capture the spirit of a warrior in battle and bring it to politics. How might this spirit be described in contemporary terms related to political thought and movement? The two elements that come to my mind are *indigenous*, evoking cultural and spiritual rootedness in this land and the Onkwehonwe[10] struggle for justice and freedom, and the political philosophy and movement that is fundamentally anti-institutional,

---

10 Alfred (2005, 288) offers the following as a definition of Onkwehonwe in the Mohawk language: "'the original people'... referring to the First Peoples of North America."

radically democratic, and committed to taking action to force change: *anarchism* (Alfred, 2005, 45).

Alfred's work described here brings together the core Indigenous and anarchist elements of anarcha-Indigenism, within a specific project of Indigenous resistance and revitalization, though I think his summary here points to the potential points of contact between anarchism and Indigenous theory and practice. He points to a focus on decentralization, direct democracy and several other commonalities that might link anarchist and Indigenous philosophies, namely:

> A rejection of alliances with legalized systems of oppression, non-participation in the institutions that structure the colonial relationship and a belief in bringing about change through direct action, physical resistance, and confrontations with state power (Alfred, 2005, 46).

Alfred's work, therefore, contains a profound anti-state impulse that is essential for working towards decentralization, autonomy and self-determination for Indigenous communities.

Alfred's work has been picked up by a number of settler anarchists as well. The work of Richard Day (2008) and Jacqueline Lasky (2011), in particular have sought to expand work on anarcha-Indigenism, with a particular view to bringing in Indigenous and anarchist feminisms as core and essential components. Day (2003) draws from the work of Indigenous writers Marie Smallface Marule,

Patricia Monture-Angus and Taiaiake Alfred, in conjunction with anarchist theorists, to suggest a convergence of
values to organize outside the state—towards non-coercive direct democratic forms of decision making and organization and away from entrenched forms of hierarchy.
Here Day argues that there are similarities, or more prop-
erly-termed, *affinities*, between some aspects of Indigenous political theory and anarchism (see also Day, 2005).
In addition to the authors suggested above, we might add,
for example, Indigenous theorists such as Andrea Smith
(2005), Leanne Simpson (2011) and Glen Coulthard
(2010, 2001) who have argued for resistance to and outside the state; or suggest to see also those whose work appeared in a recent issue of *Affinities: A Radical Journal of
Theory, Culture and Action* devoted to the particular topic
of anarcha-Indigenism. The work of these writers presents
a number of places from which to draw to continue developing what this thing anarcha-Indigenism might be and
how its comprehensive critique might be strengthened
and promote new forms of resistance.

Richard Day (2008, 3) provides the following summar-
ies of anarcha-Indigenism as "a meeting place, a site of
possibilities, a potential for mutual aid in common projects within, outside, and against the dominant order. It is
not an ideology or a party," he continues, "but an emer-
gent and ever-changing network of autonomous subjects,
organizations, and institutions": a meeting point of "an-
archisms, indigenisms and feminisms," not some form of
rigid, limited or homogenous set of political possibilities,

but something broadly defined, dynamic and evolving (Day, 2008, 3). An intersectional analysis is foundational to anarcha-Indigenism and cannot be overstated and so it warrants quoting Day at length:

> an anarcha-indigenist perspective is based on an interlocking analysis of oppression, which includes every site that has been raised as an antagonism, and privileges none over the others, in terms of their importance, intensity, or the order in which they are addressed in any work involving social change. [...] Since as all beings are interrelated and dependent upon the earth, we must also work to minimize the human domination of nature and ensure that our practices are ecologically sustainable in the short, medium, and long terms, both locally and globally. This work needs to be carried out within and against the dominant order, and within our own communities. It needs to operate both at a structural level, and at the level of daily practice (Day, 2008, 19).

The work of anarcha-Indigenism, therefore, requires a commitment to root out injustice, oppression and domination at all of the levels, whether within bodies and minds, in the dynamics of the political groups that we engage in resistance with, in the broader cultures of resistance that we seek to cultivate or in the larger structures and institutions that we struggle against. It is a relational possibility of resistance that is contextualized to the particularities of place. "It is," as Jacqueline Lasky (2011, 7) argues, "relational...plural, multiple, contingent, transient, indeterminate and thoroughly unfixed." This multiple nature of anarcha-Indigenism invites multiple perspectives to strengthen this commitment to resistance to all forms of oppression and domination. This is one possible way forward that begins to foreground colonialism as a core logic of power and domination within the US/Canada context, but also within the wider context of settler colonial states.

Anarcha-Indigenism engages in the kind of project that Olson and others suggested above, where no form of oppression is construed to be morally worse or condemnable than any other but the particularities of the settler colonial and white supremacist realities of "North America" require a specific focus on these forms of oppression and domination as foundational and what condition other forms. They are also the forms that need much more concerted attention on the part of anarchists. Olson, Crass, Martinez, Smith and Simpson, among countless others, have all noted a general lack of analysis of white supremacy or colonization within social movements and anarchist movements. Anarcha-Indigenism, by taking up Indigenous critiques of colonialism and seeking out points of contact between anarchism and Indigenous resistance is perhaps one way forward. Certainly a greater anti-racist impulse needs to be developed within anarcha-Indigenism as well to reflect the close ties between colonization, white supremacy and racism within understandings such as Smith's three pillars.

Conclusion

This chapter has been mostly theoretical in outlook, and therefore we must begin to turn, as well, to examining the possibilities for an anti-racist and decolonizing anarchism in practice. We might look to solidarity with Black liberation, APOC, migrant justice and Indigenous struggles, but also must look inwardly at rooting the privileges that we continue to accrue from these systems of oppression and domination. I have argued that anarchism, as a primarily white settler dominated movement in Canada and the US, needs to begin to take much more seriously the white supremacist and settler colonial context within which it seeks to enact resistance to all forms of oppression and domination. The first step is to view the three pillars of white supremacy, of which colonization is one piece, as the strategically central elements that fundamentally structure the particular context that we, as settlers find ourselves in. This fundamental grounding, as well as naming as important the binary of settler and Indigenous, is essential for anarchists to take up; otherwise we run the risk of continuing processes of colonization, and refuse to assess our complicity in these systems of oppression. Relationships to land, which settlers have lost, are the kinds of relations that anarchists need to carefully consider, especially if we are seeking to construct autonomous alternatives to the state and capital, without doing so at the expense of Indigenous peoples. Finally, I have suggested that anarcha-Indigenism, in bringing together both anarchist and Indigenous theory and practice, might serve as one way forward to begin to think about creating new forms of relationships to both land and Indigenous peoples. At its most basic, this chapter has argued for a committed anarchist turn to understanding and engaging with the realities of settler colonization, as it structures our context of struggle and resistance. The imperative for anarchists to think about decolonization comes, in part, from the commitment to resist all forms of oppression and domination that anarchists claim; from the challenges issued by Indigenous communities; and from our situation on lands that are narrated by processes of Indigenous dispossession for the benefit of settlers. As Maia Ramnath (2011, 256) argues:

> If we recognize colonialism as an interconnected global power system in which we're all differently located, then we're all engaged in a multifronted battle to dismantle and replace that system.

This is the way forward for anarchism, to locate ourselves within the particularities of the context of white supremacy and colonization, and begin to conceive of ways to resist and decolonize.

References

Alfred, T. (2005). *Wasase: Indigenous Pathways of Action and Freedom.* Peterborough: Broadview.

Amadahy, Z., & Lawrence, B. (2010). "Indigenous Peoples and Black People in Canada: Settlers or Allies?" In A. Kempf, *Breaching the Colonial Contract: Anti-Colonialism in Canada and the US* (pp. 105-136). New York: Springer Science+Business Media.

Barker, A. (2009). "The contemporary reality of Canadian

imperialism: Settler Colonialism and the hybrid colonial state." *American Indian Quarterly,* 33(3), 325-351.

Barker, A. (2010). "From Adversaries to Allies: Forging Respectful Alliances between Indigenous and Settler Peoples." In L. Davis, *Alliances: Re/Envisioning Indigenous-non-Indigenous Relationships,* (pp. 316-333). Toronto: U of T Press.

Barker, A. (2012). "Already Occupied: Indigenous Peoples, Settler Colonialism and the Occupy Movements in North America." *Social Movement Studies: Journal of Social, Cultural and Political Protest,* 11(3-4), 327-334.

Barker, A. J., & Pickerill, J. (2012). "Radicalizing Relationships To and Through Shared Geographies: Why Anarchists Need to Understand Indigenous Connections to Land and Place." *Antipode,* 44(5), 1705-1725.

Ciccariello-Maher, G. (2011). "An Anarchism That is Not Anarchism: Notes Toward a Critique of Anarchist Imperialism" In J. C. Klausen, & J. Martel, *How Not To Be Goverened: Readings and Interpretations from a Critical Anarchist Left* (pp. 19-46). Lanham, MA: Lexington Books.

Coulthard, G. (2010). "Place Against Empire: Understanding Indigenous Anti-Colonialism" *Affinities: A Journal of Radical Theory, Culture and Action,* 4(2), 79-83.

Crass, C. (2013). *Towards Collective Liberation: Anti-Racist Organizing, Feminist Praxis, and Movement Building Strategy.* Oakland, CA: PM Press .

Day, R. J. (2003). "Anarchism, Indigenism, and Anti-Globalization in North American Social Movements." *DeriveApprodi,* December 2003 (in Italian, copy received from author), 1-20.

Day, R. J. (2005). *Gramsci Is Dead: Anarchist Currents in the Newest Social Movements.* Toronto, ON: Between The Lines.

Day, R. J. (2008). "Anarcha-Indigenism: Encounters, Resonances,

184 | *New Developments in Anarchist Studies*

and Tensions." *International Studies Association 2008 Conference*, (pp. 1-30). San Francisco.

Gordon, U. (2008). *Anarchy Alive! Anti-Authoritarian Politics From Practice to Theory.* London: Pluto Press.

Khasnabish, A. (2011). "Anarch@-Zapatismo: Anti-Capitalism, Anti-Power and the Insurgent Imagination." (G. Coulthard, J. Lasky, A. Lewis, & V. Watts, Eds.) *Affinities: A Journal of Radical Theory, Culture and Action,* 5(1), 70-95.

Kilibarda, K. (2012). "Lessons from #Occupy in Canada: Contesting space, settler consciousness and erasures within the 99%." *Journal of Critical Globalisation Studies,* 5, 24-41.

Kom'boa Ervin, L. (1994). *Anarchism and the Black Revolution and Other Essays.* Philadelphia, PA: Monkeywrench Press.

Lasky, J. (2011). "Indigenism, Anarchism, Feminism: An Emerging Framework for Exploring Post-Imperial Futures." (G. Coulthard, J. Lasky, A. Lewis, & V. Watts, Eds.) *Affinities: A Journal of Radical Theory, Culture and Action,* 5(1), 3-36.

Lawrence, B., & Dua, E. (2005). "Decolonizing Antiracism." *Social Justice,* 32(4), 120-143.

Lewis, A. G. (2012a). "Decolonizing Anarchism: Expanding Anarcha-Indigenism in Theory and Practice." *MA Thesis.* Cultural Studies, Queens University.

Lewis, A. G. (2012b). "Ethics, Activism and the Anti-Colonial: Social Movement Research as Resistance." *Social Movement Studies: Jorunal of Social, Cultural and Political Protest,* 11(2), 227-240.

Mar, T. B., & Edmonds, P. (2010). "Introduction: Making Space in Settler Colonies." In T. B. Mar, & P. Edmonds, *Making Settler Colonial Space* (pp. 1-24). New York: Palgrave Macmillan.

Martinez, E. B. (2000, March 10). "Where Was the Color in Seattle? Looking for reasons why the Great Battle was so white."

Retrieved from *Colourlines*:
http://colorlines.com/archives/2000/03/where_was_the_color_in_seattlelooking_for_reasons_why_the_great_battle_was_so_white.html

Milstein, C. (2010). *Anarchism and Its Aspirations*. Oakland, CA: AK Press.

Nangwaya, A. (2011). "Race, Oppositional Politics, and the Challenges of Post-9/11 Mass Movement-Building Spaces." *Anarchist Developments in Cultural Studies*, 2011(1), 171-209.

Olson, J. (2009). "The Problem With Infoshops and Insurrection: US Anarchism, Movement Building and the Racial Order. In R. Amster, A. DeLeon, L. A. Fernandez, A. J. Nocella II, & S. Deric, *Contemporary Anarchist Studies: An Introductory Anthology to Anarchy in the Academy* (pp. 35-45). New York, NY: Routledge.

Ramnath, M. (2011). *Decolonizing Anarchism*. Oakland, CA: AK Press.

Regan, P. (2010). *Unsettling the Settler Within: Indian Residential Schools, Truth Telling, and Reconciliation in Canada*. Vancouver: UBC Press.

Schmidt, M., & Van Der Walt, L. (2009). *Black Flame: The Revolutionary Class Politics of Anarchism and Syndicalism*. Oakland, CA: AK Press.

Simpson, L. (2011). *Dancing on our Turtle's Back: Stories of Nishnaabeg Re-Creation, Resurgence and A New Emergence*. Winnipeg, MB: Arbeiter Ring Publishing.

Smith, A. (2005). *Conquest: Sexual Violence and American Indian Genocide*. Cambridge, MA: South End Press.

Smith, A. (2006). "Heteropatriarchy and The Three Pillars of White Supremacy: Rethinking Women of Colour Organizing." In I. W. Violence, *The Colour of Violence: The INCITE! Anthology* (pp. 66-73). Cambridge, MA: South End Press.

Smith, A. (2008). *Native Americans and the Christian Right: The Gendered Politics of Unlikely Alliances.* Durham & London: Duke University Press.

Wolfe, P. (2006). "Settler Colonialism and the Elimination of the Native." *Journal of Genocide Research,* 8(4), 387–409.

Wolfe, P. (2013). "Recuperating Binarism: A Heretical Introduction." *Settler Colonial Studies,* 3(3-4), 257-279.

THE COMMUNITY ASSEMBLY

Representatives of communities affected by Project Mesoamerica gather in a circle at the center of the poster to discuss their common struggles and plans for collective action. Some of the characters bring items from their homes, signaling that they've traveled far to be here, and that organizing efforts have been coordinated across the region. Unlike the top-down decision making that governs the "official" plans for the region, many voices are valued in this process of participatory, horizontal communication. The stories transmitted at this gathering join together in a spiral that symbolizes the conversation taking place. Documenting and spreading the word is also essential; recording equipment appears around the circle to foster communication between generations and across cultures.

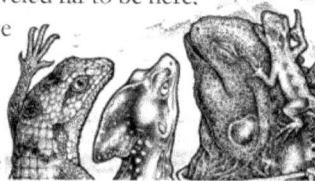

[▲ ARTwork: '¡Mesoamerica Resiste!' detail, Beehive Design Collective, see p.357]

8 | A Diversity of Media Tactics: Grassroots Autonomous Media in Montreal*

Sandra Jeppesen, Anna Kruzynski, Aaron Lakoff and Rachel Sarrasin—Collectif de recherche sur l'autonomie collective (CRAC)

Sandra: I'm going to talk about my work in an anarchist-feminist activist-researcher collective, on social movement media activism in Montreal Canada.[1]

---

* A larger version including some of this material appeared as: Jeppesen, Sandra, Anna Kruzynski. Aaron Lakoff and Rachel Serrasin. 2014. "Grassroots Autonomous Media Practices: A Diversity of Tactics." *Journal of Media Practice* 1–18

1   Presentation at NAASN5 by Sandra Jeppesen

Introduction — Theoretical Framework

Bailey, Cammaerts and Carpentier suggest that "the exist-ing genealogy of alternative media relies on an unsustain-able set of distinctions such as that between non-commer-cial and commercial or radical and non-radical alternative media," and that the characteristics and uses of "alternat-ive media should be articulated as relational and contin-gent on the particularities of the contexts of production, distribution and consumption" (xii). This chapter analyzes autonomous grassroots media activists rooted in anarchist and anti-authoritarian social movements. According to Scott Uzelman (2005), autonomous media activists are "fostering new forms of participatory and democratic communication" (17), creating alternative institutions in-dependent of corporations and the state. Their anti-author-itarian horizontal structures for organizing production are consistent with the politics of their content. How do these politics influence what Alice Mattoni (2013) calls, "reper-toires of communication," or the strategies engaged to create media? We have found the strategy, a 'diversity of tactics', first agreed to during the consultas and spokescouncils of the Quebec FTAA protests in 2001, ap-plies to social movement media as well as it does to social movements they are rooted within.

Methodology - Participatory Action Research (PAR)

We used a Participatory Action Research methodology from 2005-2012, as members of CRAC are all rooted with the anti-authoritarian movement in Quebec.

In phase one, anti-authoritarian feminist researchers collaborated with activist groups to develop interview questions, and conduct one-on-one interviews that were recorded, transcribed and coded in NVivo. In phase two, still collaborating with the groups, results were compiled into a monograph, along with images, flyers, posters and other ephemera. An iterative validation process included workshops, and a participatory launch. The third and final phase was a transverse analysis across all groups on specific themes.

We interviewed 127 participants from ten Quebec anti-authoritarian pro-feminist groups and networks. This paper is a transverse analysis of the theme 'alternative media'.

Findings—Grassroots Autonomous Media in Montreal

We found that anti-authoritarian activists use the term 'alternative media' to refer to a specific type of *social movement media* produced within, by, for and about grassroots autonomous social movements, what we are therefore calling "grassroots autonomous media". Four specific tactics emerged.

Affinities: overlapping social circles

The first tactic targets a small subcultural audience. A participant in the radical queer collective QTeam mentioned that some alternative media are disseminated through overlapping circles of friend groups, such as activist groups, student groups, housing collectives, etc. Media produced to promote events such as anarchist-feminist workshops or radical queer dance parties circulated from person to person or group to group. This tactic creates the sense of an anarchist-feminist 'scene', a radical queer 'scene', or an queer people of colour (QPOC) 'scene', all three of which are strong social movement micro-cohorts in Montreal.

Spaces: anchor points for sowing the seeds of dissent

Engaging slightly larger audiences, activist media spaces serve as anchor points for sowing the seeds of dissent. A participant in Ainsi Squat-Elles mentioned that their radio show seemed to be an "anchor point" within the Quebec feminist movement, with a core group of anarchist-feminists producing the show, and a larger group of generally feminist listeners. The 'seeds of dissent' from the show were 'sown' by listeners through subsequent informal discussions of each broadcast within the broader feminist movement. This tactic is used within a specific milieu to deepen and extend their analysis. Participants said they were trying to 'anarchize feminism'. In workshop discussions, some were concerned that the 'anchor point' tactic risks consolidating power among a small group. It was noted that spaces use skill-sharing and open collectives to better horizontalize communicative power, fostering what Starhawk, Uri Gordon and others have called, 'power-with' or empowerment of communities of shared interest.

Both affinity and anchor tactics are based on the principle Chanan calls "we talk to each other about us" (Alt Med Hbook 42), intentionally opening spaces of limited reach to foster safe spaces and develop political analysis among individuals who are like-minded based on identities or political commitments.

Mass Mobilizations: the snowball effect

Activists mobilizing mass protest convergences will use 'the snowball effect' to build momentum. A participant in the *Convergence des Luttes Anti-Capitalistes* or the CLAC (Convergence of anti-capitalist struggles) mentioned this media tactic was used to inform and mobilize the general public to participate in the Quebec City anti-FTAA protests in 2001. Their media committee debated the need to simplify language for a general audience who might be unfamiliar or uneasy with anti-capitalist ideas, the goal nonetheless being to render anti-capitalism comprehensible to a mainstream audience, and build relationships among single-issue groups into a mass mobilization. Some were concerned that simplifying language would water down their revolutionary politics, risking cooptation by reformists.

Solidarity: global dialogues

The fourth tactic, expanding beyond local or regional mobilizations, was to reach out across global networks. A participant in the anarcha-queer collective, *Les Panthères roses*, (pink panthers), mentioned dialogues with global queer anarchist communities, as zines on transphobia and sex-worker-phobia were shared, and other global radical queer groups found information on the bilingual (English/French) website and got in touch with the *Panthères*. The tactic of global media dialogues is used to share and co-produce knowledge in solidarity with global struggles, establishing relationships based on the anarchist concept of mutual aid.

Debates by Media Activists

Several debates arose around these tactics, which we have grouped loosely into content and production (or process).

Content

a. Self-representation

Activists argued that self-representation is crucial to correct mainstream misrepresentations of anarchists, to give voice to marginalized groups, and to disseminate a deeper, intersectional feminist anti-capitalist political analysis. Questions arose around the possibility of speaking for a small group or a broader social movement. Writers wondered how they should acknowledge ideas from experiences within a collective. Some noted that group self-representations did not always ring true for their own experience, as the group was romanticized or described uncritically, omitting questions of internal power, with gendered and racialized implications. We found that straight white males tended to do more writing, in effect taking credit for collectively generated ideas and actions.

b. Complexity of Issues

Media activists also spoke of the challenge of representing complex issues, such as feminist intersectionality theory, on specific campaigns where they had produced in-depth knowledge. For example, in mining justice movements, resource extraction and environmental concerns intersect with indigenous sovereignty, colonialism, racism, gender, and capitalist globalization. Activist worked hard to find strategies for articulating links among all of these issues in a straightforward and concise way for a general audience.

c. Accessibility of Discourses

Complexity of issues is also related to accessibility of discourses. Media activists are committed to keeping the media accessible. Sometimes however, discourse created an insider/outsider dynamic, where people new to activism didn't know what specific discourses meant, and felt excluded or judged if they had questions, disagreed, or used incorrect words. Autonomous garden activists, for example, provided a lot of time for discussion of pamphlets on autonomous gardening and food security disseminated at rural community events, to reach common ground with local organic farmers who shared an affinity with the group once they could bridge discursive gaps. Many groups mentioned that media productions were only one facet of communicative action, emphasizing face-to-face communication, particularly popular education workshops.

Process

a. Access to Production

Accessibility of access to media production is also key. Some felt it was easy to get involved in autonomous media. Specifically radio participants liked that it was just talking, and they didn't have to be good writers, or take time to write a lengthy article. ASE members felt that producing their radio show was convivial, and the collective was easy to join because of its open structure.

There was no consensus: some activists felt autonomous media was accessible, whereas others found it less so.

b. Prefiguration

There was, on the other hand, a strong consensus that the **context** and **process** of producing autonomous media were as important as the product, supporting the findings of Atton, Downing, Cammaerts, Mattoni and many others. Activists found peer-to-peer skill-sharing to be an important form of anti-authoritarian knowledge circulation, such as Ste-Emilie Skillshare's silk-screening workshops, or CKUT radio station peer training, which **prefigure** horizontal knowledge production relationships.

c. Power Dynamics

As in any group, internal power dynamics can be racialized, gendered, heteronormative, able-bodied, etc.. For example, people of colour in predominantly white anarchist or student activist groups were sometimes figure-headed as media spokesperson, felt tokenized, and became the target of journalists' racism (e.g. being told 'You speak English so well') or of intensified police repression and violence. Others were held up as evidence of the group's success at anti-racist politics, though this success was seen by POC themselves to be somewhat limited. On the other hand, some activists felt that seeing another POC take on the role of media spokesperson motivated and empowered them to do so.

Power hierarchies were addressed by the formation of identity-based collectives, or 'non-mixt' spaces (e.g. LPR and QTeam were radical queer activist groups; Ste-Emilie Skill-Share is a queer and trans people of colour art collective space, etc.). Non-mixed groups seem to be better at horizontality because of shared experiences of oppression, and the ability to create a safer space for media activism.

Conclusions

This understanding of the diversity of grassroots autonomous media tactics allows us to move away from genre-related interpretations of tactics such as culture jamming, and a scholarly fetishization of social media use by social movements, to understand the wide diversity of communicative action to be driven by the desired audience and actions.

Affinity group media invites people into safer spaces, such as radical queer sex parties, queer and trans people of colour art spaces, or anti-racist art and activism shows. This media links sociality, culture, politics, and everyday life, producing spaces for friendships, alliances, intimacies and understandings to develop that will ground and motivate the political organizing.

Mass mobilization media, on the other hand, reaches out to the general public to see if there is a possibility of motivating them to participate in a protest, attend a talk, or get involved in media production. Rather than creating safer spaces, this kind of media is about shifting consciousness and encouraging people to think and act beyond their comfort zone.

These diverse communicative tactics, used in a very sophisticated and nuanced way to target different audiences to compel them to take action, disabuse us of the notion that autonomous media only reaches small activist audiences.

For each communicative tactic, activists spoke about the desired audience and actions, acknowledging that there are many types of relationships being developed within anti-authoritarian communities and collectives, but also in relationships being nurtured and developed with others in the broader social justice movement, the community at large, and global movements.

For anti-authoritarians, political communication is about building relationships and taking action with others. Engaging a diversity of communicative tactics is necessary for media activists to develop a range of grassroots social and political relationships in multi-issue movements with intersectional analyses of feminist, queer, anti-racist and anti-colonial politics. This diversity of media tactics is connected to a deeper understanding and acceptance of the diversity of tactics in social movements, based on mutual aid, respect and egalitarianism in practice.

Youth are recording historic memory by interviewing their elders and broadcasting to the public.

▲ ART: '¡Mesoamerica Resiste!' detail, Beehive Design Collective, see p.357]

9 | Radical Politics in a Conservative Capital: Anarchist Groups and Projects in Edmonton

Robert Hlatky[1]

"It can be alienating to be a leftist in general when it is not accepted in an extremely conservative environment, so it's important to have organizations and events to come together and realize we have power together. Also to see that we provide food, childcare, like all that stuff [at the anarchist bookfair], it's not just a book, we're creating a microcosm of what we'd like the world to be."

—Thomas, interviewee

---

1 Submitted as presented to the January 2014 NAASN conference (so "current" dates included are from then.)

Introduction

A narchist theories and practices have been taken up in a variety of different places around the world, though they are often understudied in local contexts. This lack of academic research on anarchism includes anarchist projects in Alberta, Canada. Most people in Edmonton, the capital of Alberta, are unaware of the local anarchist organizations; nonetheless, there has been a considerable amount of anarchist activity in the city. In addition to individuals who identify with and advocate anarchism, there are anarchist groups, public events and numerous outlets for the production and distribution of anarchist literature in Edmonton. Except for this research project, there has not been an academic study of anarchism in Edmonton. Even at the Edmonton Anarchist Bookfair there has been no literature specifically concerning anarchism in Edmonton. Additionally, the University of Alberta's print and online libraries, as well as the Edmonton Public Library, do not have any material concerning anarchism in Edmonton.

At first anarchism in Alberta may seem surprising, as it is the most conservative province in Canada. The Government of Alberta has been consecutively ruled by a majority Progressive Conservative Party for over four decades. No other provincial government in the country has held such solid political dominance. Nonetheless, Edmonton can be viewed as an island of liberalism in Alberta, since the majority of non-conservative MLAs, and the only non-conservative MP, represent the city.

This chapter will provide an overview of the history of the various anarchists groups in Edmonton, including their tactics and purposes. The research conducted for this chapter was originally undertaken for my Master of Arts degree in sociology at the University of Alberta. My thesis studied anarchist theorizing and organizing in Edmonton, in which I conducted ten semi-structured interviews with self-identified anarchists from the city. Considerable detail about many of the groups discussed in this chapter was provided by the interviewees, some of whom were founding members, while others were participants. For other groups, I have relied on document analysis of electronic material discussing their purpose and activities. Eight of the interviewees have been assigned pseudonyms[1] to maintain anonymity, while two interviewees, Eugene Plawiuk and Malcolm Archibald, preferred to have their roles directly acknowledged.

A Brief Historical Overview of Anarchism in Edmonton

The first record of an anarchist visiting Edmonton was Peter Kropotkin in 1898 (Kropotkin, 1898). The railroad had recently been extended to Edmonton, which had been incorporated as a town earlier that decade. The first group in Edmonton which had a relationship with anarchism

---

1   The interviewees' pseudonyms are Thomas, Fabian Graves, Claire, Blaine, Phinneas Gage, Eric, Jake and Rob Caballero. They had the opportunity to select their own pseudonyms.

was The Industrial Workers of the World (IWW). The IWW became active in Edmonton in 1912, when they supported striking sewer construction workers (Edmonton Public Library, n.d.). In an effort to halt the IWW, the police arrested the secretary of the Edmonton IWW, and charged him with vagrancy (Caragata, 1979), which was a tactic used against multiple Edmonton IWW members during that period (McCormack, 1991). During the 1913-1914 depression, the Edmonton IWW organized unskilled and transient workers, as well as held numerous marches and rallies that attracted approximately one thousand participants (Chubb, 2012; Schulze, 1990). In February 1914, after the Edmonton IWW had been agitating railroad workers to use direct action, the police "raided the IWW hall and evicted two hundred jobless men who had been living there" (McCormack, 1991, p. 111). The IWW in Edmonton and Calgary consisted mainly of Marxists and it appears that Canadian IWW members were unaware of the anarchist influences in their tactics and in the founding of the IWW (Chubb, 2012). The One Big Union (OBU) was organized after the IWW was banned in Canada under the War Measures Act. The OBU organized the Edmonton General Strike of 1919 in conjunction with the Winnipeg General Strike. The Edmonton General Strike lasted one month and largely brought local production to a standstill (Plawiuk, 1994).

In 1927, Emma Goldman spent more than a week in Edmonton. She presented over a dozen lectures on a variety of topics, including anarchism, to an array of audiences, including University of Alberta (U of A) professors, Jewish groups, a women's club and labor meetings (Goldman, 1931/1970). At one of her lectures she spoke to an audience of 1500 (Plawiuk, 2007). Even though Goldman was a radical, she was allowed to speak in Edmonton because she was critical of the Soviet Union (Moritz & Moritz, 2001).

The first anarchist groups that appeared in Edmonton formed during the early 1970s. Black Cat Press, an anarchist printer and publisher, and Erewhon Books, an anarchist bookstore, were the primary expressions of anarchism in the city. They made anarchist literature available in Edmonton and produced their own material about theory and local issues. During this time, local anarchists printed *News from Nowhere*, an anarchist paper printed by Black Cat Press, which was one of the first anarchist journals in Canada. The IWW in Edmonton was reformed in the early 1970s. With the expansion of neoliberal policies and cultural attitudes, local leftwing groups became largely inactive until the 1990s, in connection with student organizing and the development of the anti-globalization movement. During the early 2000s, as this chapter will describe, anarchism has become increasingly popular in Edmonton, with the development of various anarchist groups. Most of the anarchist projects discussed in this chapter are volunteer-based, subverting the wage system and promoting a community of anarchists and activists. Thomas' quote, at the beginning of this chapter, is indicative of the role of prefiguration in anarchist practice, in which anarchists are setting up alternative social structures outside mainstream capitalist political and economic institutions.

The organizations discussed in this chapter have explicitly and implicitly practiced and promoted anarchist theory. The first section describes the various local anarchist groups, with the exception of the IWW which is included because of the influence of the Edmonton branch on local anarchists. The second section discusses groups and events which have anarchistic elements, though they are not necessarily explicitly motivated by anarchist theory. Both sections review each group or project chronologically. The dates recorded are as accurate as I could ascertain; however, some of the dates are estimations, as they have not been documented before.

Anarchist Organizations, Collectives, Affinity Groups and Projects

Black Cat Press, 1972 - current

Black Cat Press is a commercial printer and anarchist publisher in Edmonton, founded by Malcolm Archibald. Initially, Black Cat Press started as an IWW shop in the 1970s. It was originally a hobby for Malcolm, but in the early 1990s he decided to work full-time at the press. Black Cat Press employs several unionized staff members. The majority of its business is commercial printing, including printing for unions and non-profit organizations. Yet, it also publishes classical and contemporary anarchist theory as well as histories on anarchism and labor organizing. The main reason Malcolm started Black Cat Press was because there was not a local anarchist printer. Malcolm recollected:

> I used to work in the underground press in the sixties and early seventies and it was always a problem getting our newspapers printed... Usually the commercial printers weren't the worst ones; it was the left-wing printers that wanted to censor our paper. They wanted to read every line and make sure that it was politically correct from their point of view.

Other leftwing groups, including communists and social democrats, were unwelcoming to the influence of anarchism in the 1970s. From Malcolm's perspective, it was important for anarchists to have their own literature published and available in the community. Black Cat Press temporarily stopped publishing in the early 1980s because there was declining interest in the subject matter. As Malcolm noted, unlike in the 1970s when there was a network of radical publishers, during the 1980s these publishers and bookstores were closing in Canada. They returned to publishing in the 2000s.

When Black Cat Press started, they sold a considerable amount of their material through mail-order, which is now done online. There are currently twenty-two books, including several short books, in the publications section on their website. The catalogue includes classical anarchist theorists, such as Peter Kropotkin, Michael Bakunin and Errico Malatesta. Malcolm has translated into English, for the first time, and published the three volumes of Nestor Makhno's memoirs (2007; 2009; 2011), the leader of the Ukrainian anarchist military during the Russian Revolution and Civil War. Contemporary anarchist literature which they have published includes a book by Graham Purchase (2011), an Australian anarchist mainly interested in ecology, and two books by Arthur J. Miller (2012a; 2012b), an IWW member, on the maritime and mining industries. Malcolm has translated studies into English, including one on 20th century anarcho-syndicalism (Damier, 2009) and another on the Makhnovist movement (Azarov, 2008). Malcolm is currently working on translating a study of Kropotkin's travels in Canada.

The Black Cat Press table has been set up at dozens of anarchist bookfairs across Canada. In an interview with AK Press, Malcolm commented that, "Nowadays with this network of bookfairs, if you publish something at least you're going to reach some kind of an audience" (Zach, 2009). Black Cat Press has inspired many anarchists in the city, including many of the interviewees, who have been influenced by work published by the press.

Industrial Workers of the World, Edmonton General Membership Branch, 1972 - early 1980s

The Industrial Workers of World (IWW) was reformed in Edmonton in the summer of 1972 (Chubb, 2012). Unlike the first Edmonton IWW in the 1910s, by the 1970s there were anarchist members, including Malcolm Archibald and Eugene Plawiuk. Chubb (2012) notes that, "The numbers in the branch were always small at this point, never exceeding more than a dozen" (p. 53). The IWW was mostly involved in solidarity and educational programs during this time. They printed IWW signs and supported labor strikes in the city (Chubb, 2012). Chubb notes that they "ran educational programs targeting unorganized workers and students" as well as hospitality workers (2012, p. 53). Malcolm iterated that anarchists in Edmonton have sought the IWW as the primary organization involved in action, even though the IWW is not an anarchist organization. This is because anarchists in Edmonton have not been able to sustain an anarchist group which practices anarchist actions in the community, besides printing and publishing anarchist literature, whereas the IWW reaches out to more than just the anarchist community. The IWW ended in the early 1980s because important core members moved away (Chubb, 2012).

Erewhon Books, 1973 - 1984

Erewhon Books was an anarchist bookstore in Edmonton which started in the early 1970s and was organized as a volunteer-run collective. Malcolm Archibald and Eugene Plawiuk were co-founders of Erewhon Books. It "ran for more than ten years and was the only gay- and- lesbian friendly bookstore in the city" (Chubb, 2012, p. 53). Eugene recalled that it started because there was not a bookstore in Edmonton which explicitly carried anarchist material. The only other leftwing bookstore in Edmonton was the Trotskyist Vanguard Books, but it was not sympathetic to anarchism.

Erewhon Books originally started as a literature table at the U of A campus once a week, although they soon secured a storefront in downtown Edmonton. As a bookstore it was initially open only on Saturdays, but expanded to running Thursdays to Sundays. Malcolm recalled that, "We absorbed more people into the collective and started to carry a wider range of material and kept it open more hours." The bookstore was relocated approximately six times in Edmonton, mostly in the downtown area.

In order to join the bookstore collective, each member agreed to volunteer once a week at the bookstore and pay a collective fee which contributed to books and rent. There were typically six people in the collective and they did not have paid workers. They met once a week to decide what to order for the bookstore. Members could start their own section at the bookstore if they wanted. Malcolm noted that they "always had a big anarchist section but not everyone in the collective was an anarchist by any means." Erewhon Books initially carried mostly pamphlets and newspapers, though it eventually expanded into being a more general left-wing bookstore, featuring recent literature and academic journals that were requested as well as self-produced material. The bookstore also silkscreened shirts, pressed buttons and printed posters.

Harold Barclay (2005), an anarchist theorist and University of Alberta Professor Emeritus of Anthropology, wrote about Erewhon Books in his autobiography. In the early 1980s Barclay frequently went to Erewhon; however,

> Most of the time... there was only the store clerk to converse with... Many days there were no customers at all. At last, the collective which operated the store became tired of the operation and it folded. During its existence I found it one of the few places where I could go and spend time with those who considered themselves anarchists. (2005, p. 249)

Eugene recalled that, "We slowly declined as people moved away and people got less involved. The stock declined as well..." Eventually they were not able to generate a large enough return and at the end were offsetting the rent from personal income.

Students Organized Resistance Movement, 1994 - 1998

The Students Organized Resistance Movement (STORM) was a campus based group in Alberta which protested the growing neoliberal austerity cuts to social services, which they considered a basic human right (STORM, n.d.a). Their primary focus was on education and healthcare and they promoted bottom-up self-organization and collective action. Most of the information pertaining to STORM was obtained from their website, which states "STORM was active between 1994-1998 on the University of Alberta, Grant MacEwan College, University of Calgary, Mount Royal College, [and] Southern Alberta Institute for Technology campuses" (STORM, n.d.d, para. 3). Jake was a member and recollected that it was a political campus group which was largely tuition focused. STORM held meetings once a week at the U of A campus, which was open to the public. The decision-making process was based on voting where members presented motions, which could be seconded, amended or rejected.

This group is included in this chapter because STORM's resolution from both of the group's conferences explicitly promoted anarchism. The statement from their first conference, held in 1994, noted that "STORM's ultimate goal is to aid the construction of an anarcho-communist society" (STORM, n.d.a, para. 1). The following year their second conference reasserted their adherence to their original principles "with their emphasis on non-hierarchical structure and democratic decision-making as the basis for the movement's organization..." (STORM, n.d.c, para. 4).

STORM held "[v]arious teach-ins designed to stimulate critical thinking" encouraging student activism and informing students about current events (STORM, n.d.d, para. 2). Their stance on collective action is that it is "inherently politicizing," viewing it as giving voice to students (STORM, n.d.b). Their website chronicles various campaigns with which they were involved (STORM, n.d.d). In 1995, they helped deliver approximately 1200 eggs signed by students to Premier Ralph Klein, in re-

sponse to a comment he made about how students must
be fine with budget cuts because they were not throwing
eggs at the education minister. The premier called the protesters jackasses and subsequently apologized for his
comment. In 1996, STORM helped Albertans travel to
Parliament Hill to protest federal budget cuts to social
services. One STORM member was arrested for participating in "a civil disobedience action that shut down the
Indian Affairs' ministry office... to protest meager funding
for aboriginal students" (STORM, n.d.d, para. 2). In
1997, STORM participated in organizing rallies protesting the Alberta Growth Summit.

Food Not Bombs, Edmonton chapter, circa 1998 - 2009

The Edmonton chapter of Food Not Bombs (FNB) started
in the late 1990s with the purpose of subverting the capitalist hegemony of a basic human need by providing free
vegetarian meals. It was also explicitly protesting militarism and the budgetary allotment of funds towards the production of war and defense equipment instead of fighting
hunger and poverty (FNB Edmonton Blog, n.d.). Posters
printed by the Edmonton chapter read, "Food Not Bombs
because poverty is violence and scarcity is a lie" (Edmonton Activist Literature, 2004a). FNB resists the wage system by recovering edible food that had been thrown out
by businesses, including grocery stores, often still in original packaging, which is then cleaned and prepared, then
served freely to people in a public space.

The first Food Not Bombs chapter started in 1980 in Cambridge, Massachusetts, by anti-nuclear activists (Day, 2005). Richard Day (2005) asserts, "...FNB is a non-branded, decentralized network of autonomous chapters which function internally on a consensus basis" (p. 40). David Graeber (2009) observes that, "Food Not Bombs is not an organization. There is no overarching structure, no membership or annual meetings" (p. 236). It is an idea that food should be used by people who need it, noting that there is a "...shared commitment to egalitarian decision-making and a do-it-yourself (DIY) spirit" (Graeber, 2009, p. 236). Randall Amster (2009) argues that FNB is anarchistic in its structure and operation, being leaderless, spontaneous and opposing capitalist relations of propriety. In the mid 1990s chapters spread across the US and Canada (Graeber, 2009).

The Edmonton chapter sporadically provided food once a week for a decade, changing serving locations and kitchens several times. They have served food in downtown Edmonton, beside City Hall (Kirman, 1999), and in Old Strathcona (FNB Edmonton Blog, n.d.). Besides holding weekly food servings, they provided free food for various activist events and lectures, such as a teach-in on the struggle of Mumia Abu Jamal in 1999 (Plawiuk, n.d.) and the Tar Sands Realities and Resistance Conference in 2007 (Oil Sands Truth, 2007). Like other FNB chapters, The Edmonton FNB chapter has been harassed by the police (Butler & McHenry, 2000).

The majority of members of the Edmonton FNB

chapter were not explicitly anarchist. Nonetheless, both Eric and Jake participated in Food Not Bombs for about a year. Eric reflected, "It is very all over the place but very easy to jump in... we have taken carts of food and fed people." Jake recalled that, "It did some good things with food servings at public settings at key places where the homeless are often at in the winter." However, it did not sustain community involvement and Jake argued he eventually saw it as missionary and charity work, instead of political activity:

> It was able to push the envelope in some ways but at some point if you're not drawing in people from the community that you are targeting, then you are just coming in as missionaries and at some point the main people that wanted to keep doing it ended up going into a center using their kitchens and getting absorbed into that structure and Food not Bombs stopped being what it was and basically came to be individuals helping out at a soup kitchen and lost its politics.

In 2011, the Edmonton FNB web blog announced that they were active again (FNB Edmonton Blog, 2011), yet this seems to be its last record of activity.

Industrial Workers of the World, General Membership Branch, 1999 - current

The Edmonton IWW General Membership Branch (GMB) was reorganized for the third time in 1999. According to Chubb (2012), they had approximately 50 active members by 2010, which at the time made "the Edmonton Branch of the IWW... the second largest in the world" (p. 2). The Edmonton IWW has a variety of functions, including educational outreach, organizing, solidarity and information and skill-sharing. All the interviewees are either currently or have in the past been members of the IWW, though several current members do not regularly attend branch meetings.

The Edmonton IWW has an educational function as it provides workshops and training for members and the general public. They encourage workers to engage in their own workplace struggles to gain greater control of decision-making. The Edmonton IWW helps organize workers' struggles and labor actions as well as providing a considerable amount of solidarity support, often through members attending local labor pickets. The Edmonton IWW also has an information sharing function; as Blaine iterated, the IWW "also acts as a good clearing house of local activists and labor radicals and it allows a lot of networking to take place that otherwise wouldn't happen." Roles within the Edmonton IWW rotate, enabling members to learn how to participate in different roles within the IWW, as well as encouraging direct democracy and facilitating skill-sharing. The IWW offers the Train-the-Trainers program where members are trained to present and facilitate workshops.

Many of the IWW members view other labor unions as business unions, which are supporters of capitalism and the ruling class instead of protecting the interests of the working-class. The IWW considers the working-class as the only productive class, where the managers and bosses are only concerned with maintaining profit margins and controlling and exploiting workers. Nonetheless, some of the interviewees who are active in the IWW are dual card holders, being members of other unions.

The IWW Preamble advocates abolishing the wage system and capitalism as well as proposing, in classical Marxist language, that the "working-class and the employing class have nothing in common" (IWW, n.d.a, para. 1). The IWW is anti-political, rejecting the effectiveness of state politics. The Edmonton IWW, along with many other branches, has numerous anarchist members, though the IWW is not an anarchist organization. The IWW, as Chubb (2012) has asserted, though not explicitly anarchist, is ideologically within the anarcho-syndicalist tradition. Many of the interviewees took the position that even though the IWW is not an anarchist organization, it embodies many anarchist principles and tactics. Eric commented that, "The IWW is not an anarchist organization but the way we organize, in my feeling, is anarchist. The structure we created is anarchist." The Edmonton IWW reflects anarchist principles because it is self-organized and non-hierarchical, where workers control the decision-making. It also practices direct action and direct democracy. Many of the interviewees strongly identified with the idea of workplace democracy, where rank-and-file workers drive the decision-making of the structure and function of their work. As Phinneas Gage commented:

> We organize workers on the job to gain a sense of em-
> powerment and a greater share of control over the
> work that they do and a greater share of the wealth
> they create. Some of that is in the rank-and-file of
> other unions and some of that is in non-unionized
> workplaces.

To join the IWW, each member has to belong to the working-class, agree to the IWW Preamble and pay monthly
dues. The working-class is not defined as a socioeconom-
ic measure but instead as a relationship to the means of
production; therefore, membership is not based on the
amount of income but whether one is a worker and not an
employer or boss. Individuals cannot join the IWW if
they employ people or have hiring and firing managerial
responsibilities. Dues are minimal and are based on a
scale of income.

The Edmonton IWW holds monthly general meetings,
which discusses the various events they are organizing
and supporting, reports from officers and delegates, and
the business of running the branch. Three committees
usually meet once a month for organizing, solidarity and
propaganda. Organizationally, the IWW largely operates
on Robert's Rules of Order, though the Edmonton branch
operates on a modified version called Rusty's Rules.
GMB meetings are between one and two hours. A chair
and recording secretary are elected each meeting and
minutes are recorded. There are annual elections from the

rank-and-file membership for secretary positions which run specific tasks within the Edmonton branch, which are all volunteer-based. Many branch members, including many of the interviewees, have served as different secretaries. There are currently six secretary positions, designated for: the branch, finances, communication, organizing, propaganda and literature. Many smaller IWW branches do not have as many secretarial positions. Delegates are also elected to handle membership dues payments.

The Edmonton IWW is a social movement organization which has sustained itself through a constituency, from attracting a group of people, which are not necessarily anarchist, including participants in the labor, student and activist movements. It has maintained membership by creating a collective identity, mainly around direct democracy and solidarity. The IWW will likely maintain its presence in Edmonton.

Student Workers Action Group, circa 2001 - 2012

The Student Workers Action Group (SWAG) was a U of A campus group which aimed to strengthen the solidarity between students and workers. SWAG viewed students as part of the working class and "encourage[d] students to examine their situations as workers and be more assertive about their rights in the workplace" (APIRG, 2006, p. 4). According to a newspaper article, "SWAG was created to advocate accessible, democratic education and working environments..." (Olson, 2001, Nov. 8, p.1). There were several anarchist members. Membership was open to the general public if they agreed on basic issues "like bottom-up democratic organization" and dissatisfaction with current economic affairs (SWAG, 2008, para. 1). During the early 2000s, the original aim of SWAG was anarchistic, though when it was reorganized in the late 2000s it was more Marxist oriented, without explicitly anarchist members.

SWAG protested issues concerning university politics as well as supporting local protests. One of the interviewees recalled that SWAG protested tuition increases and supported the 2002 strike at the Shaw Conference Centre in Edmonton. They also worked on an unsuccessful campaign against privatizing janitorial services on campus. In 2001, SWAG opposed student tuition increases and unsuccessfully lobbied the Student Union (SU) to oppose the hikes. SWAG also worked on a successful campaign for a progressive SU presidential candidate, who was a member of SWAG. In the summer of 2012, I attended a SWAG solidarity march and information rally for the Quebec student strike, which marched from the U of A to the legislature, which was followed by a variety of speakers. However, it appears that SWAG has not been active in the past year.

Anarchist Reading Circle, circa 2000 - 2004

The Edmonton Anarchist Reading Circle was a group of

individuals who read and discussed anarchist literature. According to their website, "Topics include[d] anarchist theory and practice as well as discussions of current events from an anarchist perspective" (Anarchist Reading Circle, n.d.). The Anarchist Reading Circle was open to the public and met once a week. There were approximately six core participants, though there were often more people who would attend. Blaine commented that, "It was just a reading circle but it allowed the growth of many activists and anarchists in Edmonton. For myself, it was an early introduction to the works of anarchism." It helped anarchists become familiar with different movements and struggles and contributed to shaping the collective identity of the local anarchist community.

The reading circle mostly read chapters from books dealing with academic analyses of the anarchist movement in different places. They also read works by the workers' European autonomous movement and by situationists. The main Edmonton Anarchist Reading Circle website, which is no longer available, included pirated material which allowed the participants to read in advance the material being discussed. This was important because not everyone could afford to repeatedly purchase books.

Members of the Anarchist Reading Circle also organized the first Edmonton Anarchist Bookfair in 2002 and offered a book table there. One interviewee reflected that he had hoped the reading circle would have overlapped with more organizing dimensions, such as bringing in speakers whose work the reading circle could read in advance. One of the reasons he became disinterested in the reading circle was because it became just a book club. Another interviewee noted that the Anarchist Reading Circle was loosely organized, which became a problem at times. Meeting so frequently made it difficult to sustain participation, particularly if participants were working full-time. A lot of the people who attended the reading circle were students or partially employed, providing more time to read the chapter and attend the weekly discussion. Around 2002, the Anarchist Reading Circle intended to develop into the Edmonton Anarchist Free School, though this never materialized. The reading circle gradually declined to under six core people and soon ended.

Edmonton Anarchist Bookfair, 2002 - 2013

The Edmonton Anarchist Bookfair is the largest anarchist event in Alberta and is a meeting place for anarchists, leftists, activists, radical environmentalists and other interested people. The Edmonton Anarchist Bookfair started two years after the first Canadian bookfair in Montreal and was the largest anarchist event in Western Canada for most of the first decade of the 21st century, attracting over one thousand people. All the interviewees have in some way been involved in the Edmonton Anarchist Bookfair. Some have been instrumental in organizing it, whereas others have helped by facilitating workshops, tabling, cooking food, posting flyers or handling media coverage.

Anarchist bookfairs typically consist of left-wing book publishers and bookstores, anarchist and activist information tables, various vendors, a keynote speaker, workshops and entertainment, such as live music or dances. There are two main spaces, one where the tables are located and the other where lectures and workshops occur. The Edmonton Anarchist Bookfair has always provided free vegan food and free daycare with a certified childcare worker. All the keynote speakers have published books or articles and are either academics or anarchist organizers.

Blaine recalled the original purpose of the bookfair was to create an anarchist meeting space and a way to increase rapport between anarchists in Edmonton and elsewhere in Canada, "build[ing] a community across the Prairies with other people with different ideas. It was this idea of making Edmonton's [anarchist] community more open to the world and less insular." Thomas' quote at the beginning of this chapter refers to the quality of prefiguration of the bookfair: "it's not just a book, we're creating a microcosm of what we'd like the world to be." Over three days the bookfair offers free food, free daycare, free education (lectures and workshops), free entertainment (musicians and dances), free literature (usually pamphlets) and free space for conversation. The bookfair operates on a volunteer basis, underpinning the need to provide the social provisions of life without an incentive for profit.

The bookfair is as much a political event as a social

event. Politically, it promotes a common framework and collective action strategies. The bookfair also encourages people to be educated and critical of authority as well as fostering political and anarchist theory. The bookfair generally has grassroots groups which coalesce around it, such as the Edmonton Anarchist Reading Circle, Occupy Edmonton and the Free School. Socially, the bookfair is a culture-building event where people interact with others who have similar interests, while others are introduced to radical ideas for the first time. Since 2004, the Edmonton bookfair has hosted numerous parties and dances, which are a significant part of the social aspect of the bookfair, as well as music nights, described as "An evening of music fused with revolutionary politics" (Redmonton-Radical Edmonton Network, 2009, para. 2)—with various genres, including folk, punk, hip-hop and metal.

The first Edmonton Anarchist Bookfair, organized by people in the Edmonton Anarchist Reading Circle with help from Anti-Capitalist Edmonton, occurred in December 2002. The first year of organizing the bookfair was on an ad hoc basis. The second bookfair was organized by Anti-Capitalist Edmonton. The third Edmonton Anarchist Bookfair in 2005 was organized by a new group of people, who have continued to organize it, with a series of member changes, until 2012.

The organizing process of the Edmonton Anarchist Bookfair has changed several times. For the past several bookfairs there has been a core group of about five organizers, in addition to people helping out on the periphery.

The collective organizing the bookfair originally ran on a modified consensus decision-making model, changing to a voting based process several years ago. Blaine argued that, "Theoretically we had meetings that ran on consensus but a lot of the real decision-making wasn't taking place in meetings." In effect, various people took care of different aspects, such as individuals taking over the kitchen, the finances, outreach to vendors or media, often making decisions prior to communicating with the collective. By 2008, there was a new group of people involved, including some of the interviewees. Several interviewees recalled that after the 2010 bookfair, the collective and volunteers who assisted in the past voted to switch to a voting decision-making process where motions could only pass with a 75% majority. Several organizers commented that there was conflict in the decision-making, demonstrated by the transition from consensus to voting, with both models causing burn out over time. There were also complaints about people showing up with suggestions but not actually helping when the bookfair was happening.

During the past several years, the minimum price to run the Edmonton model of the bookfair has been $4000. The most expensive aspect is renting the hall; originally it only cost a few hundred dollars but now it is approximately two thousand dollars for the weekend. The Edmonton Bookfair offers travel subsidies for vendors and the keynote speaker, as well as providing free food, which many other bookfairs do not offer. The Edmonton bookfair has received financial support from various anarchist and activist sources.

All the interviewees involved in organizing the bookfair expressed uncertainty and doubt that the Edmonton bookfair would happen in 2014. The main bookfair collective members have said they are taking a step back from organizing the bookfair. There is a new group of people who organized the 2013 Edmonton Anarchist Bookfair. The 2013 bookfair has changed the Edmonton model to make it more affordable. Instead of three days, it was held over two days. They have changed venues, removed a keynote speaker and likely reduced travel subsidies. The Edmonton Anarchist Bookfair was not held in 2014.[2]

Workers' Power Study Group, circa 2003 - 2005

Workers' Power was an informal study group and was affiliated with the Edmonton IWW. Eugene Plawiuk organized the study group. It met once a month and was a social evening with eight to fifteen participants meeting at various members' homes. According to one of their announcements, "Workers Power will reflect on the limitations of 'historical' Anarchism and Marxism to develop a revolutionary critique of daily life and a political practice to apply to the current crisis of capitalism" (A-Infos, 2004, para. 5). Eugene recalled the attitude of the meetings was "bring your books, bring your ideas; let's dis-

2   Editor's note: However, the Bookfair did return in 2015.

cuss it. How does it apply today? Is it still relevant? ... Has something changed?" They would occasionally have a potluck or watch a movie followed by a discussion. Blaine's participation in Workers' Power was his first introduction to council communism, which is very critical of the labor establishment and business unions, influencing a lot of the members' perspectives regarding solidarity unionism. Eugene explained that "Workers' Power was an attempt to integrate anarchism with left communism." The readings were mainly focused on left communist, council communist and anti-parliamentary communist perspectives. These branches of communism in many ways compliment anarchist theory because they are anti-imperialist and oppose running in elections, instead supporting organizing and mobilizing from below.

Black Books Distribution 2003-2013

Blaine started Black Books Distribution as a hobby to sell books at small events, including anarchist bookfairs and activist events. He started it after he had helped order and table books for the first Edmonton Anarchist Bookfair. One of Blaine's major reasons for starting Black Books was because most bookstores in Edmonton do not carry anarchist material. Blaine asserted that, "It was something that I could promote anarchism with and also to promote reading literature that I believed in." Black Books carried books on a variety of issues including anarchist theory and history, labor organizing and history, LGBT rights and various issues from a leftwing perspective. Blaine had an arrangement with Earth's General Store where Black Books stocked several bookshelves. Blaine remarked that he enjoyed running the Black Books in the 2000s but he is now phasing it out, citing that it is becoming difficult to sell books and he no longer has enough time. Additionally, during the past decade more outlets for anarchist literature have become available, particularly online sources, making anarchist literature more accessible.

Thoughtcrime Ink, 2006 - current

On their website, Thoughtcrime Ink (n.d.a) describes themselves as "a non-profit anarchist collective that raises funds for anarchist education projects, mainly through printing, publishing, and solidarity packages." Co-founded by Fabian Graves in 2006, and based in Edmonton, Thoughtcrime Ink is a registered non-profit organization and a volunteer-based collective. They sell merchandise with a revolutionary sentiment and donate the profits to various anarchist projects. Thoughtcrime Ink originally started by producing and selling t-shirts, buttons and patches, but it has gradually changed its activities to printing essays and pamphlets and publishing books. The literature they print focuses mainly on classical and contemporary anarchist theory and grassroots labor organizing. Fabian reflected, "Thoughtcrime has made class-struggle literature easier to find and some stuff wouldn't exist without us. I'm proud of that." All of Thoughtcrime's literature is printed at Black Cat Press

though they are separate groups which independently select what they print. There is an arrangement between the
two groups wherein Thoughtcrime tables for Black Cat at
anarchist bookfairs outside of Alberta.

Thoughtcrime Ink operates on a voting decision-making process when consensus is not met. Currently there
are seven members. There are also people who volunteer
on the periphery, such as binding pamphlets and tabling at
events. Rob Caballero argued there is a performative
quality of participating in anarchist groups, such as
Thoughtcrime, expressing his participation was instrumental for becoming involved in the anarchist movement
because it associated him with anarchist events and issues.

Thoughtcrime Ink has posted a Frequently Asked
Questions page on their website where they address the
critique that by selling merchandise they are capitalizing
on anarchism and are therefore promoting capitalism.
Specifically, the first question is, "What is an 'anti-capitalist' organization doing selling apparel, anyway?"
(Thoughtcrime, n.d.b, para. 1). Part of their answer states,
"[w]e think eschewing profit for personal gain and using
all the money we make for community projects is one
way to be anti-capitalist in practice, to divert money from
'the system' into an alternative social economy"
(Thoughtcrime, n.d.b, para. 1). This refers to promoting
prefigurative politics where community groups replace
capitalist relationships. Essentially Thoughtcrime resists
generating private profit by volunteering and by donating

their profits to anarchist groups. Their only paid worker is the web designer.

The collective meets several times a year to decide which upcoming events or groups they will donate to. The website notes their criteria for funding groups is that they "maintain oppositional stances to corporations and state [and] are doing radical work that needs to be done for healthy, connected communities..." (Thoughtcrime, n.d.b, para. 7). A 2008 blog post on their website notes they originally wanted to raise $5000 for the Edmonton bookfair, but eventually decided to donate their profit and some of their merchandise to multiple anarchist projects, including six Canadian anarchist bookfairs. Thoughtcrime also donated $1500 to the interviewers of *Anarchism: A Documentary Film* who interviewed 101 anarchists from around the world (*Anarchism: a Documentary*, 2011). They have also donated to speakers who have lectured in Edmonton.

In the past, Thoughtcrime Ink tabled fifteen events in one year, during which Fabian estimated they talked to 2000 people. He considered this important, where people see that anarchists are rational and perhaps persuasive. However, Thoughtcrime does not table nearly as much now, focusing mainly at anarchist bookfairs as well as some leftwing conferences. Thoughtcrime has tabled at the majority of the bookfairs in Canada, as well as at bookfairs in the US and in Europe.

Thoughtcrime mainly sells pamphlets, some by classical anarchists like Kropotkin, Malatesta, Emma Goldman and Alexander Berkman, which are often essays or a section of a book. This type of material is no longer protected by copyright and can be freely distributed. They also print material from individuals and groups that have given consent for it to be reproduced. Books they have published include a collection of essays by Wayne Price (2010) about anarchism and reformism, as well as the study of state capitalism in the USSR by Aufheben Collective (2013). Works by the writers of the Recomposition Blog have also been published. Rob noted that a goal for Thoughtcrime is to produce literature about current events, publishing "more contemporary pamphlets especially about things that are happening... where we have material that you can disseminate because you want to insert it into social movements."

Thoughtcrime also sells t-shirts, with 35 designs available on their website, but they are phasing out this form of merchandise. Their clothing is "sweatshop-free," though they recognize any worker in the capitalist system is exploited. Thoughtcrime has also released several musical CDs, which are no longer available on their website. Thoughtcrime also offers "Infoshop in a box" which is an assortment of anarchist material which can include shirts and other merchandise that can be tabled at events. This is particularly useful "if you live in a smaller centre where radical literature might be harder to get ahold [sic] of" (Thoughtcrime Ink, n.d.b, para. 2).

Edmonton Anarchist Black Cross, circa 2007 - 2010

The first Anarchist Black Cross (ABC) groups originated in the early 20th century as an alternative structure to the Red Cross, formed during the Russian Revolution and Civil War to supply aid to Russian anarchists (Anarchist Black Cross Federation, 2011). During the 1980s autonomous ABC groups formed in North America. The ABC in Edmonton operated in the late 2000s with the purpose of supporting political prisoners and opposing the prison system. Its ultimate aim was to dismantle the prison system, though it defended current legal rights to prevent the further erosion of freedoms by ruling elites (ABC Edmonton, 2010a). Their website asserts that prisons are not rehabilitative but instead maintain class and race privilege while reinforcing state power. The organization of the Edmonton ABC was non-hierarchical and based on consensus with membership open to the general public. They organized educational events about the prison system and supported prisoners "morally, financially and legally" (ABC Edmonton, 2010a, para. 2). They also organized a letter writing campaign for anarchist prisoners, supplying postcards, stamps and contact information.

ABC Edmonton cooperatively worked with other groups, participating in events and organizing their own events. In September 2008 when the Olympic Spirit Train arrived in the city they supported a protest with various First Nations groups against the Olympic Games and the Tar Sands (Anti-Olympics Archive, 2011). On August 10,

2008, the ABC organized a Prison Justice Day event in Edmonton, offering workshops, screening two films, arranging a benefit show (Prison Justice, n.d.). The following year for Prisoner Justice Day, the Edmonton ABC and the Edmonton John Howard Society organized a protest at the Alberta Legislature (Edmonton Social Planning Council, 2009). As a way to support female prisoners, ABC Edmonton received a $670 grant from APIRG for the Books Behind Bars campaign, which purchased "books for the library at the Edmonton Institution for Women" (ABC Edmonton, 2010b). ABC Edmonton also partnered with the U of A's Community Service Learning (CSL) in 2008, which connects student with voluntary community groups (Community Service Learning, n.d.). ABC Edmonton appears to have become inactive after 2010.

Workers' Solidarity Alliance, 2010 - 2011

The Edmonton chapter of the Workers Solidarity Alliance (WSA) was short lived. Many of the members were anarchists in the Edmonton IWW who wanted an explicitly anarchist organization. After joining the WSA, which requires affordable membership dues, members were added to an email list service which networks information. It is up to local WSA members to organize local meetings under their own direction. The Edmonton chapter of the WSA held meetings for the purpose of organization-building and reaching common points of agreement. Blaine recalled that, "In our local group we tried to build more of a coherent local theoretical background. We did a lot of reading together; a lot of discussion."

The WSA started in the US in 1984 and is anti-capitalist, anti-authoritarian and anti-statist (Workers Solidarity Alliance, n.d.). The "WSA is not a union but an organization of activists" (Workers Solidarity Alliance, n.d., para 18). Some of the interviewees were disappointed with the Edmonton WSA, specifically with the lack of defined roles for members and the lack of meeting procedures. Blaine recalled that they were impressed by the efforts of the WSA in the US but locally they were not inspired and most of the members eventually left the organization, which ended the meetings in Edmonton, though some are still members.

The Free Thinkers Market, 2012 - current

The Free Thinkers Market was initially a monthly anarchist market based in Edmonton, which started in 2012. It is free for people to vend and attend, and includes a variety of vendors, mostly an assortment of local artists and craftspeople. According to their website, their purpose is to "[s]upport local artists and help build a community outside of the system" (Free Thinkers Market, n.d., para. 1). People are producing their own products, including jewelry, paintings, food and clothing, which encourages creativity and independence of workers. The Free Thinkers Market has been held in bars as well as several other venues, including a cafe which allowed the market to be open to all ages. The market usually offers some free vegan food. They encourage bartering and other "alternative methods of exchange" (Free Thinkers Market, n.d., para. 2). A poster for the market notes they offer "great art, handmade goods, live music and open mic, books and zines, crystals and stones, bold brews, treats, sweets, buttons and trinkets" (Free Thinkers Market, 2013). In 2014, the Free Thinkers Market was held less frequently.

Anarchistic Groups in Edmonton

Direct Action Groups

There are a number of groups in Edmonton, many short-lived, which have had an implicit relationship with anarchism. The most prominent of these groups is the Animal Liberation Front (ALF), which was active in Edmonton in the early 1990s. ALF is a leaderless movement which started in the early 1970s in the UK. Unlike every other group discussed in this chapter, ALF is the only group which has committed criminal acts of protest, including property destruction and arson. ALF activists in Edmonton committed two actions causing property damage over $100 000, targeting sources of animal cruelty (Animal Liberation Front, n.d.). Other actions included activists rescuing 29 cats from a research lab at the U of A, in June 1992 (Animal Liberation Front, n.d.).

Reclaim the Streets (RTS) and Anti-Racist Action are two anarchistic affinity groups that have organized direct actions in Edmonton. Besides ALF, both groups use more confrontational tactics than other local anarchist groups. There has been at least one RTS event, held in Edmonton on August 25, 2000 (Edmonton Activist Literature, 2004b). RTS coordinates unpermitted street parties, incorporating elements of the anarchist, environmental and rave movements. RTS originated in the UK in the 1990s by activists in the anti-roads movement, protesting the detrimental effects of the privatization of urban space and the heavy reliance on automobiles (Graeber, 2009). RTS is a non-branded and non-hierarchical action which has autonomously operated in multiple urban centres (Day, 2005).

Anti-Racist Action originated in the US in the late 1980s, coordinating direct actions against racism and oppression (Anti-Racist Action Network, 2009). There was an Anti-Racist Action event protesting a white supremacist demonstration in Edmonton in March 2012. It took only a few minutes for the white power rally, with a few dozen fascist supporters, to be disrupted by 300 anti-racist activists and anarchists (Libcom, 2012). The Edmonton police protected the white supremacists, separating them from the anti-racist protesters, causing the police to be criticized in the Edmonton anarchist community for protecting fascists. There were also Anti-Racist Action inspired events in Edmonton in the early 1990s, protesting a local white supremacist gang (Anti-Racist Action Network, 2009).

Affinity Groups, Study Groups and Coalitions

Other Edmonton groups involved in anarchistic tactics were the Radical Cheerleaders and the Free School. The Radical Cheerleaders operated in the late 1990s and was regrouped about a decade later. The Radical Cheerleaders "aren't practising for the next sporting event. You're more likely to see them in front of the legislature or marching down the streets with fellow protesters" (Edmonton Journal, Sept. 7, 2007, para. 3). They attended protests, often dressed in red and black, and chanted revolutionary slogans for the purpose of building morale amongst protesters. In the early 1970s there was a Free University, organized by students at the U of A. Eugene Plawiuk was a participant in it and recalled that it was involved in the local radical anti-war movement and offered classes in revolutionary struggle. There was talk of starting an Anarchist Free School in the early 2000s but this never materialized. The Free School was organized in the mid-2000s and has had various group readings and discussions, although it used a Marxist instead of an anarchist framework, yet they hosted a workshop at the 2012 Edmonton Anarchist Bookfair.

The People's Action Network (PAN) in Edmonton was a coalition group which was involved in the early anti-neoliberal globalization movement, operating in the late 1990s and early 2000s. It was involved with organizing solidarity protests in Edmonton against the Free Trade Agreement of the Americas, coinciding with the protests in Quebec City in 2001. PAN Edmonton offered teach-ins about various issues concerning globalization. It was one of the first activist groups in Edmonton which formally ran on the consensus model of decision-making. One PAN Edmonton protest marched to the Alberta legislature with approximately 200 people and then featured speakers from community groups, musical performances and a play (K-1ine, 2001). Two of the interviewees were members of PAN Edmonton, though their experiences were generally negative. One interviewee's impression was that many of the members were activists from the university who favored academic language which alienated people from working-class backgrounds.

The Edmonton Coalition Against War and Racism (ECAWAR), which started in 2003, is an activist group which has had anarchist participants, though today it is influenced more by the Communist Party and by liberalism. One interviewee was a founding member of the coalition and another interviewee was also active in the group. ECAWAR organized the largest anti-war protests in Edmonton opposing the Iraq and Afghanistan Wars, also protesting militarism and war profiteering (ECAWAR, n.d.). The group has held various solidarity demonstrations for issues in the Middle East, including the Occupations of Palestine and Lebanon as well as the importance of avoiding military intervention in Iran and Syria.

Alternatives to Capitalism and Anti-Capitalist Edmonton (ACE) are two discussion groups which were influenced by anarchist theory. Alternatives to Capitalism was a leftwing study and discussion group which met once a week for approximately one year. It was originally a group which discussed books, but it became more of a general discussion group. Blaine was a member and recalled that they would "read and discuss alternatives to capitalism, influenced by anarchist thought." They also tried having a dinner once a month at somebody's house. Blaine argued that Alternatives to Capitalism came out of the anti-globalization movement of the early 2000s and was full of hope but lacked "...a real vision aside from a wistful desire for a new society." ACE started in 2002 and continued for a couple of years and was "concerned with a number of issues, including international trade agreements, legal rights, and community selfsufficiency [sic]" (APIRG, 2006, p. 3). Jake was a member of ACE and recollected that it educated members about anti-capitalist politics, mostly through readings. ACE helped organize the first and second Edmonton Anarchist Bookfairs. Jake argued that there "comes a point where you should use the reading to engage the community and that wasn't happening."

Occupy Edmonton, 2011 - current

Occupy Edmonton was organized approximately one month after the mobilization of Occupy Wall Street (OWS). OWS is based on anarchist principles, including non-hierarchical social relationships, prefigurative politics and rejection of the legitimacy of current political and legal institutions (Graeber, 2011). Occupy Edmonton had its first public event on October 15, 2011, which was planned as a day for solidarity for the Occupy movement, in which 1500 cities participated internationally (Occupy Edmonton, 2012b). Occupy Edmonton (2012a) supports "direct action and participatory frameworks" and has bi-weekly general assemblies. It is a consensus based organization and is a leaderless movement. Rob Caballero was involved in Occupy Edmonton for its first year. Eric and Jake were also involved in Occupy Edmonton for a short time.

After Occupy Edmonton's first march through the downtown core, they marched to Melcor Park and set up an Occupy encampment for 42 days. The encampment temporarily created common property in a privately owned park, resisting the capitalist appropriation of land while targeting Melcor Developments, which is involved in the real estate industry. Rob Caballero asserted, "Occupy was a space that was temporarily liberated from the mediation of security, the state, landlords and bosses; it was a free open space." Rob was very enthused with the rapid development of Occupy Edmonton: "One day there wasn't anybody in the park and then the next day there were 200 people talking about political ideas that are in some ways radical. It was something really worth supporting." Eric argued that Occupy Edmonton raised important issues including anti-capitalism, anti-oppression and autonomy, as well as creating self-identified anarchists or people who organize along anarchist principles.

Occupy Edmonton's encampment received and ignored several notices of eviction by Melcor. Occupy Edmonton established a police committee to meet with the police and at one point two detectives threatened several participants with criminal charges if they remained in Occupy, although no one was charged. This was seen as a way to individualize blame and falsely portray the notion that several leaders were responsible for Occupy Edmonton. Rob Caballero recalled that the media had a narrative about the danger of having people in the park at night. Occupy Edmonton framed their response as their presence making the area safer. Rob related his own experience, saying "I used to live in the neighbourhood and... [Melcor Park] is so dark and empty... but now that there are people here it's a really good community space." The encampment was raided by the police shortly after 4 AM on November 25, 2011, as approximately 45 officers dislodged nine people from the park, arresting three people who refused to leave.

Rob Caballero asserted that the encampment was a difficult project for people, since many of the participants did not have previous experience in political activity. People entered a communal living situation with some similar values, such as fairness and social justice, "but very different strategies and notions of proper political activity." Rob felt like he ended up struggling with liberal and state tendencies within Occupy Edmonton, asserting "there're a lot of people involved that are trying to tone it down that come from very specific liberal perspectives."

Occupy Edmonton (2012b) participated in 100 actions during their first year of operation. During and after the encampment, Occupy Edmonton worked on various campaigns, such as protesting federal funding cuts, a proposed oil pipeline and the continuation of Guantanamo Bay prison. They also had an Occupy U of A march where there were suggestions that there would be a new Occupy camp on campus; however, the police did not allow the protesters on campus grounds (Williamson, 2012, Feb. 2). In the summer of 2012, Occupy Edmonton held solidarity protests for the Quebec Student Strikes and supported weekly "casserole nights" in May and June 2012, an activity which started in Montreal where protesters used pots and pans during their marches. Occupy Edmonton has also engaged in banner drops and guerilla art. Occupy Edmonton has become a general coalition group providing support and organizing protests for a variety of causes that members support. They continue to hold weekly general assemblies and have recently started a food cooperative.

Conclusion

This chapter has chronicled the various Edmonton groups and projects that have implicitly or explicitly practiced and promoted anarchism. Many of the local anarchist groups described in this chapter have not been documented before. There is an anarchist community in the city which fosters an anarchist collective identity and shared solidarity. Events such as the anarchist bookfair, anarchist study groups and grassroots organizations practicing anarchist principles, have contributed to generating an anarchist collective identity in Edmonton.

Anarchist social movement organizations and tactics are often modular, meaning they can be "easily transported to many locales and situations, rather than being tied to local communities and rituals" (Staggenborg, 2008, p. 4). Modular tactics used by anarchist projects in Edmonton include the Anarchist Bookfair, the Anarchist Reading Circle, the Anarchist Black Cross, Food Not Bombs, Reclaim the Streets, Radical Cheerleaders and the Occupy movement. These groups have autonomously operated in many North American cities and can be easily replicated in new places. These groups can also be considered banners, which are "a convenient label for a certain goal or type of political activity" which may operate in networks that communicate with other autonomous groups using the same name or tactics (Gordon, 2008, p. 15). The Edmonton anarchists have been active in creating anarchist projects, though often short-lived, to promote and practice their political beliefs and will likely continue to impact the social and cultural terrain in the city.

References

A-Infos. (2004). *Workers Power! Study group in Edmonton Alberta Canada*. Retrieved from: http://www.ainfos.ca/04/may/ainfos00384.html

ABC Edmonton. (2010a). *Welcome to Edmonton Anarchist Black Cross*. Retrieved from:

http://abcedmonton.wordpress.com/2010/01/24/hello-world/

ABC Edmonton. (2010b). *Thank you, APIRG!* Retrieved from: http://abcedmonton.wordpress.com/thank-you-apirg/

Amster, R. (2012). *Anarchism Today.* Santa Barbra, CA: Praeger.

Anarchism a Documentary. (2011). *The end of our travels, for now...* Retrieved from: http://anarchismdocumentary.net/indexwp.php/?paged=2

Anarchist Black Cross Federation. (2011). *What is the Anarchist Black Cross (ABC)?* Retrieved from: http://www.abcf.net/abcf.asp?page=whats1

Anarchist Reading Circle. (n.d.). *Description.* Retrieved from: http://groups.yahoo.com/group/arc-e/? v=1&t=directory&ch=web&pub=groups&sec=dir&slk=504

Animal Liberation Front. (n.d.). *Animal Liberation Front actions —Canada.* Retrieved from: http://www.animalliberationfront.com/ALFront/Actions-Canada/alfcanada.htm

Anti-Olympics Archive. (2011). *Edmonton report back on Spirit Train action.* Retrieved from: http://vancouver.mediacoop.ca/olympics/edmonton-report-back-spirit-train-action/6167

Anti-Racist Action Network. (2009). *History.* Retrieved from: http://antiracistaction.org/?page_id=30

APIRG. (2006). *Annual Report.* Retrieved from: http://www.ualberta.ca/~apirg/assets/APIRG%20Info %20Sheet.pdf

Archibald, M. (2007). *Atamansha: The story of Maria Nikiforova —the anarchist Joan of Arc.* Edmonton, AB: Black Cat Press.

Aufheben Collective. (2013). *What was the USSR? Towards a theory of the deformation of value under state capitalism.*

Edmonton: Thoughtcrime Ink.

Azarov, V. (2008). *Kontrrazvedka: The story of the Makhnovist intelligence service.* Edmonton: Black Cat Press.

Barclay, H. B. (2005b). *Longing for Arcadia: Memoirs of an anarcho-cynicalist anthropologist.* Victoria, BC: Trafford Publishing.

Butler, L., & McHenry, K. (2000). *Food not Bombs.* Tucson, AZ: See Sharp Press.

Caragata, W. (1979). *Alberta labour: A heritage untold.* Toronto, ON: James Lorimer & Company.

Chubb, A. D. (2012). *A critical ethnography of education in the Edmonton Industrial Workers of the World (IWW).* Master's Thesis. Edmonton: University of Alberta.

Community Service Learning. (n.d.). *Our community partners.* Retrieved from: http://www.csl.ualberta.ca/en/About %20Us/Our%20Community%20Partners.aspx

Damier, V. V. (2009). *Anarcho-syndicalism in the 20th century.* Edmonton: Black Cat Press.

Day, R. J. F. (2005). *Gramsci is dead: Anarchist currents in the newest social movements.* Ann Arbor, MI: Pluto Press.

ECAWAR. (n.d.). *About.* Retrieved from: http://www.ecawar.org/? page_id=55

Edmonton Activist Literature. (2004a). *FNB flier (2).* Retrieved from: http://www.crcstudio.org/activist/viewtext.php? s=browse&author=Food+Not+Bombs&tid=39&route=bythisa uthor.php

Edmonton Activist Literature. (2004b). *Street party.* Retrieved from: http://www.crcstudio.org/activist/viewtext.php? s=browse&author=Reclaim+the+Streets&tid=72&route=bythi sauthor.php

Edmonton Anarchist Bookfair Blog. (2006). *Volunteers needed!* Retrieved from: http://edmontonanarchistbookfair.blogspot.ca/2006_08_01_arc hive.html

Edmonton Journal. (2007, Sept. 7). *Rah-rah-radicals.* Retrieved from: http://www.canada.com/edmontonjournal/news/ed/story.html? id=96db584f-d46d-4e34-9b0a-dc79b058a76e&k=85305

Edmonton Public Library. (n.d.). *Edmonton timeline.* Retrieved from: http://www.epl.ca/edmontonacitycalledhome/EPLEdmontonCi tyCalledTimeline.cfm

Edmonton Social Planning Council. (2009). *Event: 'Prisoners' Justice Day'.* Retrieved from: http://www.edmontonsocialplanning.ca/index.php? option=com_jcalpro&Itemid=257&extmode=view&extid=166 &date=2011-09-01

FNB Edmonton Blog. (2009). *Reports of our death have been greatly exaggerated...* Retrieved from: http://foodnotbombsedmonton.blogspot.ca/

FNB Edmonton Blog. (n.d.). *Food not Bombs Edmonton.* Retrieved from: http://foodnotbombsedmonton.blogspot.ca/

Free Thinkers Market. (2013). *Free Thinkers' Market - August 2013.* Retrieved from: https://www.facebook.com/photo.php? fbid=10152025204408765&set=oa.1389777331239591&type =1&theater

Free Thinkers Market. (n.d.). *Free Thinkers Market.* Retrieved from: http://freethinkersmarket.org/home

Goldman, E. (1931/1970). *Living my life: Volume 2.* Mineola: Dover.

Gordon, U. (2008). *Anarchy alive: Anti-authoritarian politics from practice to theory.* Ann Arbor: Pluto Press.

Graeber, D. (2009). *Direct action: An ethnography.* Oakland: AK Press.

Graeber, D. (2011). *Occupy Wall Street's anarchist roots.* Retrieved from: http://www.aljazeera.com/indepth/opinion/2011/11/201111287 2835904508.html

IWW. (n.d.a). *Preamble to the IWW Constitution.* Retrieved from: http://www.iww.org/culture/official/preamble.shtml

K-1ine. (2001). News: FTAA protest—Edmonton. *K-1ine, 4*(14). Retrieved from: http://web.textfiles.com/ezines/K1INE/k-1ine_14.txt

Kirman, P. (1999). *Food not Bombs.* Retrieved from: http://www.inside-edmonton.com/library/weekly/aa100499.htm

Kropotkin, P. (1898). Some of the resources of Canada. *The Nineteenth Century.* Retrieved from: http://dwardmac.pitzer.edu/Anarchist_Archives/kropotkin/cana da.html

Libcom. (2012, Mar. 25). *Anarchists and locals send Nazis packing in Edmonton, Canada.* Retrieved from: http://libcom.org/news/anarchists-comrades-public-send-nazis-packing-edmonton-alberta-25032012

Makhno, N. (2007). *The Russian Revolution in Ukraine.* Edmonton: Black Cat Press.

Makhno, N. (2009). *Under the Blows of the Counterrevolution.* Edmonton: Black Cat Press.

Makhno, N. (2011). *The Ukrainian Revolution.* Edmonton: Black Cat Press.

McCormack, R. (1977). *Reformers, rebels, and revolutionaries:*

The Western Canadian radical movement 1899-1919. Toronto: University of Toronto Press.

Miller, A. J. (2012a). *Yardbird Blues: 25 Years of a wobbly in the maritime industry.* Edmonton: Black Cat Press.

Miller, A. J. (2012b). *Upon the backs of labour: Unruly working class essays.* Edmonton: Black Cat Press.

Moritz, T., & Moritz, A. (2001). *The world's most dangerous woman: A new biography of Emma Goldman.* Vancouver: Subway Books.

Occupy Edmonton. (2012a). *For immediate release: Occupy Edmonton hosts free BBQ to help raise awareness of hunger*. Retrieved from: http://occupyedmonton.org

Occupy Edmonton. (2012b). *Occupy Edmonton: One year in review.* Retrieved from: https://www.facebook.com/OccupyEdmonton/posts/47214191 9497393

Oil Sands Truth. (2007). *Everyone's downstream: Tar sands realities and resistance.* Retrieved from: http://oilsandstruth.org/everyones-downstream

Olson, A. (2001, Nov. 8). Statement for Samuel, SWAG. *The Gateway.* Retrieved from: peel.library.ualberta.ca/newspapers/GAT/2001/11/08/1/Ar0010 0.html?query=newspapers

Plawiuk, E. (1994). *The Edmonton General Strike of 1919.* Retrieved from: http://www.reocities.com/CapitolHill/5202/Edm1919.htm

Plawiuk, E. (2007). *Black and Redmonton.* Retrieved from: http://carnival-of-anarchy.blogspot.ca/2007_02_01_archive.html

Price, W. (2010). *Anarchism & socialism: Reformism or*

revolution? Edmonton: Thoughtcrime Ink.

Prison Justice. (n.d.) *Calendar of events.* Retrieved from: http://www.prisonjustice.ca/current/calendar.html

Purchase, G. (2011). *Anarchism & environmental survival.* Edmonton: Black Cat Press.

Redmonton-Radical Edmonton Network. (2009). *Reminder: 2009 Edmonton Anarchist Bookfair this weekend!* Retrieved from: http://groups.yahoo.com/group/redmonton/message/3924

Schulze, D. (1990). "The Industrial Workers of the World and the unemployed in Edmonton and Calgary in the depression of 1913-1915." *Labour/ Le Travail,* 25(1), 47-75.

Staggenborg, S. (2008). *Social movements.* New York: Oxford University Press.

STORM. (n.d.a). *First STORM conference - November 26, 1994.* Retrieved from: http://www.geocities.ws/pmoore26/novcon.htm

STORM. (n.d.b). *How to organize a protest rally.* Retrieved from: http://www.geocities.ws/pmoore26/guide.htm

STORM. (n.d.c). *Summary of the February 1995 STORM conference.* Retrieved from: http://www.geocities.ws/pmoore26/febcon.htm

STORM. (n.d.d). *Student Organized Resistance Movement.* Retrieved from: http://www.geocities.ws/pmoore26/stormindex.htm

SWAG. (2008). *Join.* Retrieved from: http://swag.apirg.org/index.php?slug=join

Thoughtcrime Ink. (2008). *Your purchases: Helping to power a-bookfairs, other radical projects.* Retrieved from: http://thoughtcrimeink.com/weblog/2008/08

Thoughtcrime Ink. (n.d.a). *Thought Crime F.A.Q.* Retrieved from:

http://thoughtcrimeink.com/about/faq

Thoughtcrime Ink. (n.d.b). *Infoshop in a box.* Retrieved from: http://thoughtcrimeink.com/infoshop

Williamson, S. (2012, Feb. 2). "U of A still unoccupied." *Edmonton Metro.* p. A1.

Workers Solidarity Alliance. (n.d.). *About WSA.* Retrieved from: http://workersolidarity.org/?page_id=11#WSAunion

Zach. (2009). *Black Cat Press: An interview.* Retrieved from: http://www.revolutionbythebook.akpress.org/black-cat-press-an-interview/

▲ Artwork by Beehive Design Collective, see pg.357

10 | The Right to the City Begins on the Street*

Dr. Katherine Dunster[1]

Introduction

David Harvey defines the "right to the city" as a "right to change ourselves by changing the city".[2] Streets can be, and should be, vibrant public open spaces for engaging all kinds of ever-changing human interac-

---

* This chapter builds on the visual presentation Dr. Dunster delivered at NAASN5 and was submitted for the current volume on February 2, 2015. All images are either courtesy of the author, or are accessible via WikiCommons, Creative Commons or are in the public domain. See them in colour at http://thoughtcrimespress.org

1 Urban Ecosystems Program, School of Horticulture, Faculty of Science and Horticulture, Kwantlen Polytechnic University

2 David Harvey (2008) "The Right to the City." *New Left Review* 53: 23-40. p. 23

tions—whether a quiet conversation between a few, for street art, pickets, performances, or protests. As a public space for democratic engagement, streets are again spontaneously (and rightly) changing the city without planning, design, or permission.

Roads have historically been designed by transportation engineers and planners to perform the function of efficiently moving people and things in vehicles through a landscape. The primary goal of such efficiency is to aid and abet commerce and capitalism. Looking at London in the Victorian period[3], the street though, was not a road, but a place where people, commerce, recreation, and social interaction occurred, resulting in a vibrant community that sometimes moved along the pavement, and oftentimes did not. Today, open space is always planned —programming where, when, and how people should use their leisure time when in the public realm. Boundaries between public and private space blur in the trade-off between the want for new land and building development and the needs for public amenities. Politicians surrender; social space disappears.

Streets are an open and common space being reclaimed by people of all ages, in all kinds of weather, at all times of day and night for purposes never envisioned

---

3 I use this time and place as an example because colonial expansion during the Victorian period brought customs, practices, and contemporary engineering to the new cities developing in all corners of the British Empire. For example, during the colonial period in BC the Royal Engineers were responsible for laying out the street grid systems in Victoria and Colonial New Westminster.

by planners and designers nor permitted by politicians. Streets are being used in creative ways to individually and collectively express opinion about issues relevant to life on this planet. Whether eluding control as an anarchistic act, or asserting control by occupying the street, the street is again a common symbolic space[4] that facilitates confrontation as Mouffe argues, but more importantly, creativity. Declared or not, temporary autonomous zones[5] and temporary autonomous spaces are visibly holding space on the street, demonstrating many long-forgotten purposes for the street. This chapter is a visual exploration of recent front-line experiences on the street and in street events that occurred primarily in Montreal, Vancouver, Paris, Berlin, and London, UK between 2011 and 2014.

The Street is Not a Road

The word street (Figure 1) originated in the Late Latin[6] as *strāta via* "a way paved or laid down in stones," which

---

4   Chantal Mouffe (2005) *On the Political* (New York, Routledge, p. 52)

5   As described by Hakim Bey in *T.A.Z.: The Temporary Autonomous Zone, Ontological Anarchy, Poetic Terrorism* (Automedia, 1991). I further refine TAZ to the Temporary Autonomous Space (TAS) which acknowledges the space occupied by an individual for a creative use.

6   *Collins English Dictionary* (2014) 12th edition. Glasgow, HarperCollins Publishers Ltd. sometime between 200 and 600 BCE when the spoken language was being formalized into the written form

morphed into the Old English or Anglo-Saxon *strǣt* between 400 and 1100 CE to describe the ways paved by the Roman, and eventually became the "street" we are familiar with today. The word road originates in the Anglo-Saxon[7] and by the Middle English period it usually referred to a rural way as contrasted with an urban street, which originated in the Latin *strāta via*. Historically then, a road's main function is for transportation, while the street facilitates public interaction.

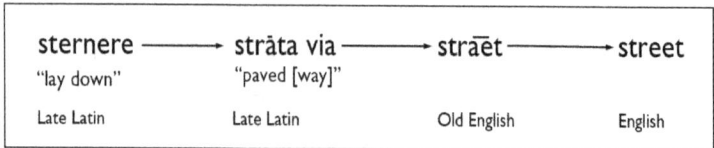

sternere ⟶ strāta via ⟶ strāēt ⟶ street
"lay down"   "paved [way]"

Late Latin   Late Latin   Old English   English

▲Figure 1. Evolution of the word 'street'

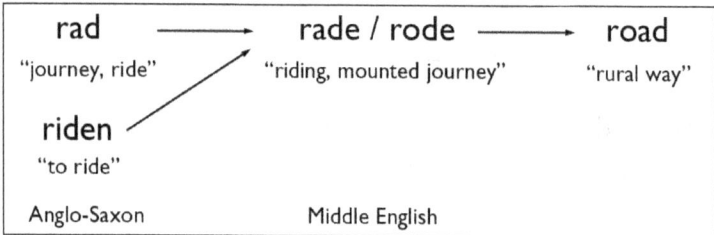

rad ⟶ rade / rode ⟶ road
"journey, ride"   "riding, mounted journey"   "rural way"

riden
"to ride"

Anglo-Saxon   Middle English

▲Figure 2. Evolution of the word 'road'

Historically, a street is defined and characterized by the degree and quality of street life it encourages. A road however has always been designed to serve primarily as a through passage for vehicles or (less frequently) pedestrians. Time, with the assistance of engineers, has blurred

7   Albert Rose (1953) *Public Roads of the Past*, Washington, DC: American Association of Highway Officials.

the distinction to the point where the common right to the street has frequently arrived in a dead end of bureaucracy and policy that favours the vehicle over the pedestrian. Jane Jacobs[8] observed street life in New York City and observed that

> Streets in cities serve many purposes besides carrying vehicles, and city sidewalks—the pedestrian parts of the streets—serve many purposes besides carrying pedestrians.

As Figure 3 illustrates, the contemporary street is the paved or gravelled space between two rows of buildings in a city and includes the sidewalks. It contains trees and light poles, parking meters, mail boxes, cars, bikes, buses and bus stops, sleeping places, sitting places, mail boxes, telephones (or not), eating places, walking places, and socializing places. And most of all the street "contains" people who share space and places in the space. Buskers, artists, beggars, patrons of pavement cafés, people watchers, flâneurs and flâneuses[9], and a diversity of other characters are habitual users of a street; the same people would not typically be found on a road. Streets that are shared by all are therefore a form of urban commons, but

---

8   Jane Jacobs (1961) *The Life and Death of Great American Cities* New York: RandomHouse. p. 29

9   Much is written about the flâneur (see Figure 4) and his ramblings about town. The published works of the 19th century flâneuse are more obscure; two examples being George Sand and Frances Trollope, and Sand had to disguise herself as a man in order to wander freely throughout the streets of Paris and publish her observations.

as the generic example in Figure 3 illustrates, who controls or manages the street is a complicated business in whatever city you live in.

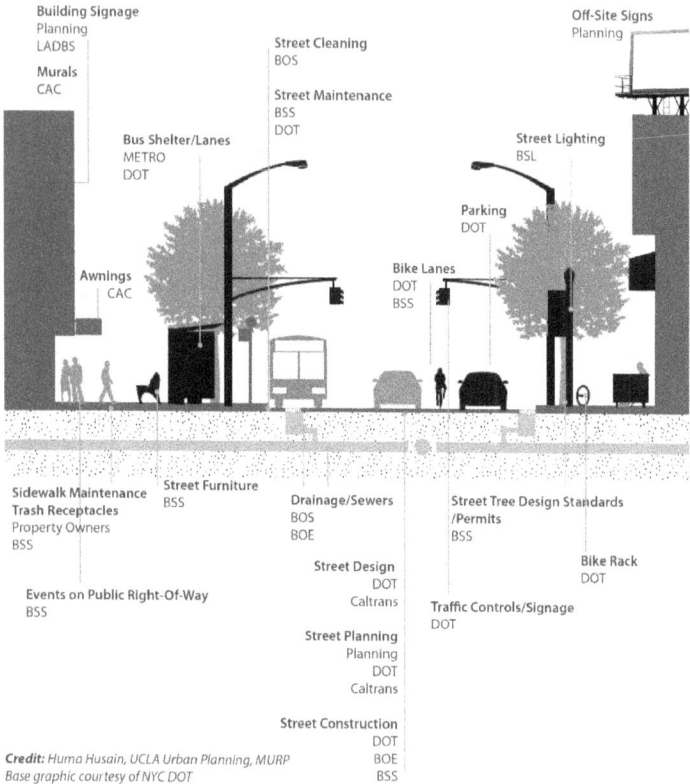

Building Signage
Planning
LADBS

Murals
CAC

Off-Site Signs
Planning

Street Cleaning
BOS

Street Maintenance
BSS
DOT

Bus Shelter/Lanes
METRO
DOT

Street Lighting
BSL

Parking
DOT

Awnings
CAC

Bike Lanes
DOT
BSS

Sidewalk Maintenance
Trash Receptacles
Property Owners
BSS

Street Furniture
BSS

Drainage/Sewers
BOS
BOE

Street Tree Design Standards
/Permits
BSS

Street Design
DOT
Caltrans

Bike Rack
DOT

Events on Public Right-Of-Way
BSS

Traffic Controls/Signage
DOT

Street Planning
Planning
DOT
Caltrans

Street Construction
DOT
BOE
BSS

Credit: *Huma Husain, UCLA Urban Planning, MURP*
Base graphic courtesy of NYC DOT

▲ **Figure 3. A typical and generic city street cross-section, showing how jurisdiction in different places can account for every element, including humans.**

"Streets and their sidewalks are the main public places of a city; they are its most vital organs.

Think of the city and what comes to the mind? Its
streets." —Jane Jacobs (1961 p.29)

The Historical Street in a Few Images

Prior to the invention and mass use of vehicles to convey
people and goods, the street was very much a people
place, alive with every sort of urban activity that required
human interaction, or not, and as Figure 4 illustrates, at
any time of the day in Victorian London.[10] Not all was
pleasant as urban populations increased. In 1654 the
chaos and conflict of horses and carriages became somewhat regulated,[11] however the street was very much alive
with other animals, contributing to the sounds, smells,
and sights of the city for its half million inhabitants. Prior
to the invention of the automobile, the necessity of horse

---

10 I use London during this time period for comparative purposes
because mass migration to the British colonies began during the
Industrial Revolution (c1760-1840) and continued into the
Victorian period (1837-1901) had a significant influence on how
Canadian cities and towns were shaped, both physically and
socially.

11 The number of hackneys on the London street had become so
unmanageable by the mid-17th Century that Oliver Cromwell
instructed the City to enact an ordinance to restrict the number of
hackney-men to 200, hackney-coaches to 300, and horses to 600,
allowing the small group to form a fellowship, which eventually
became the Worshipful Company of Hackney Carriage Drivers in
2004. After the Stage Carriages Act of 1832 the hackney cab
became the hansom-cab for hire, which was gradually replaced by
the omnibus as a means of moving about the city. See
http://www.british-history.ac.uk/no-series/acts-ordinances-
interregnum/pp922-924

and cart to move goods, and the reliance on horse and carriage (hackneys) to move wealthier people resulted in the accumulation of manure piles on the street and general chaos on the street, as stationary and pedestrian activities encountered those in motion.

TOM & BOB, *taking a stroll down Drury Lane at five in the Morning*

▲ **Figure 4. "Tom & Bob, taking a stroll down Drury Lane at five o'clock in the Morning"**[12]

By 1800 the population of London had increased to around one million, which then grew quickly to 4.5 million in 1880, mainly in response to the need for factory workers.[13] Much of life in these times has been recorded

---

12 Two flâneurs in Victorian London. Pierce Egan (1821) *Real Life in London*, Volume 2. Illustrators: Heath, Aiken, Dighton, and Rowlandson. London: Jones & Co., p.250. Accessed January 3, 2015 http://www.gutenberg.org/files/20484/20484-h/20484-h.htm

as historical fact by researchers such as Henry Mayhew[14], and in fiction by Charles Dickens. Mayhew (1851) was a shrewd observer of Victorian London street life and was perhaps the first to note the difficulty in undertaking any census-taking on a mobile street population:

> The number of costermongers,—that is to say, of those street-sellers attending the London "green" and "fish markets,"—appears to be, from the best data at my command, now 30,000 men, women, and children. The census of 1841 gives only 2,045 "hawkers, hucksters, and pedlars," in the metropolis, and no costermongers or street-sellers, or street-performers at all. This number is absurdly small, and its absurdity is accounted for by the fact that not one in twenty of the costermongers, or of the people with whom they lodged, troubled themselves to fill up the census returns—the majority of them being unable to read and write, and others distrustful of the purpose for which the returns were wanted.[15]

---

13 Demographic data accessed January 3, 2015
http://www.visionofbritain.org.uk/data_cube_page.jsp?
data_theme=T_POP&data_cube=N_TOT_POP&u_id=10097836
&c_id=10001043&add=N

14 Henry Mayhew (1851) London labour and the London poor; a cyclopaedia of the condition and earnings of those that will work, those that cannot work, and those that will not work. Vol. 1. The London Street-Folk. London, UK: George Woodfall and Son. Accessed 5 December 2013
https://archive.org/details/cu31924092592751

15 Ibid. p. 4

The Victorian street was never quiet,[16] occupied by a large population[17] of organized and specialized groups of costermongers or street sellers (Table 1), known to Mayhew as "street-folk", selling everything from fish, game, poultry, butter, cheese, and eggs, to fruit, vegetables, flowers, trees, shrubs, seeds, roots, and "green stuff" (described as water cress, chickweed, groundsel, and turf). Street-folk sold eatables and drinkables, which today we call "street food", but in Victorian times eatables included a richness of food that could be eaten on the street or taken away. Street-drinkables included a variety of hot and cold beverages including drinking water, hot-wine but not ale or gin, for which there were "public ale-houses" and "gin-palaces".[18]

---

16 Which became the Cockney "Cries of London" in and around the East End of London, performance art at its loudest, with a purpose of attracting a purchaser for goods being sold on the street.

17 Which during Mayhew's research period the number of costermongers or street-folk had increased from 30,000 to 45,000 men, women, and children by 1861.

18 Beer was safer than water. Water was rarely sold for drinking because the street accumulated manure and was used as a slop bucket for human waste, kitchen waste, animal slaughtering, and a dump for household cesspits, all of which eventually was washed into the gutters to end up as bacteria in the fresh water supply. This resulted in major cholera epidemics (blamed on "bad air"), that killed thousands until 1854 when the source was traced to a contaminated water pump on Broad Street (near Carnaby Street) in Soho. By 1858 a proper street sewer system was under construction. See for example, http://www.umapper.com/maps/view/id/43438/

The word was on the street too: street sellers (Table 1A) provisioned the city with the printed word of long-songs, ballads, and wall-songs (known then as "pinners-up," and today as wheat-paste posters). There were sellers of play-bills, second editions of newspapers, back issues of serialized periodicals and old books, almanacs, pocket books, memorandum books, note paper, sealing-wax, pens, pencils, stenographic cards, valentines, engravings, manuscript music, images, and poetry cards. And then there were the sellers of every imaginable type of manufactured article on the street—from pins and buttons to linens and crockery, new and second-hand. The selling of live animals included dealers in dogs, squirrels, birds, fish, and tortoises. Street-artisans (Table 1D) consisted of three groups, those making things right on the street, those mending things right on the street, and those making things at home and selling them on the street.

Mayhew also noted street-buyers (Table 1B), an occupation involved in the purchasing of everything recyclable—from old clothes and umbrellas to bottles, glass and broken metal to fat and tallow that could be turned into candles and soap. And there were the street-finders (Table 1C)—those deriving income from picking up and selling the discards of others on the street—from bones and cigar ends to nuggets of coal, and treasures hunted by mud-larkers from the sewers and tidal waters of the Thames, which served (and still does) as an aquatic street.[19] Street labourers (Table 1E) were employed to clean the streets and scavenge what they could from the leavings of the street-finders. Labourers included the sweeps—chimney, street crossing cleaners, and rubbish removers.

Many of these occupations have survived to contemporary times, some becoming formalized on the payrolls of local government, as is the case of street cleaners and garbage removers. Waterers and lamplighters became utility workers in public works departments. As cities became cleaner, other street occupations shifted into private businesses, as is the case with pest control.

A) Street-sellers	B) Street-buyers	C) Street-finders or Pickers
Sellers of: Fish, poultry, game & cheese Vegetables, fruit—fresh & dry	Pur-chasing all manner of recycl-ables	Those picking up bones, dog-dung, cigar ends, rags, and other discards for recycling and up-cycling
Eatables:		Sewer-picking: anything that fell

19 A mud-lark is someone that scavenges in the tidal mud of the Thames for any items of value.

fried fish, hot eels, pickled whelks, sheep's trotters, ham sandwiches, peas'-soup, hot green peas, penny pies, plum "duff," meat-puddings, baked potatoes, spice-cakes, muffins and crumpets, Chelsea buns, sweetmeats, brandy-balls, cough drops, and cat / dog food.		into latrines or privies and ended up in the open sewers (often conduits in the course of a former stream or creek)
Drinkables: tea and coffee, ginger-beer, lemonade, sherbet, nectar, hot wine, fresh cow and ass milk, curds and whey, water.		**Mud-larking:** Salvaging anything that fell off boats in the Thames or washed into the river mud from sewers, streams or creeks.
Stationery, literature, and works of art		
Manufactured articles of all and every sort		
Live animals (mostly pets, but not livestock)		

D) Street-artisans, or Working Pedlars	E) Street Labourers	F) Street-Artists/performers, & Show-men
Makers of things on the street: Metal workers (toasting-forks, pins, engravers; textile-workers and knitters; Miscellaneous makers (wooden spoons, leather brace and garters, printers, and glass-blowers.	**Cleansers:** such as scavengers, night-men, flushermen, chimney-sweeps, dustmen, crossing-sweepers, "street-orderlies," destroyers of vermin, labourers to assist sweeping-machines and watering-carts.	**Performers:** puppeteers, clowns, acrobats, jugglers, conjurors, sword, knife, and snake swallowers, fire-eaters, using trained animals — as dancing dogs, performing with monkeys, birds, mice, cats, hares, pigs, dancing bears, and tame camels.
Menders of things on the street: broken china and glass, clocks,umbrellas, kettles, chairs, greaseremovers, hat cleaners, razor and knife grinders, glaziers, travelling bell hangers, knife cleaners.	**Lighters and Waterers:** lamplighters and turn-cocks to turn on/off gas in street lights, and waterers to control public wells and pumps.	**Showmen**: of extraordinary persons such as human giants or strong men; of extraordinary animals such as alligators; of scientific instruments such as the microscope; of measuring machines; and of miscellaneous shows such as peepshows, mechanical figures, wax- works, boxing, and fortune-telling.

D) Street-artisans, or Working Pedlars (...cont'd)	E) Street Labourers (...cont'd)	F) Street-performers, Artists, and Showmen (...cont'd)
Makers of things at home and sold on the street	Street-Advertisers: handbill-stickers and deliverers, billboard posters, wall and pavement stencillers.	Artists: silhouette cutters, blind paper-cutters, coloured chalk pavement artists, photographers.
	Street-servants: horse holders, coach-hirers, street-porters, shoe-polishers, fly-catchers.	Dancers: on foot, tight rope, stilts.
		Musicians: street bands, guitar, harp, bagpipes, hurdy-gurdy, dulcimer, musical bells, cornet, drums, whistlers.
		Singers: glees, balladeers, religious music, reciters, serenaders, and improvisers.

		Proprietors of Street Games: swings, darts, roundabouts, rifle shooting, and various types of games.

▲ **Table 1. Occupations of Street-folk in the mid-18th Century (compiled and synthesized from Mayhew 1851)[20]**

"Street vending is a global phenomenon. In cities, towns, and villages throughout the world, millions of people earn their living wholly or partly by selling a wide range of goods on the streets, sidewalks, and other public spaces"—International Labour Organization[21]

Street-sellers exist formally and informally, both as permitted weekly markets, dedicated (fixed markets such as

---

20 Henry Mayhew (1851) *London labour and the London poor; a cyclopaedia of the condition and earnings of those that will work, those that cannot work, and those that will not work*. Vol. 1. The London Street-Folk. London, UK: George Woodfall and Son, p 3-4. Accessed 5 December 2013 https://archive.org/details/cu31924092592751

21 International Labor Organization (2002) *Women and men in the informal economy: A statistical picture*. Geneva: ILO, p. 49 Accessed at: http://wiego.org/sites/wiego.org/files/publications/files/ILO-Women-Men-Informal-2002.pdf

Granville Island in Vancouver), sidewalk sales, permanent markets, or pop-up sidewalk or road-side sales without a permit (Figure 4). Street buyers and pickers have manifested as bottle collectors, dumpster divers, scavengers, up-cyclers, and recyclers of many materials.

▲ **Figure 5. Pop-up water seller on the steps of Sacré-Cœur Basilica, Paris**

Outside the public and private markets, informal street food sales (eatables and drinkables) remains a part of any vibrant modern street scene on the planet and the set-up for a hot chestnut seller of 1900 is not that different from 2015 (Figure 6). In the Northern Hemisphere though, street food has become highly regulated and licensed, typically resulting in higher costs to the producer and purchaser. Besides the portable hot dog stand (Figure 7), the "food truck" concept of taking an indoor restaurant outside to serve eatables and drinkables that meet health regulations is costly, which ensures that the street food of today in Vancouver, for example, is highly contrived. Fortunately spontaneous street food sales (e.g. lemonade or bake sales) are mostly ignored (Figure 8).

City of Toronto Archives, Fonds 1244, Item 130

Today, Food Not Bombs operates as a collective of loosely affiliated groups in many cities, bringing free vegan and vegetarian food to the street during community protests (Figure 9), events, and times of need such as natural disasters since 1980.[22] Most recently the Love Activists direct action group in London, UK have asserted their right to the street by setting up a street kitchen in Trafalgar Square to serve hot eatables and drinkables to the homeless.[23] This essentially, and for as long as it lasts, is a Temporary Autonomous Zone (TAZ) on the street.

◀Figures 6a,b: Selling hot chestnuts on the street: a) Toronto c1900 (City of Toronto Archives Fonds 1244, Item 130) and b) Wakefield, Yorkshire

---

22 Keith McHenry (2012) *Hungry for Peace: How you can help end poverty and war with Food Not Bombs.* Tucson: See Sharp Press. To connect with an affinity group see for example,the social media page for Food Not Bombs Vancouver https://www.facebook.com/vancouverfnb?fref=ts

23 Love Activists initially occupied an empty bank building on 23 December 2014, for the purposes of preparing a hot Christmas lunch for anyone. They were evicted on 24 December, and served a cold Christmas lunch on the street while reorganizing a more substantial setup to serve hot food in Trafalgar Square. See The Guardian online, accessed 26 December 2014 http://www.theguardian.com/commentisfree/2014/dec/26/love-activists-empty-buildings-direct-action-homelessness The Trafalgar Square action continues as Homeless Kitchen London while Love Activists have expanded to other cities and helped set up more street kitchens. See their main social networking page for more information https://www.facebook.com/pages/Love-Activists/1500718110212573?fref=ts

▲ Figure 7. The ubiquitous hot dog stand, could
be anywhere; this is downtown Vancouver

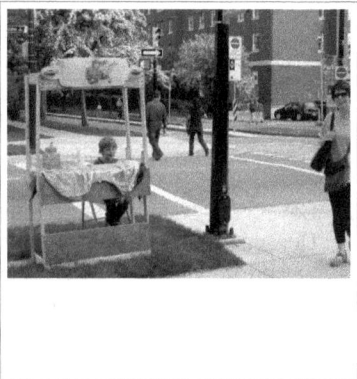

▲ Figure 8a,b. Competing lemonade stands on the
same street, West End of Vancouver

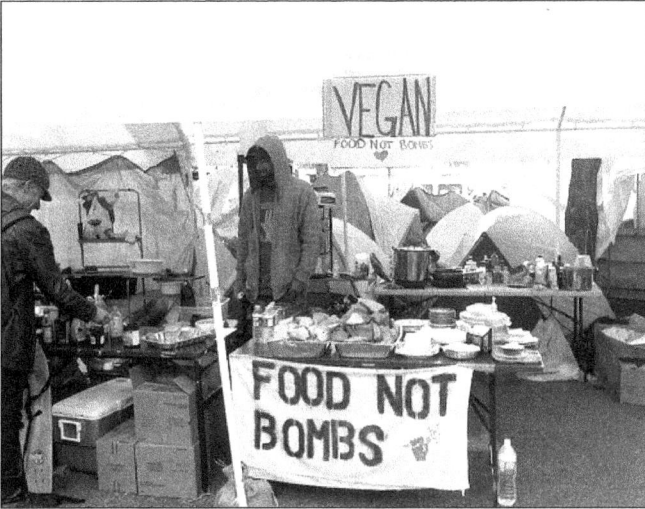

▲ **Figure 9. Food Not Bombs, Occupy Vancouver (October 25, 2011)**

Today in most cities, selling stuff on the street requires permits. Selling activities either become pop-up and mobile enough to run if the by-law officer is approaching (Figure 10), or are moved to a side lane to set up a TAS. Organize a few friends with stuff to sell and you create a TAZ flea market for a few hours (Figure 11).

▲ Figure 10a,b. **Stuff for sale on the street, Vancouver**

▲ Figure 11. **Montreal back lane TAZ pop-up flea market**

Givers of Stuff

Street corners and intersections are collectively used to advertise yard sales elsewhere (Figure 12). Using the street to give away things is much easier because it can be done as an anonymous action (Figure 13) or as a collective TAZ action as is the case with the Commercial Drive free street store in Vancouver (Figure 14).

◀**Figure 12. Street intersection used collectively to place yard sale signs**

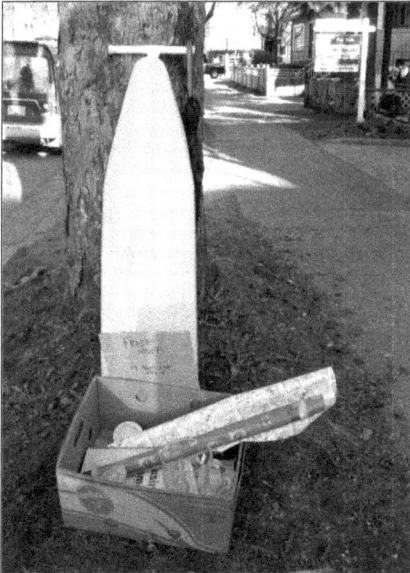

◀**Figure 13. Free stuff on the street, Vancouver**

▲ **Figure 14. Stuff at the Commercial Drive free street market, Vancouver**

Literature on the Street

The use of the street to distribute literature (the printed word in all its forms) continues today, whether as flyers on lamp posts, or as newspapers (Figure 15) and magazines sold from kiosks (Figure 16), or given to commuters for free at the entrances to public transit during rush hours. Sometimes the newspaper box finds a new form of expression (Figure 17).

City of Toronto Archives, Fonds 1266, Item 6981

▲ Figure 15. Toronto Newspaper Seller, 1880 (City of Toronto Archives, Fonds 1266, Item 6981)

▲ Figure 16. News stand and info kiosk in London

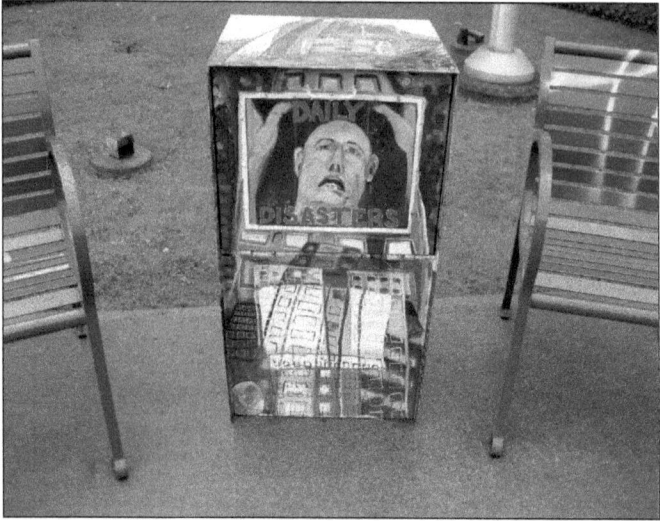

▲ **Figure 17. Altered newspaper box in Vancouver**

Postering and wheat-pasting on doors, wall, trees, benches, and poles—all forms of street furniture—gets messages onto the street quickly, and quietly (Figure 18a). Street furniture is also used to disseminate the printed word, capturing the zeitgeist of social opinion through individual (Figure 18b), or the collective expression of frustration about an injustice committed on the unceded ancestral village lands and burial grounds of a First Nation (Figure 18c).

Figure 18. ▲ a) Postering on a wall, Berlin; {following page} ▶ b) Mail distribution box used as a blackboard, Vancouver; and ▶ c) Postering under the Arthur Laing bridge in Vancouver, a message from the xʷməθkʷəy̓əm (Musqueam First

Nation) during the occupation of a property development site in Marpole after discovery of ancestral graves at c̓əsnaʔəm, 2012.

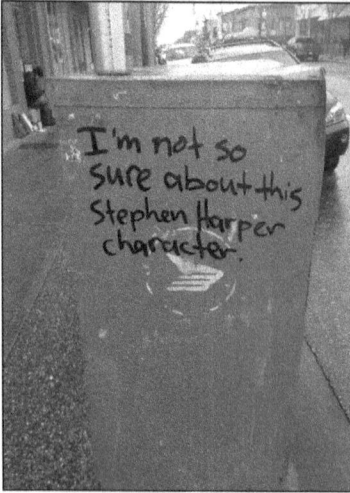

◀18.b) and ▼c)

Street libraries are created through neighbourhood grass-roots action with the common goal to freely share reading material by lending, borrowing, exchanging, or simply giving away literature no longer needed, or sharing a well-loved book with someone else. Street libraries can also connect neighbourhoods along a bike route by providing a street-side meeting space, or a meet-up space.

Most include a bulletin board (Figure 19) and some in Vancouver are expanding to include community gardens in the boulevards (Figure 20).

Figures 19a ▲,b ▼. Street libraries in Vancouver

▲ **Figure 20. New community garden constructed next to street library on West 10ᵗʰ, Vancouver**

Street Music and Performance

Besides street-folk occupied in buying, selling, making, picking, and labouring, the Victorian street was also a vibrant place for performance as a way to make a living. Self-employed street-folk used their talents, or employed others with talents to entertain both street-folk and others visiting the street (Table 1F, Figure 21). Mayhew interviews many and presents their stories in great detail in order to ascertain what exactly their occupation required in skills, what it actually did, and what kind of wages were earned.[24] Many of the activities listed in Table 1F became formalized or regulated as circus acts, or circus sideshows, however, vestiges of Victorian street art remain today, ensuring the rights to the street are upheld by any citizen.

STREET-PERFORMERS ON STILTS.
[From a Sketch.]

▲ **Figure 21. Street performers on stilts, hurdy-gurdy man in the background (Mayhew 1861:150)**

---

24 Henry Mayhew (1861) *The London Street-Folk comprising: Street sellers, street buyers, street finders, street performers, street artizans, street labourers.* Vol. 3. London, UK: Griffin, Bohn, and Company, p 43-Accessed 5 December 2013 https://archive.org/details/cu31924092592785

Busking for money occurs across many cultures and countries; sometimes legal, sometimes prohibited, sometimes regulated. The street performance that Mayhew writes about in the London of 1861 was all about busking for a living; today it is completely prohibited in the City of London, the square mile in central London that was originally surrounded by a Roman wall, and where the British financial industry is currently based.[25] Busking is slowly being pushed out or discouraged in other Greater London boroughs despite the time-honoured use of busking as a stepping stone to artistic success and fame.[26] In cities where busking and street performance are allowed with no rules (Figures 22 and 23), the street is alive with harmless individual and collective creativity on an ever-changing street stage. The acceptance of TAS reflects the collective creativity within a city and would eliminate perceived problems expressed in other places:

> Maybe it is because busking is so free and unregu-
> lated that it has also been a source of anxiety for the
> authorities. Fear of political opinion and activism, an-
> ti-social behaviour and crime, have always been asso-
> ciated with the tradition.[27]

---

25 The City of London is a corporation with different powers than other local governments in metropolitan London http://www.cityoflondon.gov.uk/Pages/default.aspx

26 See for example this article in *The Guardian* online, Accessed 15 May 2014 http://www.theguardian.com/local-government-network/2014/apr/23/support-londons-buskers

27 Ibid.

While busking above ground on the street is under political scrutiny and limited to set spots and specific rules (Figure 23), below ground on the London Underground for example, busking permits are provided for performance of all musical genres in most stations, where the acoustics can be superb. And of course buskers that hop from train car to train car are declaring TAS and keep on moving to avoid getting caught, and to find new listeners that might flip a coin. Mimes (Figure 24) assert their use of a TAS to ply their silent trade.

▲ **Figure 22. Music from a hammered dulcimer on the street, Haarlem, Netherlands**

◄Figure 23. Jazz musicians busking in Amsterdam, Netherlands

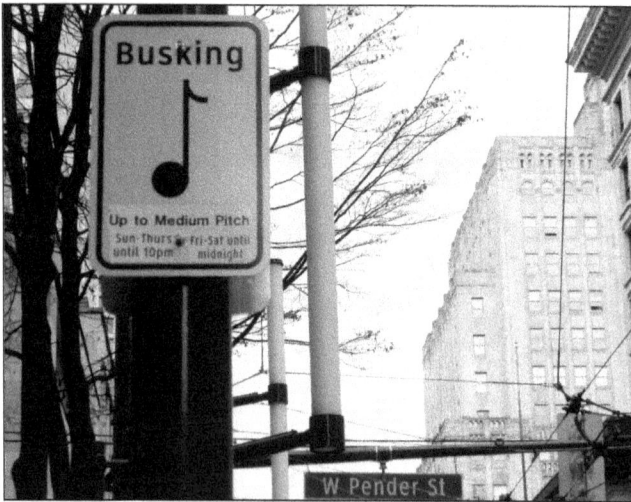

▲Figure 24. Street Busking rules on Granville Street, Vancouver

▲ **Figure 25. Mimes in Cologne, Germany**

Visual Art and Artists

Street art is visual art created on the street for public consumption. Media can include posters, graffiti, stickers, stencilling, and installations such as yarn bombing. Visual artists use the street for both business (Figure 26), as was the typical activity in Victorian London, and as a source of creative inspiration (Figure 27). Chalk artists (screevers) of all ages use the street as a blackboard, to create ephemeral pieces of art that last until the next rainfall (Figure 28), and to leave messages (Figure 29).

▲ Figure 26. Street artist sketching in Paris

▲ Figure 27. Street tree used as a TAS art installation in Barcelona

Figures 28 ▲a,▶b. Chalk artists (screevers) in Vancouver

Figures 29

▼a: "Idle No More til we show Harper the door" & b▶ [next pg.] "We are the ones we have been waiting for"

▲ **Figures 29a,b. Chalk messages made by screevers in Vancouver**

Art in Street Protests

Any peaceful gathering of people on the street creates many opportunities for individuals to express their opinions to others. In the case of large and very large protest events artists are given the opportunity to hold TAS and present their work to 100,000 or more participants which happened at the UK National Demonstration for Gaza event organized by the Stop the War Coalition in London on August 9, 2014. At the event, art work was presented in many forms—from studio artists setting up a temporary gallery on the street (Figure 30) to friends of the political artist Carlos Latuff wearing his art on t-shirts (Figure 31).

▲ Figure 30. TAS art gallery on Oxford Street, London
Demonstration for Gaza, August 9, 2014

▲ Figure 31. T-shirt showing the work of Carlos
Latuff, London Demonstration for Gaza,
August 9, 2014.[28]

28 For more information about the artist see
http://en.wikipedia.org/wiki/Carlos_Latuff

Permitted or Not?

Today, street art and performance art are either regulated or unregulated through local government policies and by-laws. In Vancouver for example, street art is defined as "busking or entertaining" and is regulated through the city engineering department, who note "to busk on most Vancouver sidewalks, you need a street entertainment permit" which costs around $120 a year.[29] You must follow a set of conditions or suffer consequences such as: be told to lower your volume or find a new location, get a warning or fine, have your equipment confiscated, have your permit suspended or cancelled, or lose the privilege to perform on City streets for six months. With the exception of two specific locations in the City though, street entertainment is allowed anywhere, which does create opportunities for spontaneous activities provided a permit is in the pocket, provided your spontaneity occurs between 10AM and 10PM, does not last longer than 60 minutes at one location, and is not too noisy (Figure 24).

Cambridge, England has the more enlightened view that busking is a part of the culture of the town (Figure 32), and has crafted a voluntary street performers' code of practice as a solution to avoid noise complaints.

> Busking is a time-honoured tradition that dates back to medieval times, when wandering minstrels and bards travelled from place to place and acted not only

---

29 Details accessed 9 December 2014 http://vancouver.ca/doing-business/busking-and-entertainment.aspx

as entertainers but also as news reporters and message bearers. Cambridge is a unique place for buskers, with many spots in the city centre for them to stop and play, and visitors, residents and businesses enjoy the variety of entertainment.[30]

Annual festivals of buskers and street performers can be found in many cities around the globe, including Cambridge and Vancouver, and are networked through the Busker Central Cooperative on the internet.[31]

▲ **Figure 32. Charlie Cavey, busker in a litter bin, Cambridge, England**[32]

---

30 See the Cambridge local government web site https://www.cambridge.gov.uk/buskers Accessed January 2, 2015

31 A good reference is located at http://www.buskercentral.com/ Accessed January 2, 2015

The Right to the Street

The right to assemble and associate is clearly articulated as a basic human right in the Universal Declaration of Human Rights, is a fundamental freedom set down in the Canadian Charter of Rights and Freedoms, and is part of the social contract recognized in the International Covenant on Civil and Political Rights.[33] The right to assemble and associate freely and peacefully has to occur somewhere, and the street is the logical gathering place—neutral common space.

As the images above indicate, the street is being used formally, informally, legally and illegally for human interaction and expression. If humans need public places and common spaces for social interaction, an outdoor location typically might be a park, plaza, square, or other open space dedicated for recreation. The public realm and social activity is much more than programmed or un-programmed space in parks. Long before the invention of parks, the street was the place where people met and socialized.

The right to the street (all of the street—Figure 3) for

32 See also, http://www.dailymail.co.uk/news/article-1209037/Can-play-Garbage-Busker-bin-surprises-Cambridge-shoppers-rubbish-medley.html Accessed January 2, 2015

33 See Article 20, 27, and 29 of the Universal Declaration of Human Rights, Article 2 of the Canadian Charter of Rights & Freedoms, and Article 21 of the International Covenant on Civil & Political Rights (1966).

social interaction and creative purposes is currently demonstrated through TAZ, TAS, and activity that takes back the street from the regulated or permitted uses of vehicular traffic. It seems sensible that those professionals responsible for planning the street should step away from creating obstacles (physical and legal barriers) that prevent its full use to simply providing for the inevitable use of the street for everything but vehicular traffic, which is the case in central Amsterdam (Figure 33). This of course requires a return to the original definition of street, a complete reversal of contemporary thinking about the role of the street in urban life, particularly for protests, parades, and demonstrations.

▲ ► ▼ Figures 33a,b,(& on following page: c,d.) The Dam— four views of the central square in Amsterdam,

home of the Dutch monarchy and a popular place for TAS, TAZ, busking, street-selling, music events and festivals.

In Canada, this will require the revision of some key laws and any local by-laws that interfere and prohibit the right to peacefully as-

semble for the purposes of individually and collectively expressing opinions. Despite the universal right to assemble for any peaceful purpose, a march down the street in Vancouver carrying a sign and banging on a saucepan or blowing a whistle (Figure 34) can be interpreted as mischief under Section 430(1) of the Criminal Code of Canada when a participant wilfully:

> (a) destroys or damages property;

> (b) renders property dangerous, useless, inoperative or ineffective;

(c) obstructs, interrupts or interferes with the lawful use, enjoyment or operation of property; or

(d) obstructs, interrupts or interferes with any person in the lawful use, enjoyment or operation of property.[34]

In the City of Vancouver though, the Vancouver Police Department interprets 430(1) as:

Obstruction or interference with the use of property includes but is not limited to the following behaviours: shouting, screaming, or swearing at anyone that disrupts public peace or physically blocking any person from freely entering, leaving, or staying at any public place.[35]

---

34 See http://laws-lois.justice.gc.ca/eng/acts/C-46/page-204.html#h-116 Accessed January 9, 2014

35 See http://rabble.ca/blogs/bloggers/david-p-ball/2012/06/vancouver-police-arrested-seven-more-quebec-solidarity-protester and see also http://www.straight.com/news/373996/pivot-questions-vancouver-police-warning-pidgin-protesters and http://www.straight.com/news/372661/vancouver-police-warn-activists-about-crossing-line-between-protest-and-crime Accessed December 18, 2013

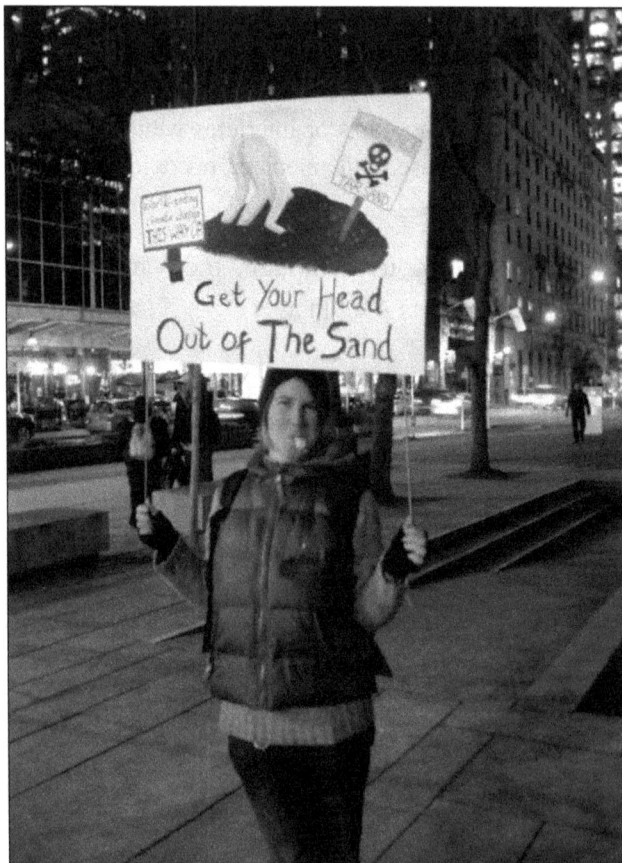

▲ **Figure 34. Street protestor and whistle-blower at the National Energy Board Joint Review Panel Hearings into the proposed Enbridge Northern Gateway Pipeline in Vancouver, January 15, 2013.**

Who defines "public peace" or "peaceful assembly" in a multi-cultural urban environment? Who defines "noise"? Is the noise of a native drum less peaceful than the constant sound of traffic on the street? What if that native drummer is drumming on a street in a city built on the unceded territory of a First Nation? Who should define public peace and peaceful assembly? The participants? Or, the onlookers? Current practice says it's the onlookers, whether police, politician, or a public outsider, that make the call. Are the onlookers actually passive participants simply annoyed they are in a minority and not occupying a TAS or TAZ for a particular moment in time on the street? Respecting the TAS of an onlooker during a protest is equally important as an onlooker respecting the TAS of a protest participant. The respective human and civil instinct of both onlooker and participant should be to step aside and avoid personal conflict that detracts from the protest itself, instead of blocking the free passage of a passer-by (Figure 35).

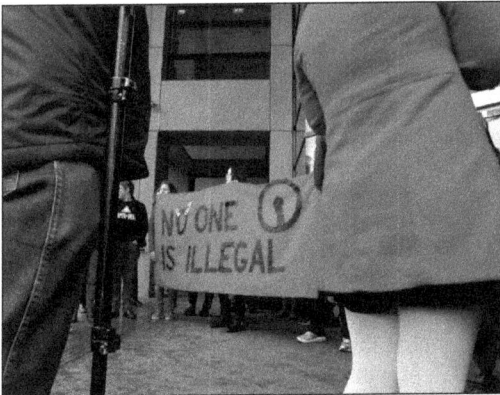

◄Figure 35. Protest against immigrant deportations from Canada, blocking access to a federal government building and the Vancouver Public Library, March 2013

Quebec 2012 and 2013

In 2012 CLASSE[36] student strike actions in Québec (Figure 36) which became known as the "Maple Spring" or "printemps érable", and subsequent 2013 protests in Montreal against the unconstitutional enactment of Bill-78 and By-law P-6[37] culminated in the fundamental human right to assemble in peaceful protest on the street being threatened and denied.

Faced with constant manifs (demonstrations), the province enacted Bill-78 to give the police extraordinary and indiscriminate powers to shoot tear gas, flashbangs,

---

36 Coalition large de l'Association pour une solidarité syndicale étudiante (CLASSÉ) temporarily united 76,000 French and English-speaking post-secondary students from across Québec in an open-ended strike to protest tuition hikes under the Charest Liberal government, which was eventually defeated in a general election. Several websites document events, all accessed January 4, 2014, see http://www.stopthehike.ca/ http://cobp.resist.ca/en http://www.asse-solidarite.qc.ca/ and https://cjfe.org/resources/features/maple-spring-impact-free-expression-quebec

37 In Québec, Bill-78 is a law that restricts protest or picketing on or near university grounds. The law further requires that organizers of a protest, consisting of 50 or more people in a public venue anywhere in Québec, submit their proposed venue and/or route to the relevant police for approval. In the Ville de Montréal, the P-6 bylaw on the prevention of breaches of the peace, public order and safety was amended to state: 1) it is prohibited for anyone to participate in a demonstration (assembly, parade or gathering) with their face covered, such as by a scarf, hood or mask; and 2) it is mandatory to disclose the location and itinerary of a demonstration to the police.

water cannons, rubber bullets, or use any type of force to break up demonstrations, beat up, arrest, and detain unarmed protestors, journalists, and passive observers, and use "l'agents provocateur" to infiltrate student events to cause unwanted trouble. The behaviour of the state and its employees was a crime against human rights and in particular the right to peaceful public assembly to express opinions, whether in favour or against the dogmas of the state. By-law P-6 was a draconian attempt by the City of Montréal to prohibit the wearing of any hats or face coverings at any street event, even in winter of 2012 when many of the manifs were held (Figure 38) By spring 2013, this had escalated to police intimidation at many other social or environmental justice events (Figure 38). The events in Québec triggered solidarity demos across the country (Figure 39).[38]

Figure 36 ◀a,▶ b (next page) Images from two CLASSÉ manifs in Montréal, 2013

---

38 See footnote 34.

▲Figure 36. b {Ed. Note: Picket sign translation: "Education is a right, not a luxury."}

►Figures 37a,b. On the streets of Montréal in 2012 and 2013.

►a) Government festival poster advertising "Celebrate our creativity" with a fleur-de-lis mask image, note graffiti with arrow pointing to the mask saying "Forbidden by P-6".

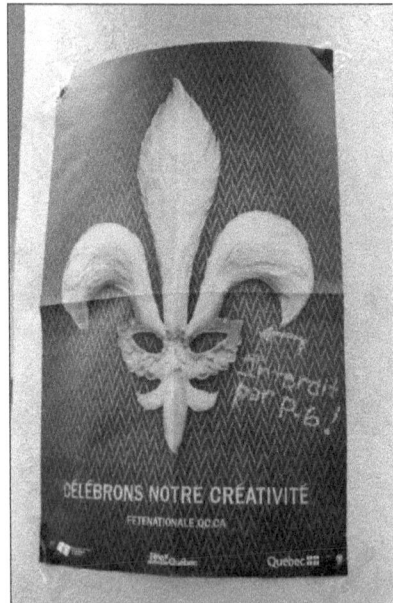

▼37b) Police surveillance at anti-poverty street occupation in the St. Henri neighbourhood, 2013

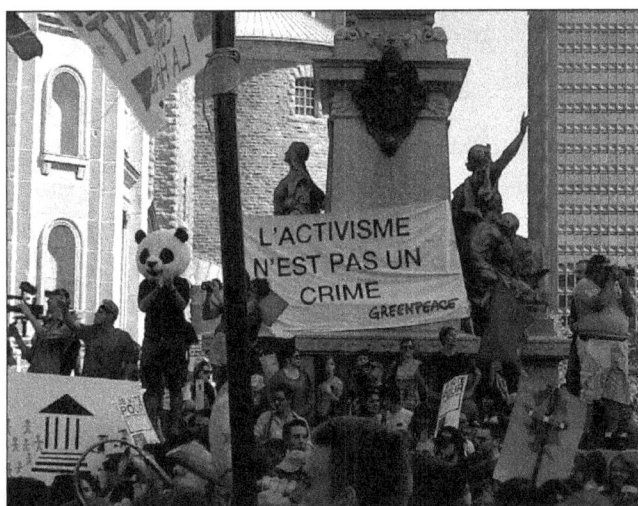

▲Figure 38. "Activism is not a Crime", Montréal May 22, 2012

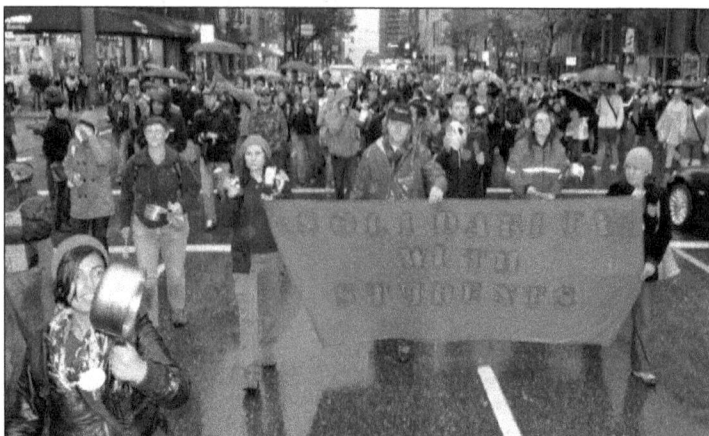

▲ **Figure 39. Vancouver demo in solidarity with Quebec students, 2013.**

Reclaiming Streets for Play

As a social animal, the human desire and need to meet and gather for collective actions and activities is strong. The street has always been a playground for individual and group play. In Canada group play often takes the form of street hockey, and there are numerous examples of local government enacting by-laws to deny assembly on the street for play (Figure 40). When the surrounding boroughs and cities amalgamated, the new City of Toronto consolidated all the by-laws into a new Municipal Code and carried forward the original draconian wording of By-law 522-78 from the former city:

> No person shall play or take part in any game or sport

upon a roadway and, where there are sidewalks, no person upon roller skates, in-line skates or a skateboard, or riding in or by means of any coaster, scooter, toy vehicle, toboggan, sleigh or similar device, shall go upon a roadway except for the purpose of crossing the road, and, when so crossing, such person shall have the rights and be subject to the obligations of a pedestrian. Toronto Municipal Code, Article III, p 950-13 [39]

Contrast Toronto with the permissive attitude of Kingston, Ontario, who set out the collective code of conduct for playing hockey on a local (neighbourhood) street with the intention of simply reducing risk of accident rather than enabling swift passage of vehicles to the detriment of the pedestrian:

Street hockey may be played on a Local Street during daylight hours when there is good visibility. Street Hockey may never be played before 9 a.m. or after 8 p.m — City of Kingston, 2008 [40]

---

39 Toronto. *Municipal Code Chapter 95, Traffic and Parking.* August 28, 2014. Accessed December 19, 2014 at http://www.toronto.ca/legdocs/municode/1184_950.pdf

40 City of Kingston (2008) *Street Hockey Policy and Code of Conduct.* Accessed December 19, 2014 http://archive.cityofkingston.ca/pdf/council/agenda/2008/A16_Rpt92.pdf

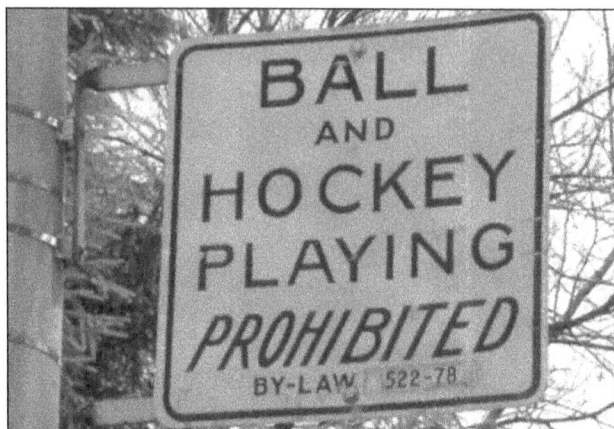

▲ **Figure 40. City of Toronto street sign prior to amalgamation and creation of the new metro Toronto.**

Play can be formal or informal, individual or collective, organized or spontaneous. Claiming the street for play is embedded in human history, and is not restricted to the activities of children. Of the many events that happen in Vancouver around the Vancouver Art Gallery between Georgia and Robson streets, two of the less structured street play events reveal how essential play and social contact is to human-kind and how easy it is to reclaim the street peacefully. While Free Hugs is now a global movement, anyone can spontaneously make up a cardboard sign and offer hugs to anyone in need of one, anywhere (Figure 40).[41]

Organizing International Pillow Fight Day consists of

41 See http://www.freehugscampaign.org/

a group in Amsterdam simply setting the date and time (for example 12 noon April 1) for their local event in The Dam Square (Figure 33). It is up to local affinity groups everywhere else to form and make the call out via social media to everyone to show up rain or shine, wait for the appointed moment in time, and when the signal is given pull pillows out from hidden locations and have all-ages, all-abilities pillow fight for fun (Figure 41).

While reclaiming a street for play of any sort is as simple as dreaming up an activity and enacting it, in some communities there is growing support from local government to help neighbourhoods shut down streets for play.[42] For example, in the London Borough of Hackney residents can apply for a Play Street Order permitting a side street to be closed to traffic for up three hours per week or month.[43] While this may not seem like much (it is only about one half a percent of the time in a 30 day month), ground has been gained and momentum towards longer closures and more closures is very much on the side of play.

---

42 See http://playingout.net/

43 See http://www.hackney.gov.uk/play-streets.htm#.VMxlCi5O2VB

Figure 40 ▲ a, ◄ b. Free Hugs, Vancouver

and Figure 41 ▼ a) see next page

Figure 41◀a▼b. Vancouver Pillow Fight Day 2013 with active and passive participants

Reclaiming the Street for Rest

Much has been written about the design of hostile street furniture and the use of urban design as a deterrent to resting and relaxing on the street.[44] While most local governments in the United Kingdom use their police powers to enact Anti-Social Behaviour Orders (ASBO) to prohib-

---

44 For overviews, see Rosenberger (2014) "How Cities Use Design to Drive Homeless People Away Saying 'you're not welcome here'—with spikes." *The Atlantic Online* June 19, 2014. Accessed June 29, 2014
http://www.theatlantic.com/business/archive/2014/06/how-cities-use-design-to-drive-homeless-people-away/373067/ and also Swain F (2013) Secret city design tricks manipulate your behaviour. *BBC Online* December 2, 2013. Accessed June 29, 2014 http://www.bbc.com/future/story/20131202-dirty-tricks-of-city-design

it the assembly of (typically) youth for what they consider rowdy behaviour (Figure 42), equally insidious efforts are initiated to stop people from sleeping or resting on the street, or on street furniture. A side benefit to local government is that the same hostile architecture denying sleeping also creates creative street uses by urban subcultures of skateboarders and parkour practitioners (Figure 43).[45]

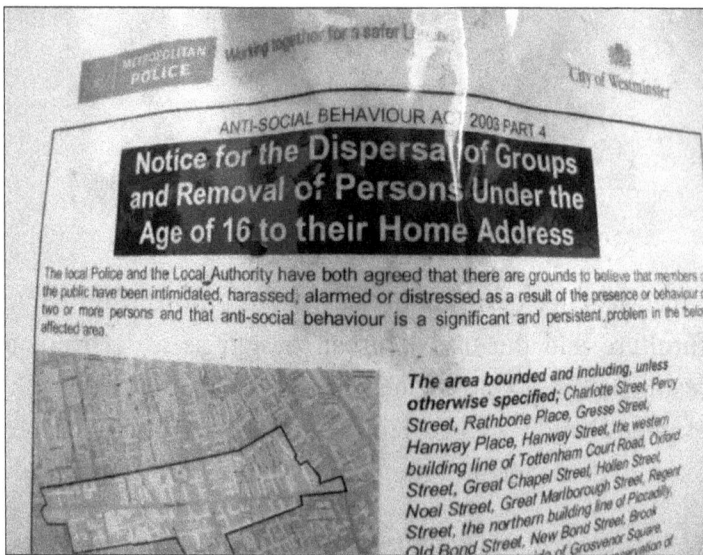

▲ **Figure 42. Posted notice of an "Anti-Social Behaviour Order" in the City of Westminster, London.**

---

45 See http://en.wikipedia.org/wiki/Parkour

▲ **Figure 43. Parkour free running in Frankfurt, Germany**[46]

Throughout human history people have slept on the street, whether because there was no other choice of accommodation and they are homeless (Figure 44), because they needed to rest (Figure 45a), or just because (Figure 45b). In 1824 the *Vagrancy Act* was enacted in Britain, prohibiting sleeping or begging on the street; this act is still in effect today and under this law the individuals sleeping in Figure 44 a) and b) and Figure 45 a) are criminals,

---

46 Image source:
   http://commons.wikimedia.org/wiki/File:Parkour_Frankfurt.jpg

whatever their reason is for sleeping in public space.

In 2008, a landmark case at the BC Supreme Court ruled that a by-law prohibiting camping in a city park in the City of Victoria was unconstitutional and a violation of the right to life, liberty, and the security of the person guaranteed by Section 7 of Canada's Charter of Rights and Freedoms.[47] The court ruled that a municipality cannot ban an activity that is biologically necessary (sleeping with at least some modest form of shelter from the elements) if the number of people who are homeless exceeds the number of spaces in municipal homeless shelters. The City of Victoria appealed this decision and lost in 2009.[48]

In her 2008 decision, Justice Ross stated that

> public properties are held for the benefit of the public, which includes the homeless. The government cannot prohibit certain activities on public property based on its ownership of that property if doing so involves a deprivation of the fundamental human right not to be deprived of the ability to protect one's own bodily integrity.[49]

Following her reasoning, the ruling should then extend to

---

47 Victoria (City) v. Adams, BC Supreme Court. 2008 BCSC 1363. Accessed December 19, 2014 at http://www.courts.gov.bc.ca/Jdb-txt/SC/08/13/2008BCSC1363.htm

48 Victoria (City) v. Adams BC Court of Appeal. 2009 BCCA 563. Accessed December 19, 2014 at http://www.courts.gov.bc.ca/jdb-txt/CA/09/05/2009BCCA0563.htm

49 2008 BCSC 1363, paragraph 131

camping or sleeping on the street, which is also public property.

Figures ▲ 44. Sleeping on the Street a) London, Trafalgar Square; b) London, Marble Arch

◄a)

◄b)

**Figures 45. Resting on the Street a) London,
Spitalfields; b) Lie-in TAS in Vancouver**

Where noise and rest collide, the typical complaint is
"disturbing the peace" which then validates police to issue a citation for violation of some sort of bylaw. But
again, is the complaint instigated by an observer outside
the activity, or by a participant? As Figure 46 clearly il-

lustrates, one child can be sound asleep 5 metres away from another child using a bullhorn to loudly lead a pro-Gaza demonstration. Both are participants occupying TAS and their rights to the street are recognized and respected.

▲ **Figures 46a) Sleeping in the middle of a pro-Gaza demonstration, London and (b) rallying the crowd 5 metres away.**

Contested Street Space:
Burnaby Mountain, November 2014

The occupation of Burnaby Mountain from September to December 2014 for the purposes of protesting the drilling of wells associated with the Kinder Morgan (KM) proposed TransMountain pipeline expansion project through un-ceded First Nations traditional territory (Figure 47). If built, the new pipeline will run close to 1000 kilometres—from the Tar Sands in northern Alberta to Westridge Marine Terminal in Burnaby where it will be loaded onto tankers headed for Asia. Contested space was central to many from the very beginning of the timeline of critical events leading to the protests, occupation, and arrests in 2014 constructed by Gray (2014).[50] Centennial Way, the street, became the central location for contesting space and

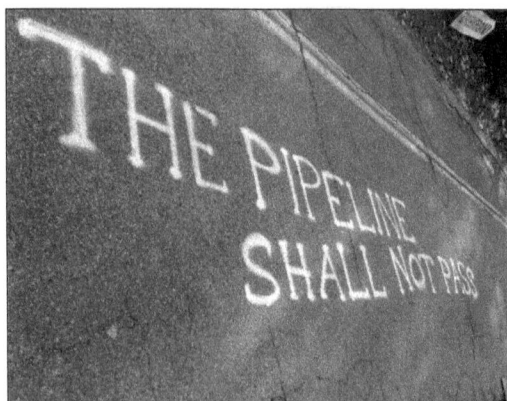

as pipeline work and protest events unfolded on Burnaby Mountain.

◄ **Figure 47. "The Pipeline Shall Not Pass"—painted on the street to mark the symbolic location of**

50 Gray C (2014) *Timeline: Burnaby Mountain pipeline protests*, November 26, 2014. Published online at http://rabble.ca/news/2014/11/timeline-burnaby-mountain-pipeline-protests-0 Accessed December 10, 2014

contested space. (previous page)

While many participants arrived at the protests to support their community affinity groups or environmental NGOs, it is important to understand that the space was contested for several independent reasons that ultimately intertwined into a highly effective collective protest (Table 2). Social media played an important role in getting out messages from events on The Mountain, where the physical location was in a wireless dead zone, and for bringing people together to inform, educate, and motivate to attend events on The Mountain. Various environmental NGOs that brought in their expertise and logistical support to help coordinate events on The Mountain included Rising Tide—Vancouver, Coast Salish Territories, Pipe Up for the Pipeline, Pipe Up Network, Beyond Boarders, No One is Illegal, Food Not Bombs, Tanker Free BC, ForestEthics, and Sea Shepherd Society.

Contestor	Reason
First Nations	Unceded overlapping traditional territories of the xʷməθkʷəy̓əm (Musqueam Nation), Sḵwx̱wú7mesh (Squamish Nation) and Tsleil-Waututh Nation. Other First Nations along the pipeline route also

Contestor	Reason
	participated.
BROKE (Burnaby Mountain Residents Opposed to Kinder Morgan Expansion)[51]	Environmental concern about tar sands (dilbit) and the shipment and storage of tar sands, particularly through Burnaby.
Caretakers of The Mountain	Protecting the environment and its people
City of Burnaby	Municipal property designated as a conservation area (highest level of protected area in the parks systems. The City of Burnaby opposes the pipeline project and has denied KM a permit for the work. In response, KM submitted a request to the National Energy Board (NEB) to confirm their rights to access City of Burnaby public lands. The NEB ruled that federal legislation gives KM the power to enter and conduct surveys and tests on any Crown or private land that lies on their intended pipeline routes. Burnaby appealed, but the appeal was dismissed. Burnaby applied for an injunction against KM, it too

51 See www.burnabypipelinewatch.ca Accessed December 10, 2014

Contestor	Reason
	was dismissed.
Stop Kinder Morgan on Burnaby Mountain	An affinity group formed through social media (Facebook, Twitter) in order to provide information about the proposed project, and has about 5,000 members that can be mobilized to action.
Stop Enbridge Stop Kinder Morgan	Another affinity group of around 2,000 members that organizes through social media (Facebook, Twitter) around the broader issues of fighting Big Oil and opposing any pipeline projects.

▲ Table 2. Key players contesting space on Burnaby Mountain.

Because of its street access, Centennial Way and the location of BH2 became the site of the largest protests, Caretakers Camp, food kitchen, sacred fire, totem carving area. I describe here the main events following the interlocutory injunction granted to KM to proceed with work supported by the RCMP.

The location of the drilling on Burnaby Mountain is known as the Burnaby Mountain Conservation Area (BMCA) and is managed by Burnaby Parks for its ecological values, including headwaters for several salmon streams. On August 19, 2014 the National Energy Board (NEB) ruled that TransMountain (TM)[52] was allowed to access the City of Burnaby (Burnaby) lands without the city's consent, subject to TM contractors being in compliance with local by-laws. TM proceeded to block Burnaby's access to BMCA. The first tree cutting contractors hired by TM were advised that they were in violation of bylaws and if they proceeded to cut on Burnaby Mountain they would likely be banned from working anywhere in the City of Burnaby (private and public lands). This contractor immediately withdrew services to TM.

On August 25th, new contractors for TM cut down thirteen alder trees and cleared many more seedlings, saplings, and shrubs in the forest at proposed borehole number 1 (BH1), and started work at proposed borehole number 2 (BH2) on the street edge of Centennial Way. Burnaby issued TM with Orders to Cease By-law Violations. A Caretaker's Camp (Figure 48) was immediately established close to the suspected location of another proposed borehole (BH2), while additional tents were set up at BH1 and in other parts of the park. The Caretakers, as they became known, came together to form a frontline for direct action to prevent the drilling from happening:

> Who are we? That depends. "We" may include you, the person reading this. "We" are anyone and every-

---

52 While Kinder Morgan and TransMountain are often used interchangeably, Kinder Morgan is the American corporation that acquired TransMountain Pipeline; TransMountain is the local operator of this pipeline project.

one who loves the earth and people more than greed, colonialism, genocide, and big oil. We call each other caretakers, as we protect and care for the land and its people - which could end up destroyed and pillaged.[53]

53 Quote from Stop Kinder Morgan — Caretakers of the Mountain Facebook Page, https://www.facebook.com/pages/Stop-Kinder-Morgan-Caretakers-Of-The-Mountain/1508198892753283?sk=timeline Accessed November 10, 2014

▲ Figures 48 a, b. Caretakers Camp at BH2.

TM applied to the NEB for an access order to BMCA on September 3, along with orders to direct and forbid Burnaby from enforcing their own bylaws. On October 9 NEB deliberated on the matter of constitutional jurisdiction (whether NEB could overrule local government by-laws), and declared through Ruling Number 40 on October 23 that Burnaby's bylaws were "inoperative or inapplicable" and that the NEB had the constitutional right (interjurisdictional immunity) to overrule local government by-laws.[54]

TM immediately gave notice to Burnaby of their intention to resume work on October 29, and on that date TM contractors began geotechnical work at three locations, Barnet Marine Park, BH1 and BH2 in the BMCA Borehole 1 on Burnaby Mountain by preparing the sites for the installation of drilling rigs. Protesters blocked TM work at BH1 and access to BH Borehole 2. The camp at BH2 grew and on November 5, a sacred fire was lit by Sut-Lut, a Sḵwx̱wú7mesh elder, and more protestors began to arrive to witness TM activity on The Mountain.

TM was granted an injunction by the BC Supreme Court on November 14, giving them the limited and temporary right (until December 1), to enforce the NEB authorization to complete their investigations on The Moun-

---

54 Transcripts of this ruling are accessed at https://docs.neb-one.gc.ca/ll-eng/llisapi.dll?func=ll&objId=2541380&objAction=browse&viewType=1

tain using geo-coordinates (GPS) to establish the work area and injunction zone. Once the injunction was granted, it was only a matter of time as to when it would be enforced. A call went out to the community at large through various social media to protest the injunction, and in defiance assemble at BH2 on November 17 for a day of drumming, singing, networking, and listening to many First Nations leaders (Figure 49).

▲ **Figures 49** ▲ **a, b) November 17 gathering of individuals, First Nations, and grassroots organizations to rally on the street against the pipeline drilling in defiance of the court injunction.**

From November 17 to 20, the street was held by many people day and night, and the camp area and sacred fire blocked TM workers from working in the vicinity of BH2. Expectations at the camp were that TM would arrive on one of those days with a surveyor to delineate the GPS coordinates of the injunction area with flagging tape so all parties would know where the line was and protestors could organize events accordingly and the injunction order could be enforced. The RCMP sent in two liaison officers to check the camp each morning.

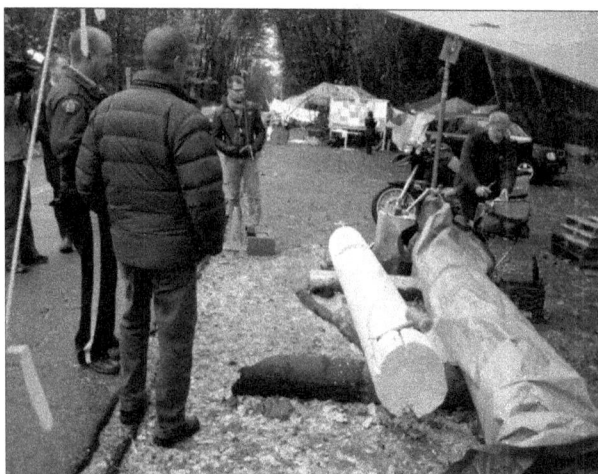

▲ **Figure 50. 8 AM on November 20, carver hold-**

ing down the street with a totem.

On November 20, at 8 AM[55] the two RCMP liaison officers assured those in the camp that the injunction would not be enforced that day and there would be no arrests until the area was marked as called for in the injunction order, and they then left The Mountain (Figure 49).

At 9:18 a convoy of black unmarked vehicles approached the camp and the RCMP immediately moved in and arbitrarily declared the camp site the location of BH2 while an officer read out the injunction order (Figure 50). He was repeatedly asked where the GPS coordinates he was reading aloud were physically located on the ground, so people could move away, or stay inside, as they desired.

▲ **Figure 51. 9:18 AM on November 20: the RCMP en-forcement convoy arrives at BH2.**

55 At this point I was in the Caretakers Camp collecting recyclables and garbage. From 8AM onwards my role turned to witnessing and recording events with a camera.

A very peaceful morning chatting around the sacred fire quickly turned into an angry crowd as police used force to immediately single out and arrest an aboriginal man. His arrest was followed over the next hour by more arrests of young and old protesters who happened to be standing in the Caretakers Camp when the RCMP arrived. They held the street by locking arms and sitting down on the street (Figure 51). None of these first arrests occurred in a marked off area as defined in the injunction order delineated injunction area, which did not occur until 9:37 AM when the yellow tape was, as it eventually transpired, arbitrarily rolled out to conveniently place the Caretakers Camp directly inside the injunction zone (Figure 52) and push witnesses and supporters away. Up until 9:45 or so, witnesses were free to wander around the street as arrests happened.

▲ **Figure 52. First batch of arrestees locked arms in a circle and hold the street.**

▲ Figure 53. The RCMP establish the "injunction zone" at 9:37 AM cutting off road access.

**Figures 54 ◄a) previous page & ▲b) Early
arrests after the police line is established.**

The arbitrary establishment of the yellow police tape on
November 20 effectively cut off through traffic on
Centennial Way, which was not in the TM plans submitted to the NEB for approval. The lines were moved further north and eventually all road access on Centennial
Way was cut off at the bottom, requiring supporters to
hike 500 metres uphill carrying food, firewood, and sup-
plies for the Caretakers who had moved camp across the
street to a field. After lengthy negotiation with the RCMP,
who initially did not believe a sacred fire is part of Coast
Salish traditions, the sacred fire was moved north, and
Sut-Lut was designated as the elder allowed to stay behind the yellow line and designate others to come behind
the line to assist with round-the-clock fire tending. The

totem stayed in its original location behind the yellow line, and carvers continued to work on it throughout the week. TM began drilling in heavy rain on November 21, and protests continued throughout that night and over the next few days, with arrests happening every hour.

When vehicular access up Centennial Way was blocked, a new tradition of inviting the public to walk up the mountain together at 10:30 each morning in violation of the injunction order and to express contempt of the court that sided with KM and TM over the wishes of the community to protect The Mountain. By November 22 the word was out and many witnesses, some new to activism, began to walk up the mountain that weekend to hold the line, see the drilling, and the behaviour of the RCMP as close to 20 arrests were made (Figure 54). Some witnessed for the first time blatant police racism as people of colour were treated more harshly than white settlers, and decolonization and white privilege were major topics of conversation on the front line.

◀Figure 55. Holding the line on November 22.

More First Nations supporters arrived to hold the line and help tend the sacred fire (Figure 55), while other Caretakers coordinated the shuttling of firewood up The Mountain.

▲ **Figure 56. First Nations supporters from Alberta hold the north line with drumming directed at the RCMP.**

A contingent arrived from Victoria on the Social Coast bus and the protests escalated into tense moments of police intimidation and protestors being grabbed and dragged over the line by the RCMP. Numerous cases of the RCMP physically harming protestors being arrested were witnessed by observers. A rally was hosted by the NGO Beyond Boarding at the south end of the police line while witnesses at the north end followed a water hose illegally laid through the forest from BH2 to BH1 outside the injunction zone, and had it removed. Some speakers at the rally and several children crossed the line in a united message of solidarity. Mirrors were held up to reflect the police line back at them (Figure 56). Night vigils were held to hold the street as the TM drilling continued at BH2 around-the-clock.

By November 24 it became clear the TM was behind schedule and had barely begun work at BH1. TM announced it would be applying to the court on November 27 for permission to expand the injunction order deadline for work completion from December 1 to December 12, but also to move the GPS coordinates described in the original injunction order. The lawyer for the RCMP also announced that police would begin laying criminal charges against people who violated the TM injunction more than once.[56]

---

56 Those who violate the injunction two or more times may be charged with "Disobeying an order of court" under section 127 of the Criminal Code. This is a criminal offence that can be prosecuted on an indictable (more serious) or summary (less serious) basis.

▲ **Figure 57. People holding the south line during the Beyond Boarding rally by holding up a mirror reflecting the faces of the RCMP back at them, Nov. 22.**

In the BC Supreme Court on November 27, TM was refused an extension to continue their work on Burnaby Mountain under the court-granted injunction. During proceedings, the TM lawyers admitted that the geo-coordinates described in the initial injunction order were inaccurate and based on desktop analysis that was not verified in the field. The coordinates placed the location of BH2 approximately 30 metres south (down Centennial Way), which effectively meant that the drilling was happening in the wrong place. All arrests to that point had thus occurred outside the court-ordered injunction zone, in a zone arbitrarily delineated by the RCMP to favour TM and harass protestors. Over 125 persons arrested between November 21 and November 27 had their charges dropped, including several that had been arrested twice, jailed, and were in contempt of court until the error was admitted in court.

Once the judgement was made to not grant a work extension, TM wrapped up its drilling at BH2 and retreated to BH1; the RCMP began to pull out and by November 30, the day of a huge celebration on The Mountain, were completely gone. At that point, all efforts between the various affinity groups, NGOs and First Nations to maintain the right to the street, hold the line, and sustain 24 hour tending of the sacred fire were completely vindicated. The additional finding of the court that the drilling had occurred in the wrong place, resulting in arrests for the wrong reason, and the dropping of charges is an important, if temporary victory, in what has been described as an issue that is "going to be a war, and it's going to be one that carries on for a number of years."[57]

The experiences on Burnaby Mountain are a good place to end this chapter as the fight for The Mountain was a fight for the right to the street, which resulted in transformative changes for many individuals who continue to collectively assemble on other streets with the intent of changing the city and its attitudes towards the environment, First Nations, and activism.

---

57 Quoted in The Province.com by Derek Corrigan, Mayor of Burnaby on November 21, 2014
http://www.theprovince.com/news/This+going+says+Burnaby+m ayor+pipeline+protesters+arrested+with+video/10400012/story.ht ml

11 | Anarchist Surrealism & Canadian Apocalyptic Modernism: Allusive Political Praxis in Elizabeth Smart's *By Grand Central Station I Sat Down And Wept*

James Gifford[1]

T his article gestures to the 1930s through 1950s international anarchist literary networks that ran from
Paris to London and Athens, Cairo and Alexandria, Shanghai, Oxford and Cambridge, New York and San Francisco,
and finally Big Sur and Vancouver. The distribution across
these nodes was intense and sustained, but this project
only hints at the historical recuperation in order to contextualize a more focused revision of critical approaches to

---

1   Associate Professor of English and Director of the University Core
    at Fairleigh Dickinson University—Vancouver Campus

the Canadian novelist Elizabeth Smart in her 1945 work *By Grand Central Station I Sat Down and Wept*. In the first instance, a significant component of the New Modernist Studies has been dominated by Marxist reading paradigms and a sense of propriety from conservative perspectives refined through a liberal helping of the vaguely liberal. This is to say, the New Modernist Studies and the recent expansion of Late Modernist Studies within it orient toward a normative reading position that is progressive in the general sense but rarely radical in its readerly interventions. Anarchist studies remain stubbornly invisible all too often, despite very fine work from Allan Antliff, Jesse Cohn, and David Kadlec, while the political neutering of anarchism by relocating its interests in purely formal matters in David Weir's Jamesonian study has taken on a normative value in literary readings. *Invisible* is also a doubly suggestive description of anarchism in the New Modernist Studies—an antiauthoritarian paradigm fails to comfortably fit the critical schema, so it becomes difficult for many scholars to recognize it even when it is near the surface or even explicit. Anarchism in effect becomes the blind spot, the scotoma, of the New Modernist Studies' methodology—anarchism hides in the hole of the optic nerve when they try to see it, persistently present but insidiously invisible. Smart, as novelist, has been misread as a result, such that her avant-garde *By Grand Central Station* degenerates into a work critically understood as embodying emotional excess in form and content because its radical politics pale from view when her allusive references to the anarchist networks of the 1930s and 40s are etiolated—this article aims to restore the red and black colours of her work and thereby a politicized reading.

The network I explore in *Personal Modernisms* began with an anarchist Post-Surrealism in Paris through the Villa Seurat group in its little magazines *Booster* and *Delta*, which proposed an organic sense of Surrealism using a conscious revision of automatism, hence returning focus to the ego between the hedonistic unconscious and the totalitarian superego. This was a non-communist Surrealism with an antiauthoritarian aim expressed through anarchism by Henry Miller in his "Open Letter to Surrealists Everywhere." This spread to the Art & Freedom group in Cairo in their "LONG LIVE DEGENERATE ART" manifesto as a reaction to the *Entartete Kunst* exhibition in Munich, and both spread to London in the New Apocalypse movement, cum New Romanticism, cum "Personalist Literature" in the journals *Bolero*, *Kingdom Come*, and *Transformation*. This meant Henry Miller, Lawrence Durrell, Herbert Read, Alex Comfort (the anarchist who wrote *Joy of Sex*), George Woodcock, the fantasy novelist Henry Treece, the Egyptian anarchist writers Albert Cossery and George Henein, and many others all began programs of mutual publication support. The London group was, entirely by chance, largely recruited together to serve in Cairo during the war rather than in Europe, where good fortune led to their meeting several Villa Seurat authors who had already fled as refugees from Greece. For a brief moment, Henry Miller ferried their works to New York and San Francisco for further publications supported by the San Francisco Renaissance writers George Leite, Kenneth Rexroth, and Robert Duncan, as well as the Libertarian Reading Circle, Circle Editions, and Jean Varda's anarchist commune in Big Sur, whose big tent had already housed many of them in Paris prior to his relocation to America. Amidst this richness of distribution, the Chinese anarchists in the London group publishing in Oxford relocated to Shanghai and there published several of these same authors again in *T'ien Hsia Monthly* before the Chinese Communist Revolution. And New York. And Woodstock. And even coastal British Columbia... Smart would go on to first write *By Grand Central Station* in Pender Harbour, British Columbia, but this migratory background to her novel is only a part of a large network for circulating literary materials, and her points of contact among the various nodes are more extensive than is recognized.

From the established narrative of the thirties, when we think of war-time writing, the dominant notions are Late Modernism, the ascendancy of the Auden generation, the "shrinking" of the British High Moderns, and bohemian anticipations of the Beats and Angry Young Men. Reading over the shoulders of the Auden generation of authors, whose histories have become normative even while the cast of participants broadens to include women and men beyond the Oxbridge networks, we find anarchism incomprehensible in a paradigm of Marxist class struggle and an end to political activity as individuals. This is to say, there were no war poets, the avant-garde eroded, realism grew in proportion to the investment in progressive politics—anarchism exited stage left after Spain, and the individual steadily diminished as the unit of worth in a creative paradigm more oriented toward surface and class consciousness. But this is the scotoma. To the Auden generation of critics, anarchism was nonsensical, and hence its role vanished from their histories, and as a consequence the politics of anarchist authors paled and made little sense to a readership coached in attending to notions of bourgeois freedom and social determinism rather than self-possession and responsibility.

Between the Auden generation and the Angry Young Men and Beats, what I call in *Personal Modernisms* the Personalist group was overshadowed by the war in which they served in either military or pacifist roles. They were overshadowed by their predecessors who attained positions of editorial authority, and they were overshadowed by their progenitors who assumed the mantle of the 1960s *avant-garde* without voicing loudly their own readerly influences, as each successive generation is wont to do. Crucially, the Personalists were disregarded because of their anarchist politics. They were of a generation too young to remain radical and rebellious after the exhaustions of the war years. Their broad networks of mutual aid rather than clearly defined schools or movements were not a Singular Modernism with a totalizing vision, aesthetic, or mode of understanding, and while this lent them flexibility the absence of manifestos and clearly defined objectives made them ostensibly diffuse or even unrelated to each other in the absence of clearly stated affiliations. In this sense, it was a movement remarkably in tune with the redevelopment of anarchism in the 1960s, even though it proved difficult for young allies to recognize this older but familiar face. Most particularly, modern readings of the misogyny of Henry Miller's obscene novels, as established in the mainstream critical tradition by Kate Millet's 1970 *Sexual Politics*, seem to find it ever increasingly difficult to notice Miller's anarchist revision to Surrealism and his pacifism, and thereby his support for the young Canadian cult novelist Elizabeth Smart during the early stages of her career in the 1930s and 40s. Before her love affair with George Barker, which is taken as the *roman à clef* for her writings and thereby stripping them of their own voice without a masculine contextualization, Smart was publishing her poetry in Miller's Parisian periodicals and experimenting in the artists commune organized by Miller's friend Jean Varda.

Where *Personal Modernisms* recuperates this network in detail and theorizes its praxis and poetics, this chapter more narrowly foregrounds what others have typically cast as background: Smart's important role in this generation and its politics from 1934 to 1949 and the recontextualization of her work from this series of affiliations, crossing from Paris to California to New York to London, and finally rural Pender Harbour on the Pacific Coast. The leap from Modernism to Kitchen Sink Realism and experimental bohemianism has led to the widespread belief in a pre- and post-war generational gap. This assumption neglects the intermediary group of writers because, out of context, their work looses its coherence. With its ideological invisibility for the progressive readers, as outlined above, its allusions and metonyms are as a consequence unintelligible in the dominant interpretive paradigms. This group's vital meetings were not in the centre of empire as occurred with the Modernists and Auden Generation—it was very much abroad and bound to the cultural lives of other nations and literary cultures, and hence Smart's participation appears secondary to the ferocious release of libidinal energy in her novel. Moreover, this group's rejection of the authoritarian elements of both fascist and Marxist movements gives a superficially passive impression; despite the ferocity of Smart's emotional excess in *By Grand Central Station*, the euphemism of quietism for anarchism leads the decontextualized reader to understand her as a passive object of the male subject's actions throughout. Returning Smart to a position of agency, a position from which her work never departs, entails by necessity overturning the strong readings that elide her politics. This means refuting Fredric Jameson's persistent refusal to engage with anarchism, and much of the critical contrasts reflect issues of selfhood, identity, and bourgeois freedom or individualism over which thirties writers disagreed. Just as George Orwell elides Miller's anarchism in his influential book-cum-essay *Inside the Whale* by referring to it as "quietism" and "defeatism" (by virtue of being pacifist), so too does Smart's critique of armed conflict and the industrialized production of war deflate under patriarchal readings that cast her as the languishing and ravenous sexualized female. Attention to allusion restores the agency of Smart's political critique in the novel and her gendered sense of female fecundity in conflict with a war effort embodying the domination-seeking elements of patriarchy—this also sets Smart into a series of relations distinct from those granted her in the established criticism, ranging from Birgitta Frojdendahl's contention that "the reader realizes that the speaker and the protagonist [in *By Grand Central Station*] lack personalities, since the main theme is passion per se" (n.p.) to Denise Heaps' contention in relation to *jouissance* that Smart was "gifted with a rhapsodic, sensual, and at times hyperbolic and overwrought poetic prose style, a style capable of ecstatic ascents and sober descents" (n.p.). Robert McGill pushes this even further and most recently by arguing Smart's novel is "predominantly a poetic rendering of her inner life, which is characterized by her desire for her lover and her agony when he eventually abandons her" (McGill 68). Rather than Smart as an allusive antiauthoritarian, the critical literature points to Smart as a passive and erotic ecstatic.

The various positions of the authors involved are by no means stable, but they found solidarity in an antiauthoritarian vision. They range from the "Anarchist Knight" Herbert Read and the mystical Robert Duncan to the violent libidinal energies of the proletarian Kenneth Patchen or the pornographer Henry Miller, and there are also the complexities of agents of empire, such as Lawrence Durrell, and licentious subjects of empire, such as Albert Cossery. Even amidst the liberally progressive groups, an antiauthoritarian vision teamed with anarchic energies before the post-war stagnation and exhaustion made several poets politely mask their politics, as was the case with university professors like J.F. Hendry (who left anarchist London groups to teach poetry at Laurentian University) and G.S. Fraser (who set aside his most active work after a nervous breakdown and suicide attempt in Japan to become a lecturer at the University of Leicester), all set in contrast to the unschooled George Barker and Dylan Thomas. Even the anarchism of *The Joy of Sex* appears in this network through Alex Comfort's poetry, novels, and anarchist theory. Despite their differences, a common core of mutual support and personal vision—a deep solidarity—unifies these authors, whether they embraced or secreted away the loaded term "anarchism," remained faithful to it, resolved it to an inoffensive antiauthoritarianism, or turned to mainstream views in middle age or in the hot conflicts of the Cold War. Returning Smart's *By Grand Central Station I Sat Down and Wept* to this network of relations troubles the apolitical approaches to her work that have privileged the intensity of her romantic excess and called out for her valuation as a desiring female subject, but that all too readily permit popularized (and inaccurate) depictions of a hysterical woman's prefeminist paroxysm of self-abasement to masculine desire in drippingly baroque prose. My central contention is that this is a wildly impoverished reading of an anarchist novel with complex formal and social preoccupations.

By Grand Central Station I Sat Down and Wept is a cult classic of Canadian literature with a significant popular following, but its ties to Smart's milieu are remarkably unexplored *despite* the extensive trend toward biographical readings. While many critics have recognized that the book's poetic diction and rich allusive structure are ripe for critiques of emotional excess, contextualization of her work and the restoration of its allusive gestures reveal this as a *deliberate* post-surrealist experiment and not reductively as an emotional paroxysm. From the opening sentence's syntactic reach to *express* excess and the feverish collapse of possibilities on the closing page, the novel's semblance of *jouissance* is never merely frenzied—it is anarchically allusive, dense with associations, and thereby shows conscious craft, which is the defining trait of the anarchist post-Surrealism theorized by Henry Miller, in tandem with the "organicism" of the London-based New Apocalypse movement that responded under Herbert Read's influence to Miller's "An Open Letter to Surrealists Everywhere" following on the 1936 London International Surrealist Exhibition. The moment when Miller and Herbert Read debated these ideas in their letters is the same as Smart's time in Paris and then Cassis with Miller's friend Jean Varda. Unsurprisingly, Smart evidences the consciously revised automatism of the Villa Seurat, New Apocalypse, and Art & Freedom movement everywhere in the novel, both in the semblance of orgiastic excess and in the chaos of images that are given order through anarchic allusions. Biographically, Smart met her lover in the novel, George Barker, through her correspondence with Lawrence Durrell. Moreover, we know Smart had ongoing contact with Henry Miller and an intense sexual relationship with Miller's post-Surrealist friend, Varda. Miller and Smart later lived in Varda's Big Sur anarchist commune in California, which is the setting for the opening of *By Grand Central Station* when Barker fled Japan. This makes it remarkable that the contextual sense of Smart's novella in the English Surrealist movement, which is based on its specific revisions to Surrealism through the New Apocalypse, has gone entirely unnoticed. Tellingly, in an otherwise excellent biography that does not include the word "anarchism," Rosemary Sullivan gestures with wordplay to the politics in Smart's life during this moment when her first sexual encounter occurred with Varda: "She had found the rhetoric of metaphor to contain her vision, surrealistic and sustaining. What is remarkable is the way she weaves the banal —'the cloistral pickings of the nose'—and the apocalyptic" (Sullivan 114). The surprise is that the surrealistic and apocalyptic were not explicitly joined given Smart's affiliations at this point in her life.

As a first point of entry, much is made by critics of the titular allusion in Smart's work to Psalm 137:1: "By the rivers of Babylon, there we sat down, yea, we wept, when we remembered Zion." This first allusion makes plain the novel's work as an act of recuperation and memory, but noting this remains easily limited through an emphasis on loss, lack, and mourning. Although Smart's narrative mourns a lost lover and completed love affair, this is not biographically true in a strict sense—as an artistic work unburdened from a strictly biographical reading of her relationship with the British poet George Barker, *By Grand Central Station* is not a remembrance of a specific lover, and its title does not gesture to lost love as one might read the Song of Solomon but rather to a lost time in the Psalm, a lost period, and a lost community. Simply noticing this reshapes our attention and emphasis for the subsequent reading beyond the title. Smart rebuilds a lost era, a lost home. In the Psalm we see a recollection of Zion by the Jews after their expulsion by the invading Babylonians followed by the articulation of the nature of the song: "For there our captors demanded of us songs, and our tormentors mirth, saying 'Sing us one of the songs of Zion.'" (Psalm 137:3). Smart's novel is such a song after war, but rather than mourning her loss of George Barker as a lover, we should read singing as a political response to exile after war and the suffering of the people in times of war. Apart from the inference of meaning from this allusion, the title also marks the importance of allusion itself, as a formal communicative mechanism, to the reader.

And allusion is very much the matter. Smart's allusion to William Blake's poem "The Question Answered" makes sudden sense of her otherwise confusing comments on state authorities. Blake offers his vision in his notebooks later collected as *Gnomic Verses*:

> What is it men in women do require?

The lineaments of Gratified Desire.

What is it women do in men require?

The lineaments of Gratified Desire. (Blake 153)

The conflict between "desire" and "require" paired in rhyme as well as the gendered division that permits only contours or lineaments of desire itself to be communicated without the reality, shifts from the satisfaction of desires or the demands of requirements to the performance for each other of the contours of consummation or semblances of satisfaction. Smart, in a fulfillment of Blake's concerns over a troubling word such as "require" turns to the wartime agent of state hegemony as her protagonist and lover cross the American south: "[the police officer] was livid with hate of our lineaments of gratified desire" and again state power with "Witches were burnt at the stake, all over New England, just for love, just for wearing the lineaments of gratified desire" (Smart, *By Grand* 50, 97). This allusion, however, is not complete with Blake. Lawrence Durrell, who introduced Smart to her lover Barker and edited her contributions to the Villa Seurat journal *Delta*,[2] uses the same allusion in *The Alex-*

---

2 Smart's poems "Comforter, Where, Where is Your Comforting" first appeared in *Delta* and the New Apocalypse literary journal *Seven* also included her "Three Poems" in a 1940 issue comprised of materials bequeathed to it after *Delta*'s closure with the outbreak of the Second World War. Both sets of poems are excluded from *The Collected Poems of Elizabeth Smart*, which is symptomatic of the critical scotoma related to her ties to the Villa Seurat generally, post-Surrealism specifically, and the New Apocalypse's understanding of organicism in particular.

andria Quartet (110) as a reference to his own and his protagonist's initials, L.G.D. Durrell began this trick with initials in 1935 in his novel *Pied Piper of Lovers* and *The Black Book* in 1938. The stock of both was lost during the war before 1945 when Smart published *By Grand Central Station* through Editions Poetry London, edited by their mutual friend James Meary Tambimuttu who published nearly everyone else in the same group of post-surrealist antiauthoritarian authors, but Smart refers at least to the latter.

While it may seem like an interpretive stretch to link Smart's allusion to Blake to Durrell's allusion to the same and further to anarchism, it becomes more plausible if we accept the reminder that Durrell introduced her to the lover whose lineaments she wears, and that she was reading Durrell's own novel of post-Surrealist stylistic excess, *The Black Book*, in late 1939 while corresponding with Durrell to discuss her poetry. The importance of this link to the Villa Seurat is cemented by another shared allusion. Durrell's first novel repeatedly alludes to the obscure Middle English poem "Quia Amore Langueo" (titled in bastardized Latin), and his protagonist Walsh sings a song setting of the work in a dramatic scene that provides the crisis of the middle section of the novel (*Pied* 203-205). Smart uses the same phrase, writing near the end of her book "I am without words. I am without thoughts. But quia amore langueo. I am dying for love. This is the language of love" (Smart, *By Grand* 109). This, nonetheless, is only a part of the allusion, and not an indication of hysterical excess of emotions. The careful phrase and its deployment as allusion is tied to another repeated image in Smart's novel: the apple plucked from the same Middle English poem. For Smart's narrator, writing of her injurious love and the vaginal wound her affair has left in her (in a direct parallel to the wounded Christ in the poem "Quia Amore Langueo," queering the relationship to a feminized and passive savior), she writes "the apples (which ben ripe in my gardayne) fall only toward that" (89). The apples "which ben ripe in my gardayne" are a direct quotation from the poem. The same parallel to Christ recurs with the same allusion in the final scenes of the novel no fewer than four times: "My love is crucified on a floating cross.... My love has a bandage like a bowel of pain... But it is not the wound that chokes him" (107). This then flows through another repetition of the title of the poem "Quia Amore Langueo" (109) and thence to the organic image of the apples of her garden: "His hand of sympathy goes out to me, soft as a dove, his cheek like early apples.... With resurrection in his eyeballs" (110) and finally on the closing page of the work "Go into your garden, for your apples are ripe" (112). All are direct allusions to the poem she discovered through Durrell and his first novel *Pied Piper of Lovers*, a poem Barker then recited at her funeral in 1986. The point bears emphasis: despite the excess of the imagery, the womb-like wound carried by the speaker, and the erotic pleasure in the blood, this is not an emotional paroxysm of *jouissance* but rather a strategic deployment of allusion to, firstly, create a poetic image with greater depth and, secondly, to tie Smart to the antiauthoritarian network of authors through which she travelled across Europe and North America during the war years. Privileging this double function of allusion is a necessary precursor to recuperating the occluded politics of her novel.

Such linkages by allusion to Durrell may seem merely convenient, but this becomes yet-more dense. Henry Miller's golden shit scene in *Tropic of Cancer* (97) is also linked by allusion (Smart, *By Grand* 75), Miller's style appears as an echo in Smart (81), Durrell's magma of history and the enormous Now in *The Black Book* (Durrell, *Black* 176, 244) appears in allusion (Smart, *By Grand* 79, 65), and Smart quite plainly quotes from Dylan Thomas' short story collection *The Burning Baby*, an excerpt from which he published in Durrell and Miller's anarchist periodical *Delta*, a journal that deeply affected the New Apocalypse and in which she published her poetry (Smart, *By Grand* 109). With this excess of allusion, not an excess of hysterical desire, the invisibility of anarchism is first noticeably operating—rather than signaling careful structure, the richness may become chaotic to a reader without the frame of reference.

While allusion is very much the formal matter at the heart of Smart's *By Grand Central Station I Sat Down and Wept*, it only informs the reader of Smart's own readings, and the meaning of an allusion may be ambiguous. The interpretive matter is that allusion operates as a formal technique through which she codes her social intervention and critique of industry versus organicism and atomic apocalypse versus sexual reproduction. The important shift is that this social critique and its allusive framework bring her work into a new politically charged context and make it intelligible through the same anarchist paradigm as this wide network to which she gestures so frequently. By taking Miller's anarchist post-Surrealism with conscious manipulation of the creative materials culled from the unconscious, and conceptualizing it in tandem with the New Apocalypse's emphasis on the organic, the politics of Smart's various comparisons and allusions then stand out strongly. Miller argues that "The age we live in is the age which suits us: its is we who make it, not God, not Capitalism, not this or that, call it by any name you like. The evil is in us…. No system of government, no belief will provide us with that liberty and justice which men whistle for with the death-rattle" (Miller, "An Open" 154–55), and in addition to this Henry Treece and Stefan Schimanski present the New Apocalypse's concept of Personalism:

> our Personalist belief rejects all politics which do not grow, organically, from living…; where lust for power and security have separated man from man, have disembodied the spirit, have disrupted the community and have made freedom the perquisite of the leisured few.

> Similarly, it rejects those fascist systems which control the defects of society by curtailing the liberty of the individual, which subordinate the destinies of men

> to the whims of a Leader…, which denies them from
> their Selves…. Personalism rejects all forms of gov-
> ernment which ignore spiritual values, which do not
> see in man an autonomously creative unit whose su-
> preme vocation is the understanding and healing of
> the Self. (Treece and Schimanski 13)

With these concepts foregrounded as among Smart's
points of reference and as collaborators in her network of
poetic collaborators, her work in the novel takes on a
greater resonance that eclipses the tendency to find in her
only a female emotional hysteria, and she finds in the un-
governed America:

> The determination of early statesmen who were mild
> but individual… No great neon face has been super-
> imposed over their minor but memorable history. Nor
> has the blood of the early settlers, spilt in feud and
> heroism, yet been bottled by a Coca-Cola firm and
> sold as ten-cent tradition. (57)

The blurring of the state and commercialism is clear, but
the addition of an anarchist or anti-authoritarian perspective broadens the rationale for combining the state and
commercialism and twinned evils. Both are anti-individu-
al and hegemonic, and the blending anticipates the kind
of fury of excess found later in Robert Duncan's anti-war
Passages—Duncan, notably, was participating in the
same anarchist reading circle that Smart visited in Berkeley after meeting Kenneth Rexroth (Hamalian 135), and
Duncan also supported the anarchist commune in which
Henry Miller lived in Big Sur, where Jean Varda from

Paris hosted both Smart and Miller as well as Barker after his arrival. The kinship between Smart and the San Francisco Renaissance made visible in this pairing of the state and consumerism is early but vital.

Smart also takes up the contest between the individual and the nation by writing "There have been men who have been more remembered than nations" (64) only to set her dismissal of "my dear country" (64) in contrast to an extended emphasis on the personal and individual on the facing page in a string of first person pronouns culminating in another parallel to Durrell's *The Black Book* through the "now" (65). These anti-state gestures (67-69) recur in a juxtaposition of the abasement of bloodied corpses of soldiers against the productive blood of her giving birth. Her fecundity is surely feminist, yet it is also more—it is a refutation of state authority begun in organicism at the opening of the novel and culminating in the reproduction at its end. It is also certainly *not* the apolitical hysterical paroxysm to which Smart is too often tied.

This then brings the politics of Smart's novel to the fore and reinvigorates our capacity for readings that move beyond biographical essentialisms and romantic excess. The industrial modernity of the state and its war-machine is set as the opposite of the individual expressing an organic and antiauthoritarian Personalism formally expressed through the concept of an anarchist post-Surrealism first developed in the Villa Seurat but disseminated rapidly around the globe. This is Smart's grand contrast in *By Grand Central Station*, and it is precisely the same conflict articulated in the anarchist works of the New Apocalypse authors who had themselves developed out of Miller's anarchist post-Surrealism and then followed by others in Egypt, London, California, and Shanghai.

This shifted interpretative paradigm can in turn make a great deal of sense from Smart's otherwise inexplicable 1945 avoidance of directly mentioning war and politics through an unpolitical stance that extols the organic, fecund, and reproductive. *Not* discussing the war that had engulfed the world is precisely the point—the praxis is to privilege the personal while barring the belicose. These are the interstices of state power between which she out-lines a life lived in the personal and productive: "a lot of *states*men will emerge twirling their moustaches, and see the birth-blood, and know that they have been foiled" (Smart, *By Grand* 66; emphasis mine). The state's defeat by organic reproduction reflects very closely the "organic form" of the New Apocalypse. Smart follows this in an anti-capitalist vein by setting her reproductive seed as sal-vation, which also disallows patriarchal interpretations of her fecundity as receptive and passive rather than active and productive, for "I shall still have a pocketful of rye, whose currency no Foreign Exchange can control, nor value be diminished by transplantation" (Smart, *By Grand* 67). Organic reproduction becomes, for Smart, the embodiment and dissemination of an antiauthoritarian politics lived in the gaps between state powers and capit-al, and as a consequence her final cry of loss in the novel's closing is not a failure to mourn the departure of her lover but an expression of terror as a new age of warfare emerges that sets organic fecundity against mechanization and an atomic sterility.

The conclusion of the novel and its titular allusion now come to life as an anti-industrial organic focus on the individual in an Apocalyptic embodied vein: "By Grand Central Station I sat down and wept: / I will *not* be placated by the mechanical motions of existence…. [My weeping] lit up Grand Central Station like a Judgment Day" (103; emphasis original). The unborn child is the Christ of this Apocalypse coming to wash away the urban world of industrialized war such that "I am going to have a child, so all my dreams are of water," an image that surrounds the watered city:

> When Lexington Avenue dissolved in my tears, and the houses and the neon lights and the nebulae fell jumbled into the flood, that child was the naked newborn babe striding the blast…. The grief trumpets its triumph (Smart, *By Grand* 104).

This unmistakably apocalyptic frame from the seven blasting trumpets of Revelations then returns to the allusions seen in "Quia Amore Langeuo" and an anarcho-pacifist vision of the Second World War. From this war, and through this allusion, and through the allusive bonds to the anarchist network of authors distributing their poetic materials globally, Smart's narrator awakes, and in this context, her love story is allegorical. For the war, her lover "sees the huge bird of catastrophe fly by. Both its wings are lined with the daily paper. Five million other voices are shrieking too.... All martyrdoms are in vain. He is drowning in the blood of too much sacrifice. / Lay aside the weapons, love, for all battles are lost" (111). The final organic call comes from Smart's pinching of Durrell's allusion when she repeats "Go into your garden, for your apples are ripe" (112), a phrase that ends this natural argument in the text before its final tragedy and recalls her own use of the apple as a figure for endless fecundity through generations in a fallen world (89, 110). Her child, the apple, is to be born, and in this knowledge of reproduction is all hope, and against it is all power seeking dominion. This cues the reader for the postwar world of inescapable modernity in the atomic age of annihilation that ends the novel:

> Odours of disinfectant wipe out love and tears. With rush and thunder the early workers overrun the world they have inherited, tramping out the stains of the wailing, bleeding past.... I myself prefer Boulder Dam to Chartres Cathedral. I prefer dogs to children. I prefer corncobs to the genitals of the male. Everything's hotsy-totsy, dandy, everything's OK. It's in the bag. It can't miss. (Smart, *By Grand* 112)

This dystopic vision is Smart's ending to the novel and the destruction of the anarchic organicism of the New Apocalypse. Without placing Smart in the context of her 1945 novel, published by Tamibmuttu under the Editions Poetry London imprint that bound this wildly international group of authors together, we could not reach such a reading. And a reading of the politics of Smart's Canadian novel is long overdue.

References

Antliff, Allan. *Anarchist Modernism: Art, Politics, and the First American Avant-Garde*. Chicago: Chicago UP, 2001. Print.

Blake, William. "The Question Answered." *The Selected Poems of William Blake*. Hertfordshire: Wordsworth Editions, 2000. Print.

Cohn, Jesse. *Anarchism and the Crisis of Representation: Hermeneutics, Aesthetics, Politics*. Selinsgrove, PA: Susquehanna UP, 2006. Print.

Duncan, Robert. *Bending the Bow*. New York: New Directions, 1968. Print.

Durrell, Lawrence. *The Alexandria Quartet*. London: Faber & Faber, 1962. Print.

———. *The Black Book*. Paris: Obelisk Press, 1938. London: Faber & Faber, 1973. Print.

———. *Pied Piper of Lovers*. Ed. James Gifford. London: Cassells, 1935. Victoria, BC: ELS Editions, 2008. Print.

Frojdendahl, Birgitta. "Passion in Elizabeth Smart's *By Grand Central Station I Sat Down and Wept*: The Sacred and the Profane." *Mosaic: a Journal for the Interdisciplinary Study of Literature* 37.2 (Jun 2004): 145-160. Print.

Gifford, James. *Personal Modernisms: Anarchist Networks and the Later Avant-Gardes*. Edmonton, AB: University of Alberta Press, 2014. Print.

Hamalian, Linda. *A Life of Kenneth Rexroth*. New York: W.W. Norton & Co., 1991. Print.

Heaps, Denise Adele. "The Inscription of 'Feminine Jouissance' in

Elizabeth Smart's *By Grand Central Station I Sat Down and Wept.*" *Studies in Canadian Literature* 19.1 (1994): 142–155. Web.

Henein, George. "Manifesto." *Black, Brown, & Beige: Surrealist Writings from Africa and the Diaspora.* Eds. Franklin Rosemont and Robin D.G. Kelley. Austin: U of Texas P, 2009. 150–51. Print.

————."LONG LIVE DEGENERATE ART!" *London Bulletin* 13 (April 1938): 16–17. *Black, Brown, & Beige: Surrealist Writings from Africa and the Diaspora.* Eds. Franklin Rosemont and Robin D.G. Kelley. Austin: U of Texas P, 2009. 148–50. Print.

Kadlec, David. *Mosaic Modernism: Anarchism, Pragmatism, Culture.* Baltimore: Johns Hopkins UP, 2000. Print.

McGill, Robert. "'A Necessary Collaboration': Biographical Desire and Elizabeth Smart." *ESC: English Studies In Canada* 33.3 (2007): 67-88. Print.

Miller, Henry. "An Open Letter to Surrealists Everywhere." *The Cosmological Eye.* New York: New Directions, 1939. 151–96. Print.

Millet, Kate. *Sexual Politics.* New York: Doubleday, 1969. Print.

Orwell, George. "Inside the Whale." *The Penguin Essays of George Orwell.* Eds. Sonia Orwell and Ian Angus. New York: Penguin Books, 1994. 101–33. Print.

Smart, Elizabeth. *By Grand Central Station I Sat Down and Wept.* London: Editions Poetry London, 1945. London: Flamingo, 1992. Print.

————. *The Collected Poems of Elizabeth Smart.* London: Paladin, 1992. Print.

————. "Comforter, Where, Where is Your Comforting?" *Delta* 3 (1939): 17. Print.

———. "Three Poems." *Seven* 8 (1940): 22–24. Print.

Sullivan, Rosemary. *By Heart: The Life of Elizabeth Smart*. London: Flamingo, 1992. Print.

Treece, Henry, and Stefan Schimanski. "Towards a Personalist Attitude." *Transformation*. Eds. Stefan Schimanski and Henry Treece. London: Victor Gollancz, 1943. 13–17. Print.

Weir, David. *Anarchy and Culture: The Aesthetic Politics of Modernism*. Amherst: U of Massachusetts P, 1997. Print.

MESOAMERICA RESISTE

Documenting stories
of resistance from
Mexico to Panama

▲ {"Huelga"::"Strike"}: Detail(s) from "¡Mesoamerica Resiste!" by the Beehive Design Collective

12 | ¡Mesoamerica Resiste!: Selected excerpts from the storybook companion to an epic illustration

Poster & Visual presentation: Beehive Design Collective[1];

The ¡Mesoamerica Resiste! graphical narrative is an immense work depicting "the struggle against corporate globalization in the Americas." Artists of the Beehive Design Collective say their first poster (2001), began a trilogy by

> celebrating the social movements that brought down
> the negotiations of the Free Trade Area of the
> Americas (FTAA) in the decade following the signing
> of NAFTA... In 2002, after traveling to Colombia and
> Ecuador to learn more about the impacts of US

---

1   Though the many Beehive Collective artists work anonymously, we would like to thank Sakura Saunders for her animated narrative to our NAASN5 visit with this massively detailed & huge cloth mural poster. She kindly brought it to the conference hall and facilitated a discussion on and around it. Gracias!

funding for the War on Drugs, we released the second poster in the trilogy. The Plan Colombia poster shows the devastating impacts of aerial fumigation of coca crops, and also digs deeper to expose the long legacy of colonialism and ongoing resource extraction in the Americas. The third and final image in the trilogy [¡Mesoamerica Resiste!] focuses on resistance to the mega-infrastructure projects that facilitate extraction and the neoliberal model of 'development.' These graphics...share stories of collective action and inspiration, stories of other worldviews and ways of life. Though the poster's details come from specific struggles in southern Mexico and Central America, the bigger picture extends to the entire Western Hemisphere and beyond, telling the story of what time it is on the planet in this era of rapid climate change and extreme loss of cultural and ecological diversity.[2]

THE TRADE WINDS

On all sides of the map, weather systems illustrate the global forces exerting pressure on the region.

The North Cloud

A dark cloud from the North puts high pressure on the world as it creates a storm of violence. This pressure system is the driving force behind military invasions and the War on Drugs, global economic policies, corporate interests, and consumerism. Pushing these agendas forward, the cloud rains down military violence, weapons, pollution, pesticides, and cultural invasion.

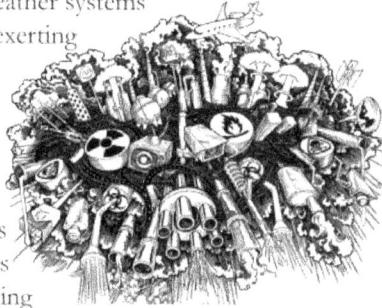

In the West: the whirlwind of disposable consumerism

The insatiable appetite for disposable goods controls the West Wind. Sucking

up container ships from the East Wind and spitting out a trash barge, the Consumer Vortex in the West creates a tornado of swirling detritus. Demand from North America and Europe, combined with accelerating mass manufacturing in East and South Asia, exert intense pressure to open up more passages through the isthmus of Central America.

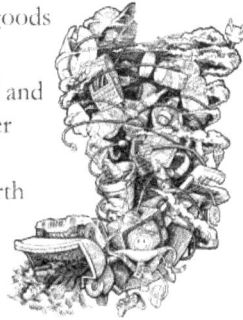

---

2   This text, along with the rest of these elements & visual details are excerpts from the Beehive Design Collective's "companion guide" to the poster, available on-line here: http://beehivecollective.org/downloads/narratives/MR_narrative_english_for_print.pdf

THE ANT SWARM

A giant swarm of ants comes down the trunk of the Ceiba tree. The ants, like so many other little critters, play an essential role in the ecosystem. Scurrying beneath the dirt, they aerate the soil, making it possible for plants to grow, essentially laying the foundations for life on earth. While these ants seem small compared to the entire forest, they outweigh all other animals and plants combined. The ants remind us that great changes are in the hands of the small and many. Working tirelessly, these miniscule creatures embody the phrase, *la revolución es el trabajo de las hormigas* (the revolution is ant's work). Little by little, their collective work has the strength to achieve great transformations, which reminds us that together, we can create tremendous changes in the world around us.

Some of the ants proudly carry messages from Indigenous communities in southern Mexico who have been slowly and steadily building autonomy for several decades. These sayings are Zapatista principles and also come from their experience of building "good government" councils, which encourage frequent rotation of leadership: "lead by obeying" the people in your community, they advise; "work from below, without seeking to rise to power;" "walk by asking questions"... Each ant is a different species, reminding us that the beauty of the world lies in its diversity, of cultures, of languages, of ways of being: "we are the same because we are different;" "a world where many worlds fit." In the face of so many threats to the diversity of life on this planet, the ants converge at the base of the Ceiba to declare, "Ya basta! Enough!"

Through this cycle of displacement, some of the bees risk their lives crossing the border to find work. They disappear off to the north, maybe never to be heard from again.

The Quetzal bird holds on to the social fabric of communities and steadily weaves cultural resistance, keeping alive textile traditions and the art of communicating through patterns and drawings in the threads.

The birds carry examples of organizing and solidarity: a childcare cooperative, saving seeds and planting hope for the future, weaving as a metaphor for the social fabric of community, mobilizing and educating through petitions and independent media. At the front of the line, two young birds carrying photos of the disappeared remind us that youth are leaders in the movement.

> ### Astronomers
>
> At the top of the hive, Melipona bees study the cosmos, learning from the cycles of the earth and moon. Informed by these natural cycles, the community can plan for planting and cultivating.
>
> ### Globalization from below
>
> Facing the serious dangers of colony collapse, over 50 bee species have come together to build an alternative economic system that emphasizes horizontal and equitable relationships, while providing the basic needs of their community.
>
> The values of an extractive economy have led us to a mass extinction crisis and climate chaos. The holistic values of a solidarity economy are part of the antidote to this crisis. Like the bees, rebuilding local and regional networks can help us deal with the challenges and consequences of a rapidly changing planet. All the critters defending their land between the roots of the Ceiba are showing us the meaning of globalization from below: reaching out across borders, cultures, and generations to link movements and support each other's struggles for survival.

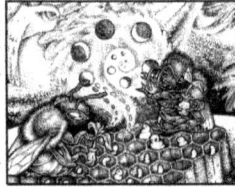

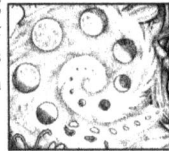

With so many artists creating this epic illustration, and so many groups involved in its production AND distribution —almost 10 years in the making!—the Beehive Collective describes it as "our most ambitious graphic to date." They thank (as do we!) the contributions of dozens of mesoamerican groups, "with support from many others along the way, including entomologists, biologists, artists, professors and students of bees, insects, animals or economies." It's truly a sight to behold, if you haven't already, you can take a closer look at it on-line (or arrange for a workshop or visit from the Collective in your locality) here: HTTP:// BEEHIVECOLLECTIVE.ORG

Appendix 1: NAASN Statement of Purpose

(January 2010 Draft | naasn.org/statement-of-purpose)

What Are We For?

The North American Anarchist Studies Network (NAASN) is intended

> 1. to serve as a means of mutual support for North American anarchists engaged in intellectual work, both theoretical and empirical;
> 2. to facilitate and promote anarchist studies by bringing together students, academics, independent scholars, and activists from across the United States, Canada, and Mexico; and
> 3. to provide a space for critical dialogue and reflection on anarchism.

What Is Anarchist Studies?

We understand "anarchist studies" as research, scholarship, education, and theorization that is

a.) about anarchism (e.g., studies of the past, present, and possible futures of anarchist thought and practice), and/or

b.) informed by anarchism (developing distinctly anarchist scholarly practices, methods of study, epistemologies, ways of knowing).

What Is Anarchism?

We understand anarchism, in general terms, as the practice of equality and freedom in every sphere of life -- life conceived and lived without domination in any form; we understand this practice to belong not only to a better future but to the here and now, where we strive to prefigure our ends in the means we choose to reach them. As such, anarchism is a distinct tradition with a specific history, rooted in the aspirations and experiences of a particular working-class movement; at the same time, it is a set of principles and possibilities that are the property of no one movement, no one thinker, and no one place or time. The many ways in which these principles have been interpreted and these possibilities realized may serve us as a continuing source of inspiration; articulating the unity within this plurality, lending it greater coherence, may be part of our continuing task.

What Is Intellectual Work?

We understand intellectual work here in terms other than "vanguardist notions of intellectual practice" (Graeber and Shukaitis) and broader than those sanctioned by officialdom and academia. It can include scholarship in a traditional sense, within and across the norms of academic disciplines; it can also include a wide variety of projects of inquiry and education, sometimes conducted under names such as "transformative studies," "militant research," "participatory action-research," and so on. We refuse the separation of intellectual and manual labor and insist that everyone has the capacity and right to share and create knowledge.

Who Is NAASN For?

Although many of us engage in anarchist studies from within existing institutions, such as universities, we do not see our projects as confined to those institutions, and we are committed to making sure that they do not share the limitations of official academia. As such, membership in the NAASN is open to all, regardless of academic affiliation or lack thereof.

While we are primarily committed to anarchist studies, in the spirit of mutual aid, we also invite the participation of anarchist intellectual workers whose intellectual work is not in this area.

What Will We Do?

To these ends, members of the NAASN will

- hold a yearly North American Anarchist Studies conference,
- organize Working Groups around our specific interests,
- pursue collaboration with other groups and institutions sharing our purposes, and
- provide a platform for other projects consistent with our purposes.

Appendix 2: NAASN5 Call for Papers (Fall, 2013)

Registration is open, and we are accepting abstracts, exhibit proposals, (or even full papers or complete individual panel proposals) for the

5th Annual North American Anarchist Studies Network (NAASN) Conference:
January 16-18, 2014 |
Kwantlen Polytechnic University

Please send in your abstracts now...
http://naasn2014.org

Over the past two decades, there's been a growing interest, both inside and outside the academy, in research done on anarchism (or by anarchists), and we have seen a resurgence in related multidisciplinary reading, study and theory.

It is hoped that this conference will build upon the work of the four successful previous NAASN conferences; first, as a wonderful opportunity for head-to-head gathering, with lively discussion and comradely debate, and then at conclusion, will leave an open archive of all published papers & presentations intended to stand as a positive contribution to the further flourishing of anarchist ideas and action.

SUBMISSION/PARTICIPATION:
▶ ▶ PUBLISHING/PERFORMANCE...

In addition to abstracts (for traditional papers you propose to present at the conference), you may also wish to submit proposals for performances, video presentations, multimedia/artistic installations, soapbox rants & raves, etc. To register (and submit abstracts!) via our website: **http://naasn2014.org** (using Open Conference Systems, first register or 'create an account', then 'create a submission'). This system is designed to organize all the conference documentation, help with scheduling, and facilitate long-term open publishing. However, you could also email your submission to **org@naasn2014.org**

*Deadline for abstracts is December 17th. *

Beehive Collective

▶ ▶ 1ˢᵗ Surrey Anarchist Book Fair: Jan. 18ᵗʰ, 2014.

There will be workshops and panels scheduled in parallel with the bookfair and we are seeking radical book & zine distributors who are interested in a table at the bookfair.

Tabling Request Deadline--for inclusion in the printed schedule--is January 6th, 2014.
We welcome all requests, questions,
comments, advice, offers of help/billeting/rides:
Please contact us at <org@naasn2014.org>

// This conference is being organized by the
Critical Criminology Working Group
(with the support of a grant from the
Faculty of Arts, Kwantlen Polytechnic University.) //

Appendix 3: Full 3-DAY Schedule[1] for NAASN5 + Indigenous Food Sovereignty Panels + Surrey Anarchist Bookfair

Thursday, January 16

2pm-3:20pm—Opening (Conference Centre)
Anarchy & Society (sociological approaches):
1/ Marginalization of Anarchist Criminology: a Content Analysis of Introductory Criminology Textbooks (Christopher Howell)
2/ ~~Liberation & Symbolic Interaction (Richard Simon)~~
3/ ~~Anarchistic Social Capital: Envisioning and Measuring Orientations Towards Horizontalism (Dana Williams)~~

3:30pm-5:00pm—**Politics and Aesthetics of Violence** and the State (Conference Centre)
1/ Stumbling in the Dark: Anarchism and Terrorism Research (Holger Marcks)
2/ Statecraft & Sexual Trust: Infiltrating the Revolutionary Left (Michael Loadenthal)
3/ ~~Aesthetics and Revolutionary Violence (Mario Tofano)~~

Friday, January 17

9:30am—Opening welcome, acknowledgement of the territories
10:00am-11:20—**Anti-racism and Anti-colonialism**

---

[1] Some scheduled presenters weren't able to make it to the conference, so these are shown here in strikethrough text.

1/ Presenting Abolition: A Movement-Relevant Journal of Politics (Brian Lovato)

2/ In Defense of Counterposed Strategic Orientations: Anarchism & Anti-racism (Jakub Burkowicz)

3/ Anti-State Resistance on Stolen Land: Expanding Anarchism's Anti-Colonial and Decolonizing Potentials Through Anarcha-Indigenism (Adam Lewis)

11:30am-1:00pm— The Forum on Indigenous Food Sovereignty

Who is your family? Stories of First Nation Food Sovereignty in the Tla-o-qui-aht Ha-houl-thee (with Johnnie Manson)

Fostering Intergenerational Resilience through the Decolonization of our Food Systems (with Galen Illerbrun & Jeska Slater)

Real Talk: on Food security, Sovereignty, and what that means to us (with Xhopakelxhit & Gwaiina)

1pm: LUNCH

2:00pm-3:20pm—Grassroots Networks: Media, Cities & Spaces

1/Grassroots Activist Media Toolkits: a diversity of media tactics (Sandra Jeppesen)

2/ Anarchism in a Conservative Capital: Groups & Projects in Edmonton (Roger Hlatky)

3/ The Right to The City Begins on the Street (Dr. Katherine Dunster)

3:30pm-5pm—ARTS & CULTURES of RESISTANCE (FIR 128)

1/ Language of Struggle, Struggle with Language (Roger Farr, Capilano U.)

2/ Anarchist Surrealism, Canadian Apocalyptic Modernism

(James Gifford)

3/ Presentation of MESOAMERICA RESISTE! banner (Beehive Collective)

Saturday, January 18

Surrey Anarchist Bookfair 10am-4pm

10am: Anarchist Interventions into Academic Conference Participation (Joanna Adamiak, Sandra Jeppesen, Sharmeen Khan, Holly Nazar)

11am: Building Cultures of Resistance (Xhopakelxhit & Gwaiina)

12 noon, LUNCH

1pm: ATI 101: Using Access to Information for investigative research (Mike Larsen)

2pm: Anarchist Tech Support for Everyone (PJ Lilley, Joe Bowser, Jeff Davis) [movement security culture & using encryption (similar to: **https://we.riseup.net/ats-mtl**)]

3pm: ~~Midwives & Alternative Health Practitioners Speak Out~~ ~~(Martha Roberts, Xhopakelxhit)~~

BIRTH*

Deep inside a womb-like cave formed by the tree roots, a scene of fertility portrays a vampire bat midwife assisting a birth. She is surrounded by medicinal herbs and plants related to fertility and women's reproductive health. Midwifery and other traditional medical practices have resiliently survived despite the biomedical model's attempts to discredit and destroy them.

*Detail from '¡Mesoamerica Resiste!' by the Beehive Collective (see page 357)

Appendix 4: A few words about Surrey[2]

S urrey is a too much reviled working class suburb of Metro Vancouver. A shadow city. Not economically peripheral, it is an epicenter of capitalist megaprojects and strip malls, a sprawling convergence of 7 superhighways and a massive port expansion.

Surrey is a city of migrant settlers on (mostly) unceded Indigenous nations' traditional territories. Besides English, it is now Punjabi and Mandarin which are the most commonly spoken languages. It is a rapidly growing suburb which became a city itself with sprawling satellite suburbs. Often outside of or marginal to the activist cultures of downtown Vancouver but with its own overlooked, unrecognized, histories of working class radicalism.

There is a long and varied history of anarchist organizing and action in the BC state context. From the intense IWW struggles in timber and mining through the Yippie riots of the 1960s, intentional communities and free schools, to the ongoing struggles against pipelines and fracking and campaigns in defense of migrants today, anarchism has taken diverse forms reflecting specific communities and circumstances. More recently recognition by anarchists has grown of the complementarity between indigenous community governance and anarchist perspectives. Current struggles pose challenges of settler anarch-

---

2   From the Introduction to the Conference Package

ists defending migrants and opposing borders or contesting oil and gas extraction on unceded indigenous territories, in a context of longstanding indigenous resistance. Surrey itself sprawls across many contested territories, lands of the Kwantlen, Katzie and Stó:lō people in the north and to the west, the Tsawassen and Musqueam Nations in the north and to the east, the Semiahmoo First Nation in the south.

Over the past two decades, there's been a growing interest, both inside and outside the academy, in research done on anarchism (or by anarchists), and we have seen a resurgence in related multidisplinary reading, study and theory.

It is hoped that this conference will build upon the work of the four successful previous NAASN conferences; first, as a wonderful opportunity for head-to-head gathering, with lively discussion and comradely debate, and then at conclusion, will leave an open archive of all published papers & presentations intended to stand as a positive contribution to the further flourishing of anarchist ideas and action. We are also looking to establish new connections within our local communities, and build toward future new infrastructures of resistance to the rule of capital. We look forward to working together with you, and thank you for your words and deeds herein...

solidarity regards,

Chris Howell, PJ Lilley & Jeff Shantz
(for the NAASN5 organizing committee)

surreywhat.info ----- # ---- # ---- naasn2014.org

Appendix 5: Forum on Indigenous Food Sovereignty

This stream ran parallel to NAASN5 on Friday, January 17, 2014, and was organized by Johnnie James Manson[1], and in co-operation with members of the Kwantlen Institute for Sustainable Food Systems.[2] The main narrative pieces began in the morning, then after lunch, there was a breakout session, which was facilitated by Dawn Morrison, who is the Chair of the BC Food Systems Network Working Group on Indigenous Food Sovereignty. (This session was not recorded, was intended for more planning and discussion with the direct participants and working on strengthening networks of support and communication amongst various communities. As Dawn Morrison put it, "a time to share information and develop some key messages for a strategic think tank and arts collective I/we are organizing to advocate for the establishment of Indigenous Bio-cultural Heritage Conservation Areas in the land and food

---

1 Johnnie Manson is a member of the Tla-o-qui-aht First Nation on the West Coast of Vancouver Island and a Masters Student at the Institute of Resource, Environment, and Sustainability at the University of British Columbia. At conference time, he was working on a project with Dawn Morrison, then Research Associate, Institute for Sustainable Food Systems, at Kwantlen. Specifically, the focus of the project, which spans across different universities and communities, is to revitalize the old grease trail network on Vancouver Island.

2 The list <landislife@naasn2014.org> was used in the planning and lead-up. Further follow-up notes and recordings may become available at http://surreywhat.info/landislife or 2014.naasn.org

systems."

Key concepts addressed around food, land and culture...

1. Health and nutritional values of Indigenous foods;
2. Gender, generations and youth perspectives in the struggle to protect, conserve and restore Indigenous food systems;
3. Strategies for protection, conservation and restoration of Indigenous food systems;
4. Indigenous Food Economies and Trade

Reinvestment

Unlike the one-way flows of the global economy, resources in the hive are cycled and reinvested.

Seed saving

Harvesting seeds and saving them to grow a new set of crops next season, the bees build sustainable sovereign food systems that will continue to feed their hives for generations. Saving seed is an example of self-sufficiency and independence from industrial agriculture.

Composting

Turning food scraps and garden waste into lush fertile soil, the bees and worms build future food systems, literally starting from the ground up.

*Detail, 'Mesoamerica Resiste' Beehive Collective, p.357

Who is your family? Stories of First Nation Food Sovereignty in the *Tla-o-qui-aht Ha-houl-thee

A narrative addressing environmental dispossession, environmental degradation, racism, and food security in the traditional territory of the Tla-o-qui-aht First Nation--with Dorothy Manson[1] and Johnnie Manson (also this track's organizer), and with Jake Gallic, a member of the Tseshaht First Nation, speaking about culture, knowledge transmission, and traditional land practices.

Fostering Intergenerational Resilience through the Decolonization of our Food Systems

(with Galen Illerbrun, Similkameen Nation; & Jeska Slater, Cree Nation and YOUNG ARTIST WARRIORS)

---

1 This visit from elder Dorothy Manson was particularly moving and memorable, and her oral historical narrative was recorded. We hope to make it available at http://surreywhat.info/landislife

Real Talk: on Food security, Sovereignty, and what that means to us

(with Xhopakelxhit & Gwaiina of Ancestral Pride, a land based movement of Nuu Chah Nulth / Ahousaht and Coast Salish / Snuneymuxw First Nations.)

We are Sovereign Ahousaht / Snuneymuxw. NYM og's, west coast warriors seeking to create a culture of resistance by asserting the jurisdiction and authority we have over our lives and lands. To empower and protect our way of life we must return home. we are in resistance to colonization, industrial land death, mining, logging, pipes and the illegally occupying military force of so called-canada. we reside on the lands and put ourselves to work for the people to ensure food sovereignty / access, and the right to house ourselves! we also are part of a larger network of decolonizing sovereign nations.

Speech Notes...

I t is hard in this day and age to be a healthy eater. This age of coca cola and potato chips, mass produced genetically modified foods is literally killing us. Food harvesting is still done but not on a scale that ensures our diets consist mainly of these foods.

I would like to address food security and sovereignty and what that means to me. In our village we have very little food security, we rely on travel to Tofino to for most of our foods and this is a $40 round trip. We are a economically depressed village with an 85% unemployment rate. This means most of our village relies on Social Assistance for help. This takes a very small food budget already and whittles it down. Coupled with HIGH food costs in Tofino for the basics it means our budget again is whittled away.

How fortunate for us, that we still know the foods of our lands intimately and have knowledge of how to harvest them. We eat salmon, crabs, clams, oysters, mussels, hiishstup, ducks and all those other amazing foods. These are natural and have been provided to us by Naas and in return for offering themselves it is our duty to care for this land and ensure that it will survive for millennia AS IT AL-WAYS HAS! Our ancestors worked hard all day every day to ensure we could inherit this bounty. What have we done to be good ancestors? It is not our fault that colonization has taken away our autonomy, and sovereignty but we can rise up from the horrors of genocide cultural break down. we can reject that which harms us and go back to the old ways. the days when we knew the value of good hard work!

You might ask what does contact and colonization have to do with gardening? everything! The foods the mulmuth-nee brought are filled with more chemicals then i can name and want to know about. We have as human beings taken personal comfort level to such a state of overkill it almost seems insurmountable but we have to abandon these ways of eating and producing foods so we can turn our collect-ive attention and work as communities to ensure the con-tinuity of the land. The foods of our oceans and lands are disappearing. Monoculture and industry is harming them, fish farms logging and pulp mills are the biggest offenders.

Food sovereignty is a big deal, more so then we know. That's why community gardens are so revolutionary, but we can take it one step further and instead of growing for-eign foods not indigenous to our areas we can focus most of our attentions to nurturing and harvesting WITH CARE our local food systems. Permaculture and wild harvesting. Healing the lands from industry and devastation due to pollution.

Evicting fish farms and shutting them down to preserve

our oceans. Stopping logging and other destructive forces. Feeding our future generations is going to take radical and revolutionary change from us as a whole. Hishak ish tsawak we are all one, connected. this planet, is our mother. not just the small bio regions we as each individual live in but the whole planet, hishak ish tsawak we are all one, the waters of the world are all connected.

What do community gardening and traditional foods have to do with the world? the fact that melting polar ice-caps and ocean acidification affect us all and care nothing for where we reside. In light of this, community gardening and traditional food harvesting may seem small BUT they are revolutionary! a tool to bring it local and keep it that way. A way to stop relying on foreign imports that devastate the lands of other indigenous people far away. I seen this first hand in Haiti, all the food went to the resorts in the Dominican Republic and south eastern USA. leaving them below poverty level and starving. We have to be conscious and mindful. If we all grew local economy and sacrificed exotic foods and put the time and money instead into food co-ops we would start regaining ground in the war on natural food. Imagine tithing food harvesters and growers once a month in exchange for boxes of local natural foods!

Community gardens and wild harvesting are focuses for the bigger picture! We need to open our eyes and gather all our resources to ensure we help those across the planet as we help ourselves.

Our village is so rich and bountiful, I want to ensure our children who are gardening and harvesting can see their grand babies do the same. We are so economically depressed and struggling to stay afloat we are vulnerable. Industry such as fish farms, logging, mining all negatively impact our way of life and these corporations use our economic depression and the greed of leadership to further oppress us. Traditional foods are revolutionary because they call for radical reform the way we govern ourselves and secure economic viability. There is other ways to secure our futures for the next millennia to come! Kleco for listening and happy growing, with respect!

[Editor's note: also shared at the NAASN5 conference was a new release of a 'zine from Ancestral Pride (available through their website...)

http://ancestralpride.ca/

Appendix 6: Bookfair Poster

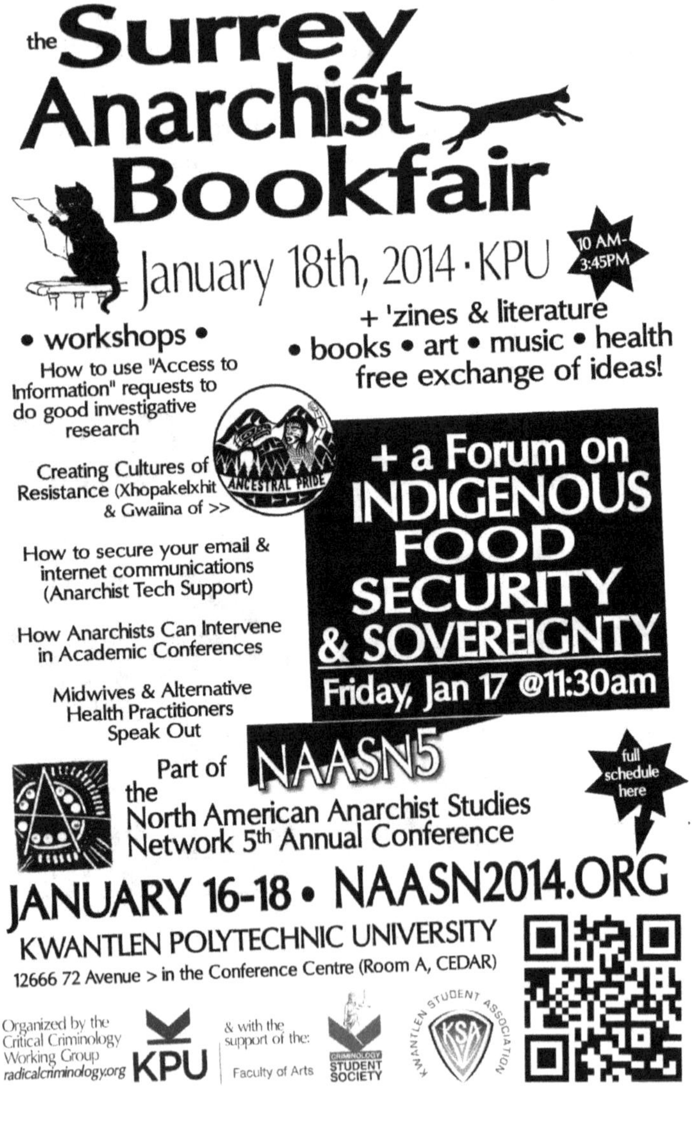

Appendix 7: Surrey Anarchist Bookfair
Tablers... (Sat., Jan 18: Conference Centre, KPU)

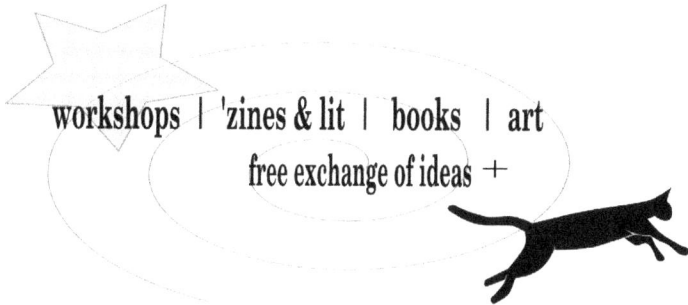

workshops | 'zines & lit | books | art
free exchange of ideas +

- **Ancestral Pride:**
  ancestralpride.ca

- **BC Blackout & Inner Island Distro:**
  bcblackout.wordpress.com

- **Black Banner Distro:**
  blackbannerdistro.
  wordpress.com

- **Critical Criminology Working Group** (with the journal *Radical Criminology*, books by **Jeff Shantz**, and 'zines from **Punching Out Press** & with ...

- **IWW Vancouver:**
  vancouverwob.blogspot.ca

- **KPIRG:**
  www.facebook.com/KPIRG

- **MENSES** (anarcha-feminists):
  mensestapes.bandcamp.com
  | mensesmixtape.tumblr.com

- **Spartacus Books:**
  www.spartacusbooks.net

- **Shout Back Festival:**
  shoutbackfest.tumblr.com

- **Upping the Anti:**
  uppingtheanti.org

...books from

Kersplebedeb:
LeftWingBooks.net
(& **Fifth Estate** magazines)

• **Robert Graham:**
robertgraham.
wordpress.com

• **Warrior Publications:**
warriorpublications.
wordpress.com

• **38 Blood Alley Square:**
38bloodalley.wordpress.com

at 7pm, there will be a fundraising dinner event
(for comrades in **Ancestral Pride**) to be held at the new
anarchist space in Vancouver: 38 Blood Alley Square >>>

www.ingramcontent.com/pod-product-compliance
Lightning Source LLC
Chambersburg PA
CBHW071728270326
41928CB00013B/2604